D1609963

THE HOSTAGE RESCUER

THE HOSTAGE RESCUER

THE RETURN OF A CHILD INTO A MOTHER'S ARMS

DARREN FRANKLIN
WITH
MARTIN PHILLIPS

PEN & SWORD
TRUE CRIME

First published in Great Britain in 2020 by
PEN AND SWORD TRUE CRIME
An imprint of
Pen & Sword Books Ltd
Yorkshire – Philadelphia

ISBN 978 1 52676 152 1

Typeset in Times New Roman 11.5/14 by
Aura Technology and Software Services, India.
Printed and bound in the UK by TJ International.

Pen & Sword Books Limited incorporates the imprints of Atlas, Archaeology,
Aviation, Discovery, Family History, Fiction, History, Maritime, Military, Military
Classics, Politics, Select, Transport, True Crime, Air World, Frontline Publishing,
Leo Cooper, Remember When, Seaforth Publishing, The Praetorian Press,
Wharncliffe Local History, Wharncliffe Transport, Wharncliffe True Crime and
White Owl.

For a complete list of Pen & Sword titles please contact
PEN & SWORD BOOKS LIMITED
47 Church Street, Barnsley, South Yorkshire, S70 2AS, England
E-mail: enquiries@pen-and-sword.co.uk
Website: www.pen-and-sword.co.uk

Or
PEN AND SWORD BOOKS
1950 Lawrence Rd, Havertown, PA 19083, USA
E-mail: Uspen-and-sword@casematepublishers.com
Website: www.penandswordbooks.com

Contents

Acknowledgements

I would like to give special thanks to Diane and Theo for their cooperation and input. Thank you to Martin Phillips for his expertise and guidance. Thanks, too, to Damien Lewis for believing in a great story and for his advice and support. I would like to thank Stephen Mastalerz who fuelled my appetite for adrenaline and who has not only been a boss, but a teacher and a friend. Oh, and thanks again for saving my life, mate! I want to thank a good friend in Ewan Ross for his wholehearted backing, without which this project would not have been made possible. Lastly, a special thanks to my parents Peter and Linda Franklin whose understanding and acceptance of whatever I told them in my most difficult times made doing what I was doing less worrying.

Picture Credits

All photos are the copyright of the author or from his personal collection, apart from the photo of the Resolute desk, courtesy of the J. F. Kennedy Arboretum, Ireland and the picture of Sir John Franklin, courtesy of the Dibner Library Portrait Collection (public domain).

Foreword

Every forty seconds in the United States a child goes missing or is abducted. In half of all those cases it is by a parent or other family member. Most cases are resolved within hours, but many are not. In Europe, more than 3,500 missing children were reported in 2016, and only seven out of ten were returned to their legal guardian within one month. That's more than 1,000 children wrongfully held. These figures are the tip of the iceberg because many cases are not reported as parents seek their own remedy to the situation. In the UK, parental child abductions are rarely recorded by police, leading charities to fear the true figures could be four times higher than official police figures suggest.

There have always been marital break-ups and, sadly, it has usually been any children involved who have borne the emotional brunt of the split, but somehow it seems to be getting worse. In today's ever-more transient world, partnerships are increasingly fragile and, whether it is for love or spite, when relationships are broken parents often fight for the legal custody of their children who get caught in the crossfire. If they go to court the judge will hear both arguments and normally decide what is in the best interests of the child, but that is rarely in the best interests of both parents and one side is usually left feeling aggrieved. If an arrangement has been made for the non-custodial parent to visit the child less often than he or she would like – or if no agreement exists – then abducting or kidnapping that child may enter their minds, and all too often it does.

When it comes to parental child abductions, it is far more prevalent in marriages where one parent may be living far from the land of his or her birth. A non-custodial parent may wish to show the child their origins and relatives and that desire only grows stronger if their access to the child is limited by a relationship break-up. Multicultural Australia has the highest per capita rate of international child abductions in the world, with many of the 250 or so children abducted every year taken abroad. The increase in marriage break-ups and the ease with which people can travel overseas, however, means no country is immune. If visiting rights are abused and the child is not returned to his or her legal guardian, then the non-custodial parent is guilty of child abduction. If the child is taken overseas, then the charge is the more serious international child abduction, but the greater seriousness of the offence does not necessarily make recovering the child any easier. Usually it is quite the opposite.

In a bid to tackle the problem, in 1980 the United Nations introduced a document called *The Hague Convention on the Civil Aspects of International Child Abduction* which was designed for the protection of children against being taken from their legal home country. Currently, more than ninety countries are signatories to the document and, in theory, abide by its rules, though some of those countries either do not enforce the rules or actively deny their existence. In the most recent year for which figures are available, around 2,600 applications were made under the Hague Convention for children to be returned to their custodial parent. More than 310 were from the USA; nearly 300 from the UK; 172 from Germany; 105 from France; ninety-two from Spain and forty-five from Australia.

Most people tend to think it will be the father who abducts a child but in seven out of ten cases it is the mother. More often than not it is a single child involved. A large majority of the applications made under the Hague Convention involve just one child, but nearly a third involve more than one. The average age for a child taken by a mother is six, while for a child taken by a father it is nearer seven. The starkest statistic, however, is that, even under the Hague Convention, fewer than half the children (forty-five per cent) are returned. If the distraught parent who has had their child or children taken away applies not to have the child returned but just to have access, the success rate drops to just one in four (twenty-seven per cent).

When the legal custodian has exhausted all official methods within their own country and within the country to which their child has been abducted, there is often no other choice but to take matters into their own hands. Child abduction organizations and child recovery specialists are companies that can help. Most child abduction organizations are non-profit making – relying on donations – and they contract child recovery attempts to specialist security companies. They also provide support and counselling to help parents cope with the ordeal. The counselling organizations and security specialists work together to provide a complete service in the planned recovery of a child and in the necessary support, but no child recovery company can guarantee success. There are a great number of things that can go wrong. Nor should they give a quote for the work after an initial consultation. Time is needed to research the recovery and to calculate an accurate cost.

Reputable child recovery specialists will make sure they are well versed in the laws of the country they are going to be operating in. Breaking and entering, taking hostages, depriving persons of their liberty, drugging people, stealing and assault are all offences in whichever part of the world you operate and are not part of the practices of a professional company. Any so-called child recovery specialist would be placing the child at risk to behave in such a manner. In most countries, any specialist who actually handles the child is committing the offence of kidnapping, despite the fact they are working for the legal parent. The handling of the child is best done by the legal parent, ensuring all laws are abided by and that there is less commotion. Successful child recoveries, sadly, are the exception rather than the rule.

Stephen Mastalerz
Managing Director
Trojan Securities International

Prologue

A single linen sheet covered the child's body where it lay in the stifling summer heat. Wisps of curly brown hair moved to and fro in the flow of warm air being pushed half-heartedly around the room by an oscillating fan. The hair, from the top of the boy's head, was all that protruded from beneath the folds of cloth which had settled protectively around him, outlining his diminutive form against the large expanse of otherwise unoccupied bed. Almost imperceptibly in the darkness of the night, the sheet rose and fell, rose and fell with every snuffled breath. The rhythmic tide of inhalations and exhalations went unheard above the noise of the whirring fan while, elsewhere in the house, much heavier snores disturbed the still night air. Slowly, the boy's murmurs faded and a new sound emerged. Rapid snatches of nasal breath grew more distinct and the irregular shudders of the sheet gave further betrayal of the staccato nature of the child's breathing. A plaintive whimper interspersed the soft, now clearly audible, sobbing. It was the same dream the boy had had before, and would have again. Searing sunlight filled his head, reflecting off whitewashed walls, the dazzling brightness blocked by the towering shadows of strangers. A blur of darkness; a flash of fluorescent yellow. Hands pulling him. Other hands reaching out to him in vain. The sounds of shouting. Screaming. A cry. His cry!

He woke with a jolt, cold sweat coating his body beneath the sheet now ruffled by his involuntary thrashing around. He looked around. He was alone and vaguely aware of his surroundings, but the nightmare chased him from sleep into fitful wakefulness and would not let go. The fan continued to whirr and his head swam with unwelcome thoughts. Who was he, really? Who did he belong to? Who should he belong to? Mum or Dad? Dad or stepdad? Where was home? This country or another? His mind raced out of control. A new thought loomed in his consciousness. Mummies and daddies sometimes took their children away because they loved them, he'd been told. But it didn't feel like love. It felt like war. A tug of war, with him in the middle. He tried to think happier thoughts, to steer his mind out of the maelstrom threatening to swamp him in the darkness. Fishing. He loved fishing. He imagined himself on a boat, gently rocking on the sea swell, the smell of the salt water in the air; the sun shining down on the bobbing craft, glinting off the silver eyelets of his fishing rod and the crests of the waves. His dad loomed large above him, leaning down to help him bait the hook on the end of his line, a smiling, comforting face. But suddenly the face changed. Unrecognizable. A blank. He tried and tried but he couldn't make out whose face it was. It just wasn't the face it was meant to be. As he wrestled to be free of this new confusion a fresh jolt woke him once more from his slumber. The night, it seemed, would not release him from his torment, and only the coming dawn could end this misery. A fresh tear traced its salty path down the olive skin of his face and, still plagued by his thoughts, he fell back into a restless doze.

Chapter One

The rainforest orchestra was in full flow now, the rhythmic 'strings' of a million insects suffusing the steamy atmosphere; the squeaks, squawks and exotic whistles of unseen birds, perched high in the palm canopy, supplying the 'woodwind' instrumentals. The temperature was already 36 degrees and the humidity eighty per cent. The drip, drip, drip of moisture rolling off giant leaves into a nearby pool of water added its own steady beat to the tropical soundtrack. Beneath the tall palms and lush fronds, the jungle musicians were not the only things warming up. I was cooking; gently stewing as I crouched in the undergrowth, peering through a shimmering heat haze at the cloud of dust being thrown up by a car fast approaching on the sun-baked clay road beyond my forest hideout.

In the distance, as if prompted by the nonchalant wave of an invisible conductor's baton, the tell-tale bark of a red howler monkey provided a bass note to nature's concerto, quickly answered by more soothing bird song. Then... chaos! Completely out of tune with the rainforest mood music came the crashing, discordant percussion of gunfire. The first half dozen rounds stitched a haphazard pattern of holes in the car's thin metal bonnet. The next two punctured the windshield before ricocheting around the inside of the onrushing vehicle. 'What the hell?' I shouted above the deafening rat-tat-tat-tat of semi-automatic weapons, but no one was listening. They were too busy opening up with everything they had on the car heading towards us – AK-47s, M16s, a few pistols like my own Browning 9mm – and that was just the firepower coming from my guys. The occupants of the car were now returning fire even as the driver slammed it sideways, wrenched up the handbrake and, in a cloud of red dust and flying stones, executed a nifty emergency turn straight out of a 1970s cops and robbers TV show. 'What happened to the fucking plan?' I thought, as bullets buzzed through the air above me like turbo-charged mosquitoes.

We were deep in the tropical outback of Ecuador's Oriente, at least a couple of hours' drive from the provincial capital Lago Agrio, and the 'bad guys' trying to shoot and drive their way out of trouble were FARC (*Fuerzes Armadas Revolucionarias de Colombia*) guerrillas – Marxist-Leninist rebels from the Revolutionary Armed Forces of Colombia – whose chief sources of funding were theft, kidnap and ransom and who weren't averse to crossing the San Miguel and Putumayo rivers into the north of Ecuador in search of easy pickings. Their politics didn't bother me but, as head of security for one of the big US oil drilling companies working in the region, their larceny did.

Some light-fingered guerrillas had been helping themselves to my client's equipment – cars, cash, drilling tools, you name it – and I had set up a roadblock to try to catch the culprits. Well, the local law enforcement, such as it was, wasn't going to – the FARC was not even classified as a terrorist organization in Ecuador. In fact, a few of the oil companies in the area who had similar problems with the rebels knew that I had a decent-sized security force and used our muscle from time to time, with my client's permission. For me, it was just business. For my men, all locals, it was different. When stuff went missing, they lost face, so they were all up for going after the pilferers and they were well-armed to do so.

My 2IC – second in command – Pedro, was ex-police intelligence and we had some decent intel on the rebels we were looking for and where we might find them, so I had chosen an ambush spot where the road narrowed as it cut its meandering route through the jungle-covered eastern slopes of the Ecuadorian Andes. Just after a bend was usually best. If you set up the roadblock on a straight stretch the rebels would obviously see you from far enough away to do a quick U-turn and hightail it out of there. Not that that stopped the rebels setting up their own roadblocks wherever they liked – they just dressed in stolen police uniforms and disguised their vehicles to look like police patrol cars to make the stop and search appear official to the unwary.

I'd run into one of those myself one time in Ecuador when we were body guarding a client. It was only when I got close enough to see the 'police' were wearing trainers and the paint was still wet on their 'patrol cars' that I realized the danger and quickly put into practice my defensive driving techniques to get us the hell out of there. It's amazing how many thoughts go through your head at moments of extreme threat like that, as if the entire scene turns to slow motion. I remember noticing that at least two of the AK-47-wielding 'police' officers were little more than boys; not a day over 14. It wasn't unusual. Up to a third of the FARC guerrillas were minors, forced to join the desperados and a life of villainy in pursuit of the cause, and I couldn't help but wonder about the pain of the families they had been taken from; their anguished but powerless fathers; their howling, heartbroken mothers. I thought, too, about the young boys themselves and the childhoods stolen from them, never to be returned, and my heart ached for them. Not that a 14 year old can't put a bullet in you just as easily as his older gang leader, which is why I wasn't keen to stick around and find out what the checkpoint was all about.

This time it was me setting the ambush, except I was not personally manning the barricades. Even if the rebels came around the bend too late to avoid the roadblock, when they saw a white face they would know there was trouble for them... or their eyes would fill with dollar signs at the thought of the ransom they could extort. Either way, they would be reaching for their weapons PDQ. So I had left Pedro and three others manning the roadblock while I took the rest of my guys into the rainforest, just off the bend of the road ahead of them, to watch for oncoming vehicles. The tropical sun blazed down on the dark red earth of the highway and though we were shaded amid the musty smell of soil and decay beneath the rainforest canopy, the air there was still and clingy and my saturated shirt was sticking to me like Elastoplast; my sweating hands struggling to hold my pistol as we waited out of sight. The hoots and squawks of brightly coloured toucans, macaws and tanagers in the trees above sounded mostly melodic but frequently like laughter at our expense. Clouds of rainforest bugs, meanwhile, were tucking into an early lunch, and I was it.

For two hours we waited among the ferns and vines and leaf litter, the occasional peasant pick-up truck the only 'customers' for our improvised checkpoint. There were quite a few civilians, as it happened, and we let them go on their way after a couple of questions. The local farmers were used to roadblocks, official or otherwise. As long as you let them through unharmed, they were happy. Well, happy enough. They didn't particularly like the oil companies or the FARC, but at least the oil companies had provided them with the road they were travelling on. They were more concerned about covering up the peccary carcass or two they might have in the back of the pick-up in case we were actually an official police roadblock. The indigenous people were allowed to hunt for bush meat to eat but not to sell. Most of the cars and trucks we stopped just assumed my guys were FARC, but the hasty rearrangement of sacks in the back as they approached us showed they weren't taking any chances.

The trickle of farm vehicles slowed and for twenty minutes we stopped none. Then I saw it. A white Chevrolet Chevette with no plates was heading towards our trap, kicking up clouds of dust in its wake. It matched the description we had been given of the car used by our pilferers and when it got closer I could make out three – maybe four – men inside, and they clearly weren't farmers. As the car neared my position at the bend, about 50 metres from the roadblock, I turned to signal to Pedro to be ready, but Pedro wasn't waiting for a signal. As soon as he saw the car he opened up, spraying it with 7.62mm rounds. The men with him followed his lead and, not to be left out, the men with me stepped from the vegetation to dish out some good news of their own.

Even without the burst of gunfire that greeted them as they rounded the bend, the rebels would have known as soon as they saw the roadblock that there would be more of us in the jungle and they weren't about to hang around to find out why. The driver, with some skill, spun the Chevy as his mate in the back seat opened fire with a semi-automatic through his open window. The front-seat passenger loosed off a few rounds of his own before the car sped away, its crazed windshield and rear window crumbling under the weight of hot metal rounds peppering the glass. Even from 30 metres away it was clear the car had been riddled with bullet holes. Whether any of the occupants had been too, I couldn't know.

'Hold your fire! Stop!' I shouted, as a last few aimless rounds chased the fast-disappearing rebels who were soon lost in the screen of dust that hid their retreat. 'Enough!' I yelled. A quick check revealed we had taken no casualties. At least that was something to be grateful for, and there was precious little else. 'Jeez, mate,' I exclaimed to Pedro when I reached him. 'I thought we were going to question them! You know, a bit of dialogue... find out if they were our thieves, what they knew about the stealing, gather a bit of intel.' Pedro looked unconcerned. 'They already reach for *sus armas* – for their guns,' he said by way of explanation for his shoot-first-ask-questions-later choice of action. 'Bien! Et definitivamente la FARC. They no rob us again. They know we know them,' he concluded. 'Tell me something I don't know,' I said, angrily.

It was a safe bet the rebels knew we were on to them already, with or without that little shoot-out. In my position as head of security for one of the big players in the region, I had regular briefings with local forces and visiting military groups. There was an American liaison officer – a captain – going on observation patrols with the local soldiers and everyone from the Ecuadorian Army to the FBI was benefitting from the intel I was providing. I was doing a lot of damage to the guerrillas and it wasn't going unnoticed. Pedro had told me recently some Colombians had come to our oil company offices. Suited and booted, they wouldn't say who they were or what they wanted but they had asked specifically for me. By name. 'You need maintain your head low,' Pedro said. I did need to keep my head down but that wasn't my nature.

Travel and adventure had always appealed to me, ever since I was a boy. Anything with an element of risk would excite me. Perhaps it runs in my blood. The Franklins are descended from Rear Admiral Sir John Franklin, from Lincolnshire, the former Lieutenant Governor of Van Diemen's Land (now Tasmania). He was the nineteenth-century explorer who disappeared on his last expedition attempting to chart and navigate the Northwest Passage of the Canadian Arctic. As it happens, more ships were lost searching for him than the two from his expedition which were crushed by the Canadian ice, leaving Sir John and his crew to die from a combination of starvation, hypothermia and scurvy as they trekked on foot in search of salvation.

HMS *Resolute* was one of the search vessels lost, and from the recovered oak timbers Queen Victoria had a desk made and given to the USA as a gift. So now there is not only a bust of my great, great, great, great, great uncle in Westminster Abbey, but a brass plaque commemorating him on the Resolute desk used by successive presidents in the Oval Office of the White House.

My maternal grandfather was in the navy too. John Nuttall, from Burnley, was an able seaman on an aircraft carrier during the Second World War, working as a butcher, and his sweetheart Elsie Hopwood, who was a weaver by trade, worked in the NAAFI (Navy, Army and Air Force Institutes) – the forces' canteen – servicing the troop trains with food and drink. Whole families joined the war effort back then and mine was no different. My great grandmother worked in a munitions factory making bullets and continued to do so even after she had half a finger blown off by a bullet which exploded. As soon as the war ended,

John and his best girl Elsie were married and my grandfather worked as a railway track layer while the family carried on their life in their little terraced house, one street back from the Leeds and Liverpool Canal in Burnley, where my mum Linda was born.

It was my grandmother's idea to escape the post-war austerity of Britain and emigrate to a new life in Australia. My grandfather wasn't so keen, probably having had enough of sailing round the world during the war, but on 13 May 1955 John and Elsie Nuttall and their 7-year-old daughter, my mum, packed their bags and left Burnley behind. They were what was known as 'Ten Pound Poms' because that was the going rate for the cheapest passage when they boarded the MS *Georgic* at Liverpool bound for Fremantle, Western Australia, en route to Sydney. My mother recalls how her dad was especially protective of her on the voyage, never letting her out of his sight, and perhaps with good reason. There were apparently some 'undesirables' on board and at Melbourne federal police officers boarded the ship for the protection of passengers on the rest of the journey to Sydney.

I still have relatives back in Burnley, but my family's new home was now Down Under and that's where I was born and grew up, though my grandmother never lost her thick northern English accent. I joined the boy scouts as a kid, then the cadets as soon as I was old enough, so the natural progression was to join the military when I left school, which I did. Having had a grandfather in the Royal Navy, and my uncle, Les Hiddins, famed for the Australian TV series *Bush Tucker Man*, in the army, I felt the military was in my blood.

I joined the Australian Army and spent nine years in service, achieving the rank of sergeant. My speciality was psychology. In fact, the highlight of my military career was conducting special operations in psychology and intelligence operations – PSYOPS. It was an intriguing subject. In due course I left the military but having not had my fill of action and adventure I joined a state police force. If I thought that would quench my thirst for excitement, I was disappointed. It was a good job, and worthwhile, but not what I was looking for.

It wasn't until I teamed up with an old ex-Australian SAS soldier that my career changed dramatically. He was offering his expertise at a decent rate, and I was a willing pupil prepared to pay to better myself. He took me to a remote location in Australia and trained me in personal protection, counter-terrorism, hostage rescue and advanced firearms training, all at a level well above what I had experienced in the army or police. To complement my training, I travelled overseas to practise surveillance, covert operations, photography... and acting. With my previous training in the army and police, and new skills from my ex-soldier mate, I was now a pretty well-trained unit and had finally found what I was looking for – the chance to offer my services as a decent security consultant.

For me, the next three years were like something you would watch in a movie. Still, to this day, I can't reveal too much, though one of my most challenging jobs was as a security manager of a US oil drilling company in the Ecuadorian jungle. Every facet of my training was utilized. Especially surveillance, which would come in useful for the career route I would later find myself on. I was not the only one who had turned on to an unexpected pathway in life.

Chapter Two

An avalanche of dazzling white apartments blanketed the rocky hillside from the tree-covered higher slopes down to the water's edge and, like so many Greek island towns, Pothia from a distance looked every inch the picture postcard image of the perfect holiday destination. Wooden-masted tall ships, cruisers, yachts and fishing boats bobbed gently in the harbour on gin-clear blue-tinted water, turned aquamarine by the fine yellow sand visible just a few metres beneath the surface. The sun-bleached whiteness of the closely built houses arrayed lazily around a labyrinth of narrow streets and even narrower passageways served only to emphasize the deep azure tone of the cloudless blue sky above the idyllic island of Kalymnos. Bright yellow lemons and purple-ripe figs hanging on terrace trees added their fragrance to the air already faintly scented by the thyme, sage and oregano growing wild on the mountain slopes above the town.

Diane's gaze, however, was attracted to colours of a different hue, transfixed as she was by a pair of soft brown eyes set in the olive-skinned face of the smiling young man before her, blinding her to the beauty around her. Diane had not set out from Scotland with any intention to do a Shirley Valentine. She was no middle-aged housewife escaping a life of drudgery, just a 21 year old with a gaggle of girlfriends from the suburbs of Glasgow in search of some cheap summer sunshine. If it had been a wild time they were after they could have picked an 18-30 package deal in Spain, or one of the bigger resorts on Crete, Rhodes, or Kos, but they had opted for quieter Kalymnos, one of the northernmost and smaller islands of the south-eastern Dodecanese archipelago favoured by so many Greeks from the mainland for their own summer getaways.

A craggy limestone outcrop just off the coast of Turkey, it had been under Turkish rule until 1912, Italian until 1943 and Greek since the end of German occupation during the Second World War, but always simply home to the core of families, fishermen and smallholders who had lived there for generations. Now the sponge-diving capital of the Aegean was discovering tourism as its new 'Kalymnian gold', though sales of sponges from virtually every other shop still brought in the drachmas.

Nikita – the owner of the captivating brown eyes – was not your stereotypical taverna waiter trying it on with every new batch of nubile girls flown in for a fortnight of sun, sea and retsina. A carpenter by trade, he'd served his time in the Greek Army and was back on his native island for an extended holiday, although the family did own one of the most popular bars on the island in which he was a partner and a frequent visitor and he clearly had an eye for the female tourists who were his customers. Curly-haired, strong-jawed and barrel-chested, he was a handsome young man. Not that he, or any other boy, would have been the first thing on the minds of the Scottish lasses as the ferry landed them on the island and they were transported to their accommodation.

For Diane, celebrating the completion of her nursing degree, and the rest of the girls, their first consideration had been to hit the shingle beaches, to swim in the hypnotically beautiful sea and to soak up at least enough sunshine to rid themselves of any peely-wally Scottish pallor. At the end of days spent gently curing like sun-dried tomatoes in the Mediterranean heat, when the wine and the dancing made them forget their sunburn and their inhibitions, some of her friends may have been on the lookout for a handsome young Adonis. Diane wasn't. It just sort of happened.

Every night she and her pals would head out in search of food and fun, spoilt for choice by the range of restaurants and tavernas. Above the tinny cacophony of motorcycles and scooters which filled the streets as much at night as during the day, the soundtracks from the different bars and eateries competed for attention, from cheesy bazouki music straight out of Zorba the Greek *to the even cheesier Bombalurina pop hit* Itsy Bitsy Teeny Weeny Yellow Polka Dot Bikini, *all of them beckoning the carefree holidaymakers. If the music, and the wafted aromas of souvlaki and pan-fried fish, didn't tempt them, the suntanned waiters and pretty waitresses did their best to, but one bar beckoned more often than others, and Diane's new admirer was usually there.*

After an initial chance encounter with the handsome local, she had been only too happy to talk to him as often as possible, charmed as much by his heavily accented English as he seemed to be by her soft Scottish brogue. Her protective pals did their best to chaperone her when they realized their friend's persistent suitor wasn't going away but they were fighting a losing battle. Nikita was no predator and Diane no pushover but, as she would say, her head was away with the pixies. Snatching moments away from the noise of the bars, she tingled with electricity just to be standing with him in the light of the oversized moon which seemed to fill the star-dotted night sky, and as they talked and talked they quickly discovered shared interests, hopes and dreams.

Strolls through the steep narrow streets, between the gleaming white neo-classical houses with their wrought iron balconies, were a joy for Diane as Nick introduced her to his hometown. Walks on the beach, with the waves lapping on the shingle, were even more romantic. It was exciting and adventurous and made Diane's heart skip but, for the young couple, it felt more than just a holiday romance and the nearer the end of her time in Kalymnos came, the more often she was hit by wild thoughts of not going home; of not getting on that plane; of quitting Glasgow and staying on to work in a taverna on the island.

That sort of thing only happened to the fictional Shirley Valentine, she chided herself, and so did her friends, but the agony of separation made the end of the holiday even more painful for Diane than for her pals, who were already dreading the return to work on Monday. Even as she buckled herself into her seat for the package tour flight home and looked out of the oval-shaped perspex window onto the Greek skyline she was leaving behind, she was determined it would not be the end of the special connection she had made. The girl who had arrived on the idyllic island was not the same girl going back and she felt sure that if she did not follow her heart she would regret it.

The phone calls and handwritten letters to and from Nick continued long after Diane had flown back to Glasgow and it was a struggle for her to concentrate on work at her desk as she plotted and planned her earliest possible return to Kalymnos. She did not have to wait long, though it seemed like forever as the days dragged by into weeks and then months. That Christmas, as all around her prepared for festive celebrations in the dirty snow-flecked streets of Clydeside, and cheered themselves with pre-holiday drinks to keep out the cold, Diane took a flight to Kos and the ferry to Kalymnos and was met by the handsome boy she'd fallen for.

The reunion was all she had dreamed it would be. This time in Pothia she was on her own, without her Praetorian Guard of girlfriends, and Kalymnos was a totally different place. Many of the restaurants and tavernas of the scorching high season were shuttered and empty, their owners having closed up and returned to the mainland for the winter. The music from dozens of different bars and the noisy revelry of happy tourists were glaring by their absence. The atmosphere, like the weather, was very different, but that suited Diane. This was real, not some fantasy seen through the distorting heat haze of a holiday getaway. Despite the lack of summer sunshine, Kalymnos still seemed like a beautiful pearl set in the sapphire surrounds of the Aegean, and the warmth of the welcome she received matched the balmiest of heatwaves.

After a week's stay with Nick and his family, who greeted her like a long-lost daughter, she was convinced more than ever of her feelings. One return visit became several and occasional weeks here and there, when work allowed, became months at a time and she began to learn Greek. Nick's family introduced her to the owners of the cafe on the corner of their street whose family had a flat to rent, and they too showered this pretty stranger, their new tenant, with kindness. Diane felt completely at home with her boyfriend and safe in the keep of his close-knit extended family who doted on their son's blue-eyed, blonde Scottish princess.

Chapter Three

Positioned discreetly behind a pillar, and well behind the jostling scrum of taxi drivers and chauffeurs holding boards with their clients' names in front of their chests, my eyes struggled to cope with the never-ending stream of people flooding through the automatic doors into the arrivals hall of Bogota's El Dorado Airport. Anyone who has ever met a loved one off a flight at a busy international terminal knows how difficult it can be to spot the person you're meant to be meeting. It's altogether more stressful when you only have a vague description of what they look like; you don't know exactly what flight they are on; but you do know they have a contract to kill you.

Trouble and I had become reacquainted and it was not a healthy relationship. This particular flirtation had begun a few weeks before in Florida, a holiday destination for many but for me the venue for a business opportunity which had started with a hotel room rendezvous, and not the fun kind. Turn right off the Dolphin Expressway from Miami International Airport towards South Beach and you are spoilt for choice among the stylish, pastel-coloured art deco hotels of the American Riviera, with their whimsical curves, porthole windows, and wood-panelled receptions where the likes of Clark Gable, Rita Hayworth and other Hollywood legends would have sauntered to the check-in desk in their heydays. Our taxi, however, had turned left.

North of the less-than-salubrious Little Haiti, we'd been dumped outside a two-storey U-shaped budget motel – the kind of place where the bad guys always go to ground in an American crime movie. The disinterested-looking caretaker in a dirty white vest had not even bothered to get up out of his easy boy chair to react to our arrival. He stayed seated to reach into the cubby holes behind him, grabbed a key attached to a sizeable lump of wood bearing the first-floor room number, and pushed it nonchalantly across the formica-topped desk at Rob and me.

Chapter Three

A cheap motor inn was all my finances stretched to, but it was on the promise of big bucks. The view from the hotel balcony on to the sparkling blue bay beyond the Biscayne Boulevard was absolutely five star. The room was definitely not. Square, functional and age-worn, it was well past its best-before date and I doubt it would have been worth writing home about even when new. The decor was from a time that fashion forgot and a lingering musty stench, like body odour or something worse, filled the air already tainted by the stale smell of cigarettes from an ashtray left uncleaned since the previous occupants. The air con was working hard but achieving little; a loud occasional clunk suggesting that it could expire at any minute.

I was sitting in the corner on the single velour-upholstered chair provided, and Rob was perched on the edge of one of the beds, as our visitor tossed a manila folder on to the coffee table in front of me like he was dealing me the king of hearts, knowing that he held the ace. He leaned forward to open the dossier and to reveal the A5 photograph on the first page. 'That's your target,' he said, with a self-satisfied grin. Out of the corner of my eye I could see the look of bewilderment creeping across Rob's face and I fought against the knot of anxiety stirring in my own stomach. Target?

Victor, our new paymaster, was a big man, 6ft 2ins, with slicked-back brown hair greying at the temples. A Canadian who'd served in the US Army before setting up his own body-guarding business, I'd bumped in to him on the personal protection circuit in South America and he'd massaged my ego, telling me how good he thought I was at my job and that he might have some work for me in future. I'll be honest, I was flattered. He was someone who had been around for a while, knew a lot of top people in the game and had earned his stripes. He was also someone who was full of bullshit; a fantasist who thought he was living his own adventure movie and kept quoting lines from the gangster film *Heat*, but he didn't just talk the talk. He had walked the walk in the past and now he was head of security for a major international conglomerate and, in my game, the sort of person you thought you wanted to be in with.

I'd been back in Australia, feeling pretty pleased with myself for the way the Ecuador job had gone in spite of the dangers, and was enjoying a relaxing break when Victor had rung and told me he had a big body-guarding gig for me if I was up for it. The client was the chief executive officer of a multi-million-dollar company whose safety was under threat and I was to keep him out of the way for a while. There were risks, of course. Some very heavy-duty bad guys had him in their sights, but that would be reflected in the money I would get for just a few weeks' work, Victor said. He didn't confirm exactly how much but the ball-park figure was upwards of $100,000.

Naively, I was hooked. I'd recruited a bouncer mate, Rob, from New Zealand, who was fairly new to the game but willing to learn, and I'd paid $5,000 for our return flights to Miami. I ought to have smelled a rat when Victor told me to ring him from the airport at exactly 11.37 am, so he'd know it was me, and to put on a fake accent to ask for him when his wife answered the phone, which he'd make sure she did. That way, he said, he could tell her some business had come up at short notice and that he had to leave their home in Tampa and drive across the state. If this job was legit, you might wonder, why was he lying to his own wife about what he was up to. The thing was, Victor lied to his wife about a lot, and about one woman in particular that I was aware of. I suppose I thought he might be combining business with a little pleasure on his trip to Miami.

Now, standing over us in his ironed jeans and cowboy boots, with sweat glistening on his upper brow and beginning to stain the underarms of his Hawaiian shirt, he was outlining a kidnap plan and the 'target' was his own boss. The CEO. In Colombia. The air con gave another clunk, or it could have been my stomach doing a somersault. We'd been duped and I could feel my lower jaw sagging as Victor thumbed enthusiastically through his dossier to illustrate his plot for a classic inside job: 'You got a map of the area, the address of his villa, here, and names of his security detail. I can maybe arrange for one of them to be called away when the time is right, so you only have to worry about the other one.' I stared at the dossier, then at the faded curtains, the shit-brown patterned carpet, anywhere but into the eyes of the madman now briefing us as if we were seasoned crooks.

As Victor looked out of the window I caught sight of Rob, a muscular, rugby-playing beast of a man who was used to looking menacing as he filled nightclub doorways but who now looked like a lost schoolboy, sitting on the floral polyester bedspread, his eyes seemingly beseeching me with: 'What the fuck is going on?' I returned a silent look which I hope said, 'Trust me.' But I hadn't a clue myself and I was desperately trying to think. Victor rumbled on, warming to his theme. 'You'll conduct surveillance on the villa, find out what time he comes and goes and the routines of his security detail and then, when the time is right, you'll lift him, incapacitate him with pills and alcohol and secure him in the safe house you'll rent on the other side of Bogota, here.'

He prodded the map with a thick finger and flicked through a few pages until he came to a scrap of paper with some addresses on. 'You'll send the ransom details to the company here and... .' He paused to allow himself a little chuckle. 'And, as per company procedures, they will leave it to the head of security – me – to negotiate with the kidnappers. I'll come down to Colombia, agree to drop the cash in the jungle at set coordinates, after which you'll release the CEO and meet me back here in Florida.' 'And why would we do this?' I asked, trying to mask my incredulity. Victor smiled. 'Five million US dollars, baby! That'll be the ransom, and they'll pay it. They'll assume it's the FARC and just business. Your cut will be $500,000. And here's your advance.' He threw an envelope with $10,000 dollars onto the bed. 'And what if it goes wrong?' I asked. Victor was clearly now in full Robert De Niro mode. 'Hey, baby,' he drawled. 'You know the risks. It rains... you get wet.'

The shock at being duped subsided as he spoke. I had now gone well past bemusement and straight on to annoyance. I'd taken a short stop at embarrassment, having been so foolish as to find myself in this position, and had arrived at full-blown anger, but if I told Victor to shove his ridiculous plan where the sun didn't shine I'd not only be left looking a mug, which I deserved, but I'd be $5,000 out of pocket, which I was not about to swallow. I was furious and that probably clouded my judgement over what to do next. If Victor wanted surveillance, we'd give him that, while we were being paid. We'd provide him with photos of the CEO at his *casa*, timings of the movement of his guards, and we'd find a safe house, all to be detailed in daily reports, in return for more cash, and when we'd got enough to cover our costs and our time, we'd be out of there. 'You've picked the right men for the job,' I told him, aware even without looking that Rob would be in a silent panic.

'Good', said Victor. From a large military-style holdall he produced a pepper spray. 'To help subdue the guards,' he said, and then pulled out a smoke grenade. 'To show exactly where in the jungle the money is to be dropped,' he added. He delved further into the holdall and brought out military ration packs, for when we were in the jungle for the recce and the money drop, and then a large green waterproof duffle bag. 'This is to transfer the money into,' he explained, though we weren't to be trusted to carry the cash away. He would be there to do that and to transport it back to Florida by his own means. Finally, like a magician pulling one more rabbit out of his hat, he dragged from the bag a blue bulletproof vest – just the one – and two pistols – a .22 and a 9mm, both of which he handed to me. 'You're all set. Keep me posted, regularly,' he said before adding for the full De Niro effect, 'And you'd better not waste my motherfucking time.'

With that he announced he had an appointment with 'a great piece of ass' over on Brickell Key, and left the room. A few more clunks of the air con was all that broke the silence until Rob was sure that Victor had gone and was not going to burst back into the room, and then he spluttered, 'What the hell have you just agreed to? You have got to be fucking joking me! I'm not getting involved in any kidnap, mate.' 'No,' I told him. 'Nor am I.' I explained that we would merely play Victor along until we had got our money and then go home. 'What's he going to do?' I said. 'Go to the cops and complain that he's been ripped off on his kidnap plot?'

After booking flights to Bogota for the next day, we grabbed a beer in the Florida sunshine and I left Rob to unscramble his brain at the motel while I jumped in a cab downtown to buy a couple of other things I felt we might need. That night we had some junk food and an early night and the next morning I stuffed the dossier and Victor's cash in my backpack, hid the two shiny new pistols in the false bottom of my suitcase, and we jumped in a cab back to the airport. I read later that there was a $25,000 fine and up to seven years' imprisonment for smuggling firearms in or out of the US but this was in the days before 9/11, when security was far more lax, and I reckoned at the time that if they had spotted the weapons on the X-rays they would have been only too grateful there were two fewer guns in the US.

The temperature at El Dorado International, Bogota, was a cool 15 degrees by the time we landed, hired a small car and headed towards the north east of the city where the CEO lived in a large *casa* or villa on a gated estate. We found ourselves a reasonably priced small hotel in the Chico Navarra barrio for the first couple of nights until we could sort ourselves out a cheap apartment, and then we settled into a routine, carrying out surveillance on Victor's 'target' in his much higher-class district north of calle 127.

The CEO lived in a four-bedroom, four-bathroom home with enviable views of the Cordillera Oriental, the widest of the three branches of the Colombian Andes which run through the country. The two-storey brick property was surrounded by a large manicured lawn, tennis court and swimming pool and set in a well-maintained estate. The whole complex was surrounded on all sides by a 6 ft-high brick wall, topped with barbed wire. Fortunately, for us, it was close to a large public park from where we could easily watch the comings and goings. Being *gringo* tourists, no one had any reason to question our cameras, but most of the time if people were close by we would kick a football or throw a Frisbee to one another. If in doubt, smile and wave. No one seemed to give us a second look.

Most of our work was done in the first few days, taking photos of the security detail in their guard house beside the main gate, noting their dress, their weapons, the times of their patrols, all information which we could feed back bit by bit to 'El Commandante' Victor in our daily reports. We noted the time of the morning the CEO was driven out of the gates by his chauffeur, which didn't change much, and the time he returned from work in the evening. If we had been planning a kidnap it would all have been useful information, but we weren't.

The house was the sort of property you would expect a man of the CEO's status to be living in but it was far too big for him alone. His family clearly lived elsewhere while he was at work during the week, and watching him stroll alone in the quiet grounds that should have echoed to the laughter of children, I felt sorry for the guy. Sure, he had power and wealth, and the trappings that went with it, but at least for the time he was on business in Bogota he didn't look to have much in the way of happiness. I imagined him sitting in the house in the evening, unwinding with a glass of whisky after the housekeeper had served him his dinner and retired for the night, with no one to talk to but the TV. No amount of money would compensate for not seeing your family, in my book, but that wasn't my concern.

We monitored the route that the CEO's chauffeur took most days to drive him to his office and, after the first week, we checked out a more remote apartment to the south east of the city which we rented as the safe house where Victor believed we would keep the kidnapped CEO. The rental receipt added to the blizzard of car hire bills, taxi receipts, food and accommodation tickets and the like which we sent to Victor to back up our daily reports. It was just as well, because El Commandante had to fly down to Bogota on business and decided to pay us a little visit to see how his scheme was progressing.

Rob played his part brilliantly, grabbing a chance for a quiet chat with Victor to let him know the 'stress' I was under trying to cover every angle, and hamming up the diligence with which we were carrying out our surveillance and plotting the best way to grab the CEO. It all served to help our case for when El Commandante had flown back to Florida and I outlined to him on the phone the further elaborate preparations we would be carrying out and asked him to send another $10,000, which he did. We were, after all, carrying out his instructions and he seemed happy with the progress. Another week or so, and another advance of cash, and I reckoned Rob and I could book ourselves on flights and get out of there with our wasted time handsomely paid for.

I don't know what it was that alerted him, but approaching the end of the third week, Victor seemed to cotton on to the fact that we might be taking him for a ride and baulked at transferring more funds. In a tense phone call I spelled out the kidnap plan we thought we might be able to put into practice in a week or so, but El Commandante was back in De Niro mode. 'If I gotta put you down, I will,' he warned. He reluctantly agreed to another, smaller, payment, but the warning signs were there and Rob and I began planning our exit from Bogota.

It was a few days later when I took a call from another acquaintance from the security circuit, Stephen Mastalerz, a Brit who used to run a body-guarding business in America and who I'd got on well with when we'd met. 'Hello, Skippy,' he said, gently mocking my Australian background. 'Who have you been upsetting now?' That knot of anxiety returned to my stomach. 'I dunno,' I said. 'Who *have* I been upsetting?' Stephen explained that he'd bumped into a couple of his former body guarding students; two South Americans who now worked for none other than our commander and who, in the course of a brief catch-up chat, let slip that they were about to fly down to Bogota to 'get rid of a couple of gringos' who had double-crossed Victor.

'They told me who their targets were,' Stephen said. 'I told them it was a bad idea, that I knew you and that you were one of the good guys. But they said they had their orders, the flight tickets had been paid for and they had to go to Colombia.' My blood was running cold by this stage. Jeez, what have I got myself into? I'd had Victor down as fantasist, but this was taking things to a whole new level. I had been furious at being conned into flying all the way to America on a false premise and wanted revenge but now he was sending a couple of hit men to Colombia to kill me? This was getting serious and I was cursing my stupidity in getting caught up in the whole charade.

Stephen tried to put my mind at rest. 'Look, it's none of my business but I thought you ought to know,' he said. 'The lads coming down there aren't bad guys and, to be honest, I think they have the same opinion of Victor as you do so you should be alright, but you might want to keep your head down.' That phrase again. If I hadn't got the message before, I was getting it loud and clear now. It was time for Rob and me to step up our surveillance, but not on the CEO, who was of no further interest to us. This time we would be watching the airport.

For two days we staked out El Dorado, watching every flight coming in from the US, armed with the names and descriptions Stephen had given me of our would-be assassins. Airports can be soulless places at the best of times and watching endless streams of passengers, alternating with glances at the mesmerizing matrix board showing the constantly updating flight times, was brain-numbing. El Dorado is one of the busiest airports in the world and had just opened its new hub, offering around 6,000 possible connections a week and carrying more than twenty million passengers a year, and at that moment it felt like I had to see, identify and categorize every single one. It certainly sharpens the mind when you know the people you are watching out for are arriving with the intention to kill you.

We'd already cancelled the rental on the 'kidnap' safe house the day after Vincent had inspected it for himself since we never had any intention of using it and why would we waste more of our cash on it? We'd checked out of our accommodation; left our football and Frisbee for the local kids in the park; and, with a hole punch and hammer, I'd tapped out the serial numbers on the pistols and buried them in case I ever needed to retrieve them. Hanging around the airport with our suitcases and backpacks, we blended in with the other travellers thronging the busy arrivals hall, except we weren't there waiting to give a welcoming hug to anyone emerging from the customs channel.

Towards the end of the second morning we spotted them, in their jeans, denim shirts and desert boots, travelling light with just a rucksack each. They clearly weren't expecting their business to keep them there for long. Outside the terminal building the yellow cabs buzzed around like orderly bees awaiting their turn to access the hive. We watched our assassins climb into one bound for the city and a quote from Victor's favourite movie came into my head: 'Don't let yourself get attached to anything you are not willing to walk out on in thirty seconds flat if you feel the heat around the corner.' I had felt a furnace and Rob and I should have walked straight back into the airport terminal and promptly booked ourselves on a flight to Australia. Instead, I hailed the next taxi and Rob and I jumped in, in pursuit of our pursuers.

Chapter Four

If Diane's family thought it had been a big step for her to leave behind her entire life in Glasgow and move to a remote Greek island for the love of a boy she had met on holiday, then they were in for an even bigger shock. Nick's time on his native Kalymnos was coming to an end. His parents had decided to follow a path previously trodden by other family members and emigrate, along with Nick, to the other side of the world; to Darwin, Australia. He invited her to join him and where Nick went, Diane was determined to follow.

The state capital of Australia's Northern Territory was named in the mid-nineteenth century by the captain of HMS Beagle, in honour of his former shipmate and evolution proponent Charles Darwin, and the place seemed to epitomize Darwin's survival of the fittest theory. It had been almost completely destroyed by cyclones in 1897, 1939 and 1974 and by Japanese bombing in the Second World War, and each time the surviving inhabitants had picked themselves up and rebuilt their city. Indeed, it was the devastation wrought by Cyclone Tracy on Christmas Day 1974 that had brought hundreds of Kalymnian workers to help with the rebuilding. Many of them had stayed to build new lives for themselves, so the links between Darwin and the tiny Greek island were strong.

Diane had tried to imagine what the place she was about to call home would be like, but on arrival she was surprised at how wrong she had been and how different it was to the picture that had formed in her mind's eye. Flat, low-lying and very modern, Darwin can nonetheless feel strangely remote. Situated at the northernmost point of the 1,700-mile Stuart Highway which bisects Australia from top to bottom, the city is closer to Jakarta, Indonesia, than it is to Australia's capital Canberra more than 1,900 miles to the south, and Dili, in East Timor, is just 400 miles away.

After temperate Glasgow and Mediterranean Greece, Diane now found herself in the tropics and, arriving at the height of the dry season, it was hot; very hot for a fair-skinned Scottish lass. It was hotter even than she had remembered the Greek islands to have been, though the cloudless blue skies, gentle breeze from the harbour and the many Greek voices in the city reminded her of Kalymnos. That, of course, was why Nick's family felt so at home there, but for Diane it was about as far from Glasgow as it was possible to be. She had never seen indigenous Australians before, and there were plenty in Darwin to remind her she was in a very different part of the world, but it was the Greek culture that she was still struggling to get used to.

At least she was not living with Nick's family, as friendly and as welcoming as they had been. Maintaining a degree of independence, Diane had rented a one-bedroom apartment in the centre of the city when she first arrived and had set about finding temporary work to pay her way. She was nothing if not resourceful. The weather was relentlessly hot and dry as she hopped on and off the buses that got her around Darwin and to different office locations each day, or transported her to Nick when she was neither working nor waiting by the phone on the off chance of work offers, but it was already getting hotter and more humid as the wet season approached. When the monsoons broke, the sun-kissed city was frequently blanketed by grey clouds during the day and lit up by spectacular lightning storms at night.

In such unfamiliar surroundings, Nick was her only constant and when she was with him she had no reason to regret her decision to put all thoughts of a nursing career on hold and follow him to the other side of the world. Her temping job just about paid for her rent and for the cost of the bus fares to see him as often as she could but, because Darwin's remoteness increased supply costs, she found the prices of everything more expensive than she had expected and home in Scotland seemed a universe away.

As soon as she could, Diane found herself a full-time job with an insurance company and moved to a cheaper rented 'unit' in the suburb of Casuarina where Nick's parents were renting their own home. Her continuing independence was at odds with the sometimes overbearing nature of Greek family life but she and Nick were happy and Diane was getting used to her new world. Getting her driving licence and her own car had helped her to acclimatize and soon enough it felt like time for her and Nick to settle down.

Having Nick's family to guide and support her was a great help, though not quite the same as having her own parents on hand, and the longer she stayed in Darwin – and she'd been there for a few years by then – the more Diane got used to the climate and the people and the more like the UK the city seemed to become so that she did not feel so remote. Her sister had visited her soon after she first arrived and now, as she planned her wedding to Nick, an aunt who was travelling around Australia had called in on her. It helped her to feel less isolated from her family in Scotland and ready to take the next big step in her life with her handsome beau.

In a beautiful white gown that showed off her slim figure and with her shiny auburn hair in flowing ringlets, topped with a white headdress, Diane's happy smile lit up the ornate soleas of St Nicholas' Greek Orthodox Church, Darwin, as she married Nick amid all the fervour and ancient ritual of a traditional Greek wedding. Two lit candles stood alongside the Holy Gospel, a cup of wine, the betrothal rings and the wedding crowns on the ceremonial table, in front of the church's holy altar, to symbolize that 'Christ would not let the happy couple walk in darkness'. After the betrothal service, the marriage service and the crowning of the bride and groom, watched proudly by Nick's family, their friends, and an array of saints and martyrs whose paintings adorned the walls and the carved wooden surrounds, Diane and Nick led the Dance of Isaiah procession before the priest's final blessing paved the way for a 'big fat Greek' wedding party.

The couple was indeed blessed. Soon after the wedding, and just four years after she had moved to Darwin, Diane was happily pregnant and convinced from the start that she would have a little boy. Nick was every inch the doting husband as his new wife blossomed and her belly swelled. Excitedly, the newlyweds prepared for the start of their family and when Diane was seven months pregnant they went along to the clinic for the ultrasound test that confirmed Diane was indeed expecting a son. If Diane was delighted then Nick, a proud Greek, was doubly so. The birth to come would not be straightforward but Diane had rarely felt as complete and as content as she did then, snuggled in at home with Nick as the monsoon rains lashed the windows, watching for the tiny kicks from inside her expanded midriff.

A few days before their baby's due date, the nervous couple drove to Darwin's private hospital for a planned Caesarean and, having arrived first thing in the morning, they had to endure an apprehensive wait until late in the afternoon before Diane was prepped and wheeled into theatre with Nick looking awkward and ill-fitted in the supplied medical scrubs.

At 4.41 pm on 20 February, the surgeon plucked an 8lbs 4oz baby boy from Diane's abdomen and held him for Diane to see before placing him gently on her chest. He was still smeared with blood and amniotic fluid, with the crinkled old-man features all newborns seem to share, but to Diane he was perfect; just beautiful, and she cried with the joy only a new mum can know, sniffled tears interspersed with embarrassed snorts of laughter at the wonder of it all. Beaming husband and new dad Nick grinned like a Cheshire cat and, in spite of feeling massively underqualified to do the job, he cut the umbilical cord with pride. The mewling infant had only just taken his first breaths but already he had a name as, in line with Greek tradition, he took his grandfather's moniker, Theo.

Diane felt overawed by the responsibility of caring for this precious, fragile bundle of life but, at the same time, she knew she was born for this task. She had met other new mums at the baby clinic and several became friends with whom she could share her concerns and new discoveries, and she also had Nick's mother on hand to offer advice. It remained hard for Diane that her own family was so far away and she was sad that her father would not get to see his grandson until he was 18 months old, but she had plenty to occupy her, bringing up this new boisterous bundle of joy.

As soon as he had grown old enough for Diane to know his frequent smiles were real and not just grimaces caused by wind, she took comfort from the fact he seemed to be happy throughout every day. If only he would sleep at night! He rarely did, which meant that Diane rarely did, but in spite of her exhaustion, nothing could dim her love for this child. Even after a sleepless night, she delighted in singing Twinkle Twinkle Little Star *to him and watching him try to make a star shape with his tiny little fingers as he gave her that infectious grin. When she wasn't cradling or feeding him she watched him for hours in his cot, singing Greek children's songs to soothe him to sleep.*

Theo was a plump little baby, prompting family and friends to want to pinch his rosy cheeks which grew redder as he began to teethe, sucking and chewing and dribbling over his favourite crocodile toy. In Darwin, it had to be a crocodile. Nick, like Diane, adored his son and could not show him off enough. Together they would push the baby buggy around the shops as fellow shoppers stopped to coo over the chubby cherub and comment on his cheeky face and gorgeous curly hair. At that moment, they seemed the perfect little family. But things would quickly change.

Chapter Five

Who hasn't wanted to jump into a taxi and tell the driver, 'Follow that cab!'? Now was my chance, but my mouth was drier than a saltpan in the Sahara and the words would not come out. We'd watched our would-be killers arrive and then leave the airport and we had the opportunity to get on the next available flight and escape. Instead we were about to chase after them. Why? As I saw it at the time, there were only three possible endings to the contract killing scenario and for me, as the target, only one of them was desirable. I didn't fancy option one – I got killed – or option two – I spent the rest of my life with a contract hanging over my head, knowing it could happen at any time. That only left option three – to sort out the issue with the hired contractors. I knew they were newly trained guys and my experience should give me the jump on them so I decided to take my chances and confront them, but that didn't make it an easy choice. It could all go horribly wrong.

It took a couple of seconds of hard swallowing before I managed to explain to our taxi driver that our friends were in the cab in front and that only they had the address of where we were going. As luck would have it, he got the picture, and stuck to them like glue. My heart was in my mouth when he jumped a red light to keep within sight of them, but every other driver seemed to treat the lights as purely advisory, so who would notice? Half an hour later we were back north of Chico Navarra barrio and I guessed where we were going even before the first taxi pulled up a discreet distance from the apartment that Rob and I had not long since vacated. I directed our cab to pull up some 50 metres behind and as the guys headed for a restaurant within watching distance of the apartment, our driver must have been more than a little bemused when I paid him his fare and Rob and I walked in completely the opposite direction from 'our friends'.

I needed to carry out a bit more surveillance on these guys before we did anything hasty. Fortunately for us, we had become familiar with our little neighbourhood and I knew there was another cafe close by where, over the previous few weeks, we had bought more of the local *arepa con queso* than was good for our waistlines. It had a table by the window from where we could see the outside seating of the restaurant our assassins had opted for. The pretty young waitress smiled in recognition as she served us two coffees but my mind was elsewhere, desperately trying to formulate a plan. Our 'friends' weren't about to make any sudden moves without getting the lie of the land – Stephen had trained them well – so I knew we had a bit of time. But after a short while I had seen enough and explained my plan to Rob who had that same nervous frown I'd seen in Florida, only now it was a permanent fixture.

Our assassins had deliberately chosen a restaurant in a public area so they could blend in as they carried out their surveillance, unaware that we were watching them watching out for us. I reckoned that could work in our favour. They wouldn't try anything while surrounded by people. At least, that's what I gambled. We waited as their restaurant filled up with punters grabbing their customary long lunch and then, after leaving enough cash to cover the cost of our unfinished coffees and a tip, we left the sanctuary of our own vantage point and walked towards our hired killers. The pavement was helpfully busy but the people walking towards me were a blur and my legs felt like jelly. What if I had miscalculated? What if these guys were more reckless than I thought? We closed the gap – 50 metres, 30 metres, 10 metres, trying to look as natural as possible but using the crowds of pedestrians as cover for our approach until the moment we arrived at the restaurant and were unavoidably exposed. I saw the startled look of recognition on the face of the first guy as he clocked us, but it was too late.

'Do you mind if we join you?' I asked, not waiting for a reply as Rob and I plonked ourselves in the two spare chairs at their table before our amigos could even get to their feet. 'Hi, I'm Darren. This is Rob. But, then, you know that, don't you?' I said. 'Perhaps we can talk about this over a beer?' The hunters had the look of prey and, somewhat sheepishly, nodded a cautious acceptance. An hour later, when a couple of beers had been followed by lunch, we had found common ground in our admiration for Stephen and our loathing for Victor and had reached an uneasy agreement. Rob and I would get out of Colombia, pronto, and they would spend a relaxing, and profitable, couple of days in Bogota before telling El Commandante that the birds had apparently flown.

With that, we hailed a taxi and very happily told the driver to take us to El Dorado Airport. Even so, I couldn't help the occasional glance over my shoulder to check whether we were being followed.

As it happened, I didn't have to worry about Victor. Not long after our escape he found himself laid up in hospital after a tandem skydive went wrong, injuring him and killing the young woman he had jumped out of a plane with; some poor innocent he had been trying to impress in the hope of later jumping into bed with. It was as he lay incapacitated in a hospital bed that his long-suffering, and clearly not-so-ignorant, wife chose to shop him to the FBI with details of his kidnap plot. I got a call out of the blue from the Feds and explained the whole story and they seemed happy with the way I had handled it. I can't say, with hindsight, that I was, but I'd emerged mercifully unscathed and with a renewed certainty that a change of career path might not be a bad thing. It really was time to keep my head down.

If nothing else, the episode had renewed my acquaintance with Stephen Mastalerz. I owed Stephen, big time, but maybe he had his own motives for calling me. His business was taking a new direction and he needed someone reliable to get on board. 'How do you fancy getting into child recovery?' he asked the next time we spoke. He told me some of the statistics for kids who are abducted each year around the world, sometimes from rich parents for ransom but more often by one parent from another after a relationship break-up. I was staggered. I had no idea of the scale of the problem, but the numbers were almost irrelevant. Behind every single statistic was an individual story of heartbreak; of a child being prevented from seeing one of their parents ever again, often fed a diet of lies to turn them against that missing parent in order to make the abduction easier; and of a loving mum or a dad going through the living bereavement that the loss of a child brings. I could not think how any person could do that to their own child, and to a former partner they had once loved enough to create that child with. I still can't. But as Stephen outlined his plan to help rescue children where the courts had ruled they had been illegally taken, it sounded to me like a chance to use all my skills on the side of justice; not just making money but putting right wrongs at the same time. I was up for it.

It was the start of an amazing series of adventures. Each fresh case became a logistical roller coaster for our small recovery team as well as an emotional roller coaster for the parent who had exhausted all official efforts to get their snatched child back and who had turned to us in desperation. What every good recovery case has in common, and the successful ones are sadly rare, is excellent pre-deployment planning, very good surveillance, an exceptionally good operation plan... and a great deal of luck. I have been involved in many abducted child recovery attempts now and, although I can generally block out my emotions for the sake of the job, it still saddens me to know that so many children throughout this world are treated like pawns in bitter relationship splits.

I enjoyed working with Stephen. He was ex-Special Boat Service (SBS) – the marine branch of the UK's elite Special Forces – but quiet and unassuming. He didn't need to shout about his Special Forces credentials. Those guys rarely do. He was short and stocky, very skilled in his craft and not someone who would stand any nonsense or suffer fools gladly. He oozed professionalism and I felt it rubbing off on me when I was in his presence. It felt good to work for Trojan Securities International, which was his company, and which reflected his very high standards. We were a small outfit but well trained and very competent and child recovery was just one aspect of our work.

We specialized in personal protection, hostage rescue, surveillance, counter-terrorism and the training of military and government personnel and I was always travelling and working in different countries. We won many contracts because of the high-class service we prided ourselves on and we had a select core of 'top shelf' clients who regularly used us because of our ability to get the job done. In some cases, parts of the US government used our services and we were known as much for the jobs we didn't take on as the ones we did because we would not agree to do something unless we were absolutely certain we could deliver. On one occasion a government body offered us two million dollars to extract a drug lord from a hacienda fortress in Mexico so he could stand trial for killing two Californian policemen. After determining that the operation required a helicopter and a diversion team as well as an extraction team, and after weighing up the risks, we turned it down.

We were good at what we did. We didn't need to oversell ourselves. No egos, no media, no advertising, no rip-offs and no illegal activities. The child recovery cases fitted in well to what we could offer. Most days were busy but it was a particularly hectic day in Trojan's Arkansas HQ one morning in June 2002 when the phone rang. On the other end of the line was a young guy called Peter, from a company in California which advises parents whose children have been abducted. They had contacted us before about our child recovery capabilities and wanted to recommend us to a client. Stephen took down the details and quizzed Peter on as much of the basic background as he could supply. We would not touch a case unless it was legit but this one seemed to have all the necessary court backing.

I wasn't in Arkansas but was with my parents in my hometown in Australia on a much-needed holiday and was sitting in the lounge catching up on news of the Filipino terror group Abu Sayyaf's latest atrocities on CNN. I had a particular interest in this region as I had knowledge of some upcoming surveillance and protection contracts in the southern Philippines for which the activities of the terrorists might well be relevant, but my attention was diverted by the ringing of my phone, with no caller ID showing. 'Hi mate, it's Stephen. How's your holiday?' he asked in that friendly way that immediately suggested it might be about to end. 'G'day, mate,' I answered, 'What's happening?' I had already been home for seven weeks and felt rejuvenated to the point of boredom. I was itching to get back in the saddle. 'I have a child recovery assignment in Greece, if you're interested,' Stephen said. I certainly was. A 5-year-old Australian boy had been abducted by his Greek father from his Scottish mother's legal custody.

Greece, where the dad had taken the boy, was a signatory to the 1980 Hague Convention (an agreement between countries to return children abducted from one member country to another). This meant it should be fairly straightforward to recover the child using legal channels, but it hadn't been so far and it would not prove to be anytime soon. The mother, who lived in Australia with her new husband, was at her wits' end trying to recover her adored son who, it transpired, hailed from Darwin.

Alarm bells began to ring in my head. I had worked in Darwin for three years doing security work and used it as a base for many of my international operations. It was full of Greek Australians and many people there knew I worked in the security industry but were unsure of my actual roles. The last thing I needed was for this job to follow me back to Australia. Greeks tend to take somewhat personally such matters as child rescue – or child kidnapping, as the father and his family would undoubtedly see it if we managed to pull this one off. But what the hell. We would be on the side of the law and I craved a new adventure, not to mention the chance to earn some money. 'What are the numbers?' I asked Stephen. 'We need to be careful with the client's money,' he said. 'She's not wealthy. She's had to take out a loan from the bank to fund this operation.' What parent wouldn't do everything they could to get their child back? I could sense her desperation already, but I had to keep emotions out of this. This was business. This was my job. 'Up to $1,000 a day,' Stephen went on, cutting to the chase. 'Capped at ten days.' The maths wasn't hard. Up to $10,000 each for the operation. 'Count me in,' I said.

Chapter Six

Perhaps love had blinded them to their differences, but the gap between Diane and Nick had widened following the birth of their son. The arguments had been petty, at first, but increasingly heated. The cultural divide was obvious and as Theo grew, the gulf separating them grew too. They both loved their son, of course, but they wanted different things for him; saw his development differently. As they each invested more of their love into their beloved toddler, they devoted less of it to each other until the chasm had become unbridgeable and the split inevitable.

None of that background had been the first consideration for those of us now being called upon to pick up the pieces. Every broken relationship has its explanations; its sad stories of human failings and lost love; its revelations, perhaps, of betrayal, jealousy, selfishness or even cruelty; or maybe just an amicable drifting apart. But when it comes to the time to call us in to recover an abducted child, things have gone way beyond that. Stephen had already begun much of the groundwork that we relied upon, starting with a list of questions for Peter to put to the mother. What court gave you legal custody? Can you send copies of the legal custodian papers with recent photos of the child and the father? What island is the child on and where is he living? If in a house, what does it look like? What other relatives have contact with the child? Does the child go to school? What is the father's name? Does he work? Does he have a criminal record? Does he own a weapon?

A flurry of emails had passed between Peter, the mother and Stephen. One from the mother, via Peter to Stephen, and forwarded to me, read: 'My son Theo is living with Nick and his grandmother on the island of Kalymnos. The nearest island to this is Kos. The population of Kalymnos is 18,000. The house is situated on a corner and the road goes in front of and then beside the house so it will be hard to do surveillance without being noticed. The local police have been ordered to pick up Theo on sight but they cannot do the job. The neighbours have been helping Nick out and sometimes look after Theo. The family use their phone often. Theo will be close to his grandmother. She absolutely adores him and will make sure that he does not leave her side.'

The mother expressed her personal opinion of the competence of the local police commissioner but we would have to judge that for ourselves. Stephen sent recent photos of the child and father on to me. The boy was a cherubic-looking kid, the spitting image of his father. What on earth was going on in the dad's head that he had decided to steal away his son knowing he was depriving the boy of his mum, never mind the pain he was causing his ex? How had things come to that? I couldn't afford to get emotionally involved but knowing the background could be useful in determining what issues we might face. I would find out, all in good time.

I busied myself chasing up and studying maps of Kalymnos and researching the local culture to give me some clue as to what to expect. Stephen was obtaining satellite images of the islands and touching base with his Greek contacts. A lot of work was being undertaken even before setting out on the operation. One thing I found out about the area that was vaguely relevant had been the 1991 disappearance of a British child from the nearby island of Kos. Ben Needham had been 21 months old when he went missing while his grandparents were babysitting him. The newspaper reports in the library didn't give me much insight into child abduction in the region, since the family was initially, and wrongly, suspected of involvement and no evidence of abduction had been found, but it did give me an insight into the workings of the local Greek police and it wasn't encouraging. Still, weighing up the risk versus the gain, I felt confident in getting involved. The mother was the sole custodian; Greece was a signatory under the Hague Convention; the police were aware of the case; and it was a small island on which to try to trace the child. There were also apparent escape routes for us if it all turned sour, as sometimes these things do.

Stephen had decided it would make sense if I escorted the mother, since we would both be coming from Australia, though escorting the parent was not something I was used to. Our normal operating procedure was to conduct surveillance for at least seven days to find a pattern of behaviour which would make recovering the child easy, and then have the parent fly over at the last minute to handle the child during the recovery – an absolute necessity because, in most countries, if we handle the child we are committing the offence of kidnap even though we are working for the legal guardian. I was always nervous about straying from tried and tested procedures but on this occasion it seemed to make sense.

Then Stephen bowled me another googly. He told me that Peter would be coming to Greece too. Peter's company had been involved in many international child recovery attempts before, I was told, and they wanted to send Peter as their representative to be part of the operation. Since the mother had contacted them and they had contracted us, they were in effect our employers, and another expert on the team would be helpful, I reasoned, particularly with his apparent experience. Stephen would still be the operation commander and I would be team member one. Though I was sceptical about conducting potentially hostile operations with people I hadn't worked with before, I accepted the benefits of having Peter along as team member two. After all, he was already involved, this stuff was his forte and he effectively held the purse strings. For a start, it was Peter's responsibility to organize the flights for the operation – for himself and Stephen from the USA to Greece and for the mother and me from Australia and back with, hopefully, an additional seat for the child on the way back.

It was by now mid-July and we would need to get arrangements made fairly promptly for the sake of the operation. It was the summer holiday season in Greece, which was relevant because Melbourne, where the mother now lived with her second husband, has a large Greek community so flight seats would quickly get booked up. After a few days, Stephen asked me to telephone the mother and introduce myself as she seemed to be getting anxious over the speed of progress. 'Hello Diane,' I said when I rang that Thursday night. 'My name is Darren. I work for Trojan Securities International and I'm currently in Australia.' She sounded relieved to hear from me. 'Oh, hello Darren,' she said. 'I'm pleased you rang. I was beginning to wonder what was happening.' The note of nervousness in her voice betrayed that much, but it was her soft Scottish accent which took me back a bit. I knew from the paperwork that she was originally from Scotland but I had just assumed she would sound more Australian.

'I wanted to introduce myself and let you know that I will be escorting you from Melbourne to Greece and back,' I went on. She sounded tense but there was a steely determination to her words and a business-like resolve forged, it would seem, through previous battles over her missing son. She expressed her concern about getting flights and I shared her anxiety, not having had any word from Peter on what bookings he had made, but I tried to put her mind at rest. 'I'll let Stephen know,' I said. 'But I want to reassure you that even though it may appear that things are not moving along, we are doing a lot of work in preparing for the recovery.' That seemed to pacify her a little. 'Oh good,' she said. 'It did seem as though nothing was being done. Do you think we will be there before the 15th of August?' I wasn't exactly sure of the significance but assumed it was to do with the school holidays. 'We should be there within the next three weeks,' I said, and I hoped I was right.

I emailed Stephen to let him know we needed the plane tickets as soon as possible or we ran the risk of not being able to get a seat. The mother, understandably, was keen to go as soon as possible though we had other considerations to bear in mind. When 15 August came and went with still no word from Peter, she emailed Stephen to say she wanted to go the following week. He suggested holding off until 9 September when the schools were back, in case Theo was attending school on the island. It would make it far easier to establish a routine if the child was coming and going to school at set times. Recovering a child while they are on holiday is more challenging as there is no set pattern to their movement.

Stephen told the mother, and Peter, that he would be in Memphis instructing the Tennessee Special Weapons and Tactics (SWAT) team for a week but would be free after that. We were all set to go but when I had still heard nothing from Peter by 25 August I rang Stephen. 'Hey mate, it's Skippy. What's the latest update?' I asked. 'I'm still waiting for Peter to organize the flights, then we are good to go,' he said. 'If he doesn't pull his finger out soon we'll be travelling from Oz by boat,' I said, trying to tone down my annoyance. 'Because there won't be any seats left on any flights.'

I was starting to get a bad feeling about Peter. His lack of organization and time management skills did not sit well with me, and it didn't bode well for the operation. Four hours later I got a telephone call from the mother. 'Hi Darren. It's Diane. I've booked the tickets. They're for tomorrow. You can leave tomorrow, can't you?' She had clearly got fed up waiting for Peter. I told her it shouldn't be a problem once I'd checked with Stephen. 'My girlfriend is a travel agent and was able to get us on the last seats available, but we are waitlisted for the return,' she explained. 'Your Virgin Blue flight to Melbourne leaves Sydney at 1 pm and we leave Melbourne at 7.10 pm with Emirates.'

Sydney? Who told her I was in Sydney? I was a couple of hours outside Brisbane and a fourteen-hour drive from Sydney! The operation was starting to go wrong and I hadn't even left my home country. With much organizing, I found my way to Sydney in time for the pre-arranged flight. If this organizational cock-up was an example of Peter's expertise I was not impressed. Sadly, it was to be an omen for things to come.

Chapter Seven

The slim blonde loitering in front of the check-in desks looked stressed. The attendant's attempts to catch her eye and beckon her forward went unheeded and she was oblivious to the steady trickle of passengers who shuffled their heavy suitcases along the floor to overtake her in the queue, if indeed she was any part of the queue. Her demeanour was fidgety and her eyes repeatedly scanned the busy departure hall, desperately looking for someone. That someone was me. I felt a pang of guilt at letting her wait but I needed to watch for a few minutes more.

I had arranged to meet the mother at the Emirates airline counter at Melbourne International Airport at 4 pm and she had told me she'd be wearing navy blue tracksuit trousers and a sky blue shirt. From force of habit I had arrived an hour early and had observed the counter from a distance until ten minutes before our scheduled meeting time when I had sat myself some 50 metres from the check-in desk in a lounge where I could watch the area from behind a magazine. It sounds melodramatic but it pays to know who might be lurking in the background. Melbourne, as I mentioned, has a large Greek community and this assignment had been discussed widely by phone and email. Had Diane told anyone beside her husband, and us, of her plan to try to recover her son? Had word slipped out to the father's extended family or friends? It was the sort of thing I needed to know.

During one child recovery we attempted in Central America, and unknown to me at the time, the abductor and the people close to him knew that the mother was in town looking for her son. She was subsequently fed misinformation that her son would be at an airport at a certain time waiting to board a particular flight and we immediately headed for the airport, split up and searched the departure terminal. The child was nowhere to be found but I'm pretty sure that we were under surveillance from the father, or the people he hired. They already knew what the mother looked like, of course, but, if they were at the airport as I suspect, then they also knew what I looked like. Needless to say, we didn't get anywhere near the child after that because the abductors were able to stay one step ahead of us at all times. Distance can be the difference between success and failure in my line of work and, in the most extreme cases, between life and death.

I knew that it was the mother looking anxious by the Emirates counter because of the navy blue tracksuit trousers and sky blue top. I couldn't be sure, yet, whether her stress was a culmination of months of battling to get her son back or because of the latest complication of trying to rendezvous with a man she had never met before and wouldn't recognize. At least she was early, which gave me a few minutes to check for any suspicious persons who might be following her. When I was satisfied that everything appeared normal, I approached the still fretful lady. 'Diane?' I asked, though I knew the answer. A nervous smile suffused her face, replacing her frown. 'Darren?' she replied.

She was of medium height, approximately 30 years old, with piercing blue eyes beneath her long blonde hair. I couldn't help but notice how attractive she was, but it was her look of relief that struck me most, though that was perhaps to be expected. She had handed over a sizeable amount of money to a foreign charity but had only had contact by emails and telephone calls from the charity and a sub-contracted security company. She had contacted Peter via the internet and sent money to him; had emailed Stephen and had spoken to me once by telephone. She had not met anyone face-to-face and now she was about to go overseas with three male strangers on a hazardous mission to try to recover her son. It was all pretty daunting. At least now she had met one of us in the flesh.

I was relieved as well. It wasn't my money on the line, and I was used to working alone, but after all the false starts and the organizational chaos, mostly conducted electronically across different time zones, it was nice to actually meet the person we were working for. I immediately took a liking to her. We checked our bags in together and collected our boarding passes. Normally I would arrange to sit a few rows back and to the side of the subject, so I could watch them without appearing to be associated with them, but for this trip I thought it better to travel sitting together so I could gather more information on the way over and, if we were to be successful, offer more security for the mother and her child on the way back.

My luggage consisted of a large backpack, which I put in the hold, and a small daysack as carry-on luggage. The selection of bags, like my casual clothes, was intended to make me look like a tourist in Greece, since there wasn't really any better way to disguise the intentions of a 6ft 4ins, blond, blue-eyed security operative. After we had checked in our luggage we sat in one of the airport cafes and chatted. I was full of questions. Probably because of my PSYOPS background, I was keen to know the psychological makeup of the father as I usually see the abductor as being the main threat in any rescue equation. I wanted to get into his shoes and know how his mind ticked, but the mother got her questions in first. 'Do you think we can get Theo back?' she asked, putting me straight on the spot. It was the $64,000 question, and the reason we were travelling around the world, after all. 'Yes, we'll get him back,' I said as confidently as I could. 'How can you be so sure?' she pressed. 'Because we have everything on our side,' I replied.

It was true. We did have everything on our side, particularly in a legal sense, although we did not necessarily have *everyone* on our side. She seemed far from convinced. I could see that the ordeal of losing her son, and her fruitless attempts to get him back, had taken its toll on her. She looked like she hadn't slept in days, had dark bags under her eyes and her fingernails were chewed short. The wedding band on her finger moved as she waved her hand to make a point, presumably because she had lost a lot of weight recently. 'So, how do you think you will do this?' she asked. It was way too early for us to have settled on a definitive plan, though we had an idea of how we would proceed. 'I'm not really sure at this early stage,' I told her. 'But we will do plenty of surveillance and find a pattern in their current lifestyle. Ultimately, we want to find a moment when Theo will be by himself, which would make our job much easier, but it might just be that we knock on the door with the authorities behind us, carrying the legal paperwork, and you walk out with Theo.' Her face fell. 'Oh not the authorities, Darren!' she said, with fear in her voice. 'They can't be trusted.'

'Well, we don't really know how we are going to do it just yet,' I continued, truthfully. 'As I said, first we do surveillance to make sure Theo is on the island, and then we work out when would be the best time to recover him. Next we arrange support and put a plan of action into place. Only then would we conduct the recovery, which is where you will come in. You will grab Theo and we will make our pre-arranged escape.'

Another look of alarm came over her. 'I grab him?' she questioned, raising her voice. 'Yes, well, if we grabbed him it would be regarded as kidnapping,' I explained. 'Only the legal custodian can recover the child under the Hague Convention, Diane.' She pulled a face. 'Oh, no. I'm scared now, Darren. No one has said anything to me about needing to grab Theo. That's what I thought you guys would be doing.'

Surely Peter had explained this to her. This was meant to be his area of expertise and this was basic stuff. I tried to calm her. 'We can't, you see. Only you can physically touch Theo. If we did that and the escape was unsuccessful, we would all go to jail, including you. We will protect you until that moment by not saying you are on the island, although it won't take long for the authorities to work out you are in Greece,' I explained gently. 'Oh my God, Darren,' she said. 'I'm not sure I can do that.'

It was clearly the fear of the authorities and the legal processes, not the thought of holding her beloved son again, that spooked her. 'Diane,' I said. 'If there is one last chance of ever being with Theo and you are presented with that chance, I know you can do it. You have come so far, done so much and risked such a lot, I'm sure. I know you can do it. If you can't, at any stage of this operation, then you can say "stop" and we will abort the recovery.' That seemed to calm her. 'OK, Darren, thanks,' she said. 'I hope I can be strong enough. We cannot stop this job at all. I want my Theo back.'

I waited for her to regain her composure before I asked her any more questions but, again, she got in first, explaining why she had not realized she would have to physically grab her son at the climax of any recovery. 'My husband said that you guys would probably kick down doors, tie Nick and his mother up and grab Theo,' she said. Now it was my turn to look surprised. 'No, that's not the way we do things,' I said, smiling at the difference between public perception and reality. 'That might be the way they do it in the movies, but we only work within the law and, besides, we have the legal documentation so there is no need for it.'

I have heard of some companies operating like this, but the results were horror stories, with no successful recoveries made. In one particular case in Russia the mafia had kidnapped a billionaire's son. When a team assembled by the father went in to recover the child, kicking down doors and the like, it quickly turned bad. They recovered the child but, as they were making their escape, all of them were shot and killed, including the child. I didn't mention that case to the mother, of course. She was anxious enough without scaring the living daylights out of her.

As she continued, it became clear that not all of her far-fetched ideas had come direct from Hollywood. Remarkably, even the child recovery charity that had contracted us seemed to have a hazy grasp of the facts. 'Peter said that you might drug Nick's drink while he is out in a bar,' she went on. 'Really?' I said, bemused, and not just because I couldn't think what drugging the father would achieve. I didn't know much about Peter – apart from his dubious organizational skills – and nor had I been contracted to work for his particular organization before, but I was starting to wonder what type of security teams he had sub-contracted to help him in the past. Russian underworld, perhaps? On top of that, why would this woman want to recover her child in such circumstances?

It was clear that she desperately wanted her son back at all costs. That bit, I understood. But was it for the love of the child or a desire for retribution against the father? I needed to know more, but this poor woman appeared more confused and nervous than vengeful. 'Darren, I'm afraid,' she said. 'What if it doesn't work out?' I really didn't have a good answer. Well, not a pre-prepared answer, anyway. I could only offer the truth. 'If it doesn't work out, I'm afraid you have probably used your last chance. Your element of surprise will have gone and Theo will likely be moved to a more secure location, making another recovery attempt very difficult,' I said. 'But I am sure it will go according to plan.'

'Oh my God, I hope so,' she said before adding: 'What if he finds out?' I looked at her. 'He?' A frown wrinkled her forehead. 'Nick!' she replied, and I understood her concern. If he was capable of abducting his son and keeping him beyond the reach of the boy's mother, what else was he capable of? 'Then the operation is aborted, Diane. What is important is the safety of Theo and all of us,' I explained as gently as I could. 'Then I will lose him forever,' she said, staring into the distance, her eyes filling with tears.

It was clear that at that moment we were having very different thoughts. An aborted operation to me meant we had been compromised and our safety and well-being, including that of the child and the mother, was in jeopardy, but an aborted operation to her meant never seeing her child again, and I could see how, in her mind, that trumped any physical danger she might face.

We continued getting to know each other as we waited to board our flight for Greece. Our cheap, last-minute tickets were going to take us from Melbourne to Athens via Singapore, Dubai and Cyprus and, collectively, take around twenty-seven hours, so I knew there would be time for plenty more searching queries. Once the captain had switched off the seat belt sign following take-off, and it felt like we were properly on our way, I said: 'So, tell me, how did all this happen? Why are you in this position?' Her eyes looked sadder than ever and, with a gentle sigh she said: 'This has been one long nightmare for me, Darren.'

She explained her background in more detail than I needed to know but I was not about to stop her. It seemed to help her to talk it through. She told me about finishing her nursing degree in Glasgow, about meeting Nick on the island of Kalymnos and about falling in love. She told me about the move to Darwin and about getting married. It was only when she told me about Theo's birth that the sparkle returned to her eyes, but the light dimmed as she explained how things had quickly turned sour. They had divorced before Theo had even started nursery school and Diane had gone on to remarry. She and her ex had gone through the Darwin law courts to decide custody of Theo and she had won, but she had remained cooperative and let Nick see his son regularly, and arrangements seemed amicable. That was until Nick had asked to take 4-year-old Theo with him on a five-week holiday to Kalymnos and she had agreed.

She was six weeks pregnant with her second child when she received a message at work to tell her that her ex was not coming back from Greece and nor, therefore, was her son. 'I was told at my workplace, Darren,' she said as she wiped welling pools of moisture from her eyes. 'My lawyer received a fax from his lawyer stating that he would not be coming back and I was notified at my workplace that my son wasn't coming home. I was absolutely gutted. My legs just collapsed under me; just buckled underneath me. It ripped my heart out.' That had been fourteen months before and she had been fighting every day since to get her son back.

I tried not to show my emotions. I needed to stay a strong and calming influence. 'So, your second child,' I began, distracting myself by doing the maths. 'My daughter is just six months old,' she said, answering my unfinished question. 'I had to stop breastfeeding her in order to make this trip. My husband, my mother-in-law and a very good friend of mine are looking after her, which is very hard for me. As a mother, it's just horrific having one child in one country and one child in another country but I had to come. I just had to, Darren. I've already missed Theo's fifth birthday. It's been fourteen months now and time is of the essence because if it's left any longer... .' She gulped as she struggled to complete her sentence. 'If it's left any longer, he might not want to come home.'

The young man to our left shuffled in his aisle seat and I turned, ready to have a word with him about listening in to other people's conversations, but he was just adjusting his headphones to better hear the in-flight movie in which he was already engrossed. I swivelled back to Diane, fighting the sting of salty water in my own eyes as she turned away to hide the evidence of more tears flowing from her own. Looking out of the window at the carpet of white clouds below us, she said: 'This really is my last chance.' Just why that was would soon become clear.

Chapter Eight

The air hostess gave me a withering look as she backed her trolley down the aisle just as I offered Diane a tissue to dry her eyes. Goodness knows what she thought I might have said to upset this fragile woman, or what she thought our relationship was. Obviously, there was no relationship, but Diane was already more than just another client; no longer simply 'the mother'. Mercifully the drone of the engines reverberating through the plane and the white noise of the air conditioning and numerous other conversations had masked our very personal conversation from any prying ears, and the arrival of the first of several in-flight meals gave Diane a chance to recover her composure.

We picked at our food in virtual silence as I gave her breathing space to get her head straight. 'I think it might have been talk of babies that made Nick flip,' she said at last, after the remnants of her barely eaten meal had been taken away by the still-suspicious stewardess. She explained how the shared care of Theo had settled into an uneasy pattern as both she and her ex moved on into different relationships after their divorce. 'It was normal access, every second weekend, Friday at 5 pm 'til Sunday at 5 pm,' she said. 'But that changed when Theo went to school. I did give Nick extra access to Theo too. I was quite... I never said "No" to him. If he wanted an extra day because they were having relatives over, or whatever, I was quite, you know, flexible. But it was never enough and I think he worried because the Australian way favours the mother, doesn't it? Mothers are usually the primary carers. I think he started to panic about his and his family's relationship with Theo. That's all I can think of,' she said, and I nodded. 'He didn't agree with Theo going to day care for a few hours every week,' she explained. 'He didn't agree with that because, you know, the Greek grandparents do everything. I think it was just a cultural thing and I think he just thought he was losing... I don't really know, but there was just no compromise with him.'

I could sense the tension that led up to the situation I now found myself tasked with resolving, and Diane was still trying, and failing, to rationalize it. 'When Theo turned 4, Nick got married again, to a Greek girl from Sydney. I thought that would have settled things down but clearly not. Her relatives had been from Kos so the pair of them had wanted to go back there for a honeymoon, to Kos and Kalymnos, which a lot of Kalymnian people do,' said Diane, and with that she gave a shrug and a wry smile. 'I mean,' she added, 'I'd rather go somewhere else on my honeymoon than go home, to be honest, but they wanted to take Theo with them and, really, according to the court orders, I couldn't say no because, as far as the court is concerned, his father is from a different country and his mother is from a different country and each parent is entitled to take the child back to their home country for a holiday. It didn't matter that I had a bad feeling about it. Nothing bad had happened previously and the court doesn't act on hearsay. Nick had taken him on holiday before and returned him, after all. I think I was just uneasy because Theo was only just 4 and it was overseas, so that's just a mother's anxiety, but I never thought in a million years Nick would not bring him home.'

Diane looked out of the window. Then, facing me again, she told me how she had found out she was pregnant only a week or so before Theo was to go away and how she and her husband had excitedly told him that he was going to have a baby brother or sister in a few months. She had consoled herself, as she lovingly packed a small suitcase for him, with the fact that she was allowed to ring Theo whenever she wanted while he was away and that, according to the solicitor's undertaking that Nick had signed vowing to bring him back after five weeks, he had to ring her once a week to let her know how Theo was. 'He rang me one time and it was OK,' she said. 'But the second time he rang he told me to make it quick and, before handing the phone to Theo, he said to me, "Theo keeps talking to me about a baby. Whose is the baby? What's this baby?" So I told him, "I'm having a baby," and that was it. He didn't call the next week and I think it was because of that conversation that he did what he did.'

Nick's decision not to return from Greece with Theo was, insisted Diane, just as much of a shock to his new wife, who had expected to be returning to Darwin on the return tickets they had. So, his decision to abduct his son didn't sound premeditated, I thought, but now Theo was back on Kalymnos and with his grandmother. How much did she know about it beforehand? I didn't get a chance to ask the question before an announcement from the stewardess told us the captain had switched on the seat belt signs, just in case we hadn't noticed the illuminated pictogram above our heads and the sudden, stomach-churning lurch as the plane flew into a patch of turbulence. I looked at Diane in case she needed reassurance but she seemed totally unfazed, perhaps because she was tougher than she looked, or because her mind was completely absorbed by her story. Or both.

As soon as we had stopped kangarooing through the sky, Diane explained how she had immediately got a ruling from the courts in Darwin that Theo must be returned and how the Greek authorities were alerted but the police on Kalymnos reported back that they could not find Theo anywhere. That was in spite of the fact Nick and Theo were spotted on a Greek TV current affairs programme, holding hands as they walked along the harbour, with a policeman writing a traffic ticket in the background. Diane clearly believed that her ex was keeping their son on the island with the full support of the local community, including the police. 'They are just one big family and everybody sticks together and this is how they have kept him for so long,' she said. 'I have had a whole island against me.'

When Diane became exasperated by the failure of the local police she sought the help of the court on the neighbouring, larger island of Kos, and was temporarily encouraged when the judge, accepting that she was the legal custodian and that Greece was a signatory to the Hague Convention, issued a finding against Nick and a court order for police to execute, demanding that Theo be handed back to her. Nick had apparently appealed, lost, and promptly disappeared, holing up with Theo in a monastery on Kos for forty or fifty days, so the court order was never executed. In desperation, Diane tried to have Nick charged and jailed for abduction in the hope he would hand over Theo. He was convicted but got a suspended sentence and still kept Theo as the Greek interpretation of the Hague Convention was that only a parent could hand over the child; that the police could not seize the boy. Since Nick was not cooperating and wouldn't let Diane anywhere near their son, the court order and the Hague Convention were worthless.

I was beginning to understand why Diane was at the end of her tether and I was becoming as concerned as she was about some of the difficulties we might face. 'So, then you contacted us?' I ventured, but she gave me a look of pity, like I didn't know the half of it. 'No, that was well after,' she said. 'I then decided to take matters into my own hands and hired some security experts in Greece.' Now it was my turn to give Diane a quizzical look. 'This should be interesting,' I thought, as we prepared for landing and a tedious change of planes. It turned out that she hired a Greek specialist security team consisting of some off-duty police officers and their buddies but their attempt to recover Theo failed when a local court secretary tipped Nick off about the operation. That had cost Diane and her husband 10,000 Australian dollars and got them absolutely nowhere.

I could understand her frustration but I wasn't especially surprised. I once set up an arrest and extraction operation with the police in the Caribbean. We had surrounded a hotel where the father and his abducted son were known to be hiding but when the police kicked down the door the man and boy were nowhere to be seen. To this day I am sure the police had an insider who tipped the father off. Nobody wants things to get messy, particularly the police, but after all the effort and pre-planning that went into the operation, it was heart-wrenching to have to break the news to the boy's mother that we had failed.

Back in Melbourne, Diane lobbied the Greek consulate, threatening them with unfavourable press coverage in the run up to the 2004 Olympic Games which were to be held in Athens, and her case had aired on CNN and a current affairs programme in Melbourne and been reported in various newspapers in Australia. Even the Australian Prime Minister, John Howard, on a visit to Greece, had been asked by the Attorney General's department to raise the case of little Theo with the Greek President. She didn't know if he had done, but she had been running out of options by the time she heard about us. 'I have tried every avenue within the law, and the law has so far failed me,' she said. 'I heard about Peter's charity after reading about it in a women's magazine and he told me about Trojan Securities so I looked you up on the internet. I knew this was my last option, that we didn't have a choice, and that I just needed to raise the money to pay for your help. I went to my bank manager to ask for a loan and he asked me what I needed the money for, so I told him.' I could just imagine the refusal she would have got from most hard-nosed bank managers. 'What did he say?' I asked. Diane smiled. 'He said, "Do it!"' She clearly had a more understanding bank manager than most of us. 'It was 60,000 dollars,' she replied in anticipation of my follow-up question.

I knew she had many legal fees and she had given $30,000 to Peter's agency for the recovery, to include the cost of hiring us. I started to do the maths in my head and concluded that the operation couldn't drag on as there was barely enough money for a fortnight at most. Diane and her new husband had mortgaged their future on a gamble that they might be able to get her son back. If I didn't realize before I certainly knew now that the stakes could hardly be higher. I could see that just telling me the case history was taking its toll on Diane, but it was something she felt she absolutely had to do.

With the cabin lights dimmed, the shutters down and passengers sleeping all around us, she finally closed her eyes and let exhaustion overtake her, but my mind was still whirring. I was sure she had told her story countless times, adding a new injustice with every update, and I sensed we were just another chapter in her horror story, but I hoped, really hoped that this was going to be the last chapter. Something inside of me wanted this operation to be successful for more than just professional pride. She had touched my heart. This was her last chance to be reunited with her child.

As Diane slept my own thoughts shifted to Theo. What does he think of all this, if he knows any of it? What does he think of his father? Where would he like to live and who with? Will he get a say in it? I hadn't met the boy but I cared about his thoughts beyond the officialdom of a court order. I remember conducting surveillance on a 13-year-old abducted boy in the Dutch Antilles. He was having a whale of a time riding jet skis, playing with remote model aeroplanes and swimming in the ocean. He was a happy boy yet there I was planning to take him away from that life and escort him back with his mother to Amsterdam. At the time I wondered if the courts always really acted in the best interests of the child.

But it wasn't my decision. I didn't know the ins and outs of Theo's current life, nor the life that he would have if our operation was successful, so I just needed to focus on the job at hand and ensure that the court order was carried out. I already knew from my long chats with Diane that it would be easier said than done, but I was determined to do all I could. This was the first time I had actually got close to a client. We had spent a great deal of time talking about the case and getting to know one another and I felt a lot more sympathy for Diane than I normally would for a client. Would that be a good thing or a bad thing? Only time would tell. It helped that I was now fully informed and aware about the case and its history. On the other hand, if you become emotionally attached you conduct the operation with your heart and not your mind, which can lead to mistakes and anything from an aborted mission to finding yourself or a team member detained or even killed.

In the Caribbean, my female client phoned my hotel room very late one night and requested I join her for a chat and bring a bottle of wine. I asked her if we would be discussing the operation and she said, 'No', she just wanted to get to know me. I apologized and told her I was busy planning the next day's mission and left it at that. Had I been unprofessional and got involved, I might have pressured myself into taking unwarranted risks just to please her and it is never good to mix business with pleasure, especially when your business is a risk to your life.

After twenty-seven hours' flying, including transfers, and getting more and more information, I was convinced that this assignment was going to be anything but a trouble-free gig. I also knew that I would need to sit down and explain a lot of background to Stephen before we could begin to formulate a plan. My thoughts were interrupted by the cabin lights coming up and a voice that took me by surprise. 'Good morning ladies and gentlemen. We will soon be serving breakfast before landing at Athens International Airport.'

Chapter Nine

The heat hit the moment we stepped off the plane. It was a stifling 38 degrees and the air was dry and hazy, like walking into a brick wall. The landscape hit me the same way as we drove into the city. It was arid and dusty and a maze of concrete walls, enlivened occasionally by the graffiti on the buildings that lay derelict, and there were plenty of them. I clearly wasn't seeing the best of Athens, but maybe I wasn't looking. In my defence, I was exhausted after the long series of flights. The city obviously had its plus points, though most of them were ancient ruins.

Our taxi dropped us off in front of a typically dilapidated edifice. Any claim it might have had to a proud heritage had been lost to the noise and fumes of the busy road that now ran past its façade on its way to the major new shopping centre just a couple of kilometres away. It was perfect. Nobody was going to be looking for us in the grubby Hotel Anatole. We checked in, with Diane's room two doors down from mine. Apart from the fact that it was cheap, so we wouldn't be eating too much into Diane's limited funds, I was happy that it was anonymous, in a particularly low-profile area of the city, though I could just about see a corner of the Acropolis if I leaned precariously out of the small window high up on the wall of my bathroom and peered at an angle.

Unlike Stephen, I hadn't worked in Greece before and my natural suspiciousness was kicking in, not helped by the shockingly lax passport checks at the airport. 'I hope they improve on that before the 2004 Olympics,' I thought after the immigration officer took my passport, stamped it and handed it back to me without once looking at me, and this was less than a year after 9/11. My normal operational kit bag consists of surveillance equipment, self-defence items and disguises, but I'd left much of it at home. Posing as a tourist on a tourist island wasn't going to require any special disguises and I'd originally been led to believe we would only be gone for ten days on a fairly straightforward case.

My long chats with Diane had put me right on that score and now I felt naked without many of the tools of my trade. That's probably why I was happy to check in to such a nondescript hotel.

What I wasn't happy about was that we were still in limbo. It was now Monday, 26 August and I didn't know when Stephen and Peter were going to arrive. Nor was I convinced that they knew either, but I was anxious to get to an internet cafe to try to find out their flight details. Diane had more reason than me to be anxious. Some guy named Peter, whom she had never met, had all the money she had borrowed for this operation and had given her no satisfactory details about when he would make contact. She remembered only that he had emailed her saying that he would arrive in Athens on Wednesday at 11.50 but that was hardly specific. Was that 11.50 am or 11.50 pm, ie 2350 hours? He was clearly not a military man and his imprecision might mean we had to make two visits to the airport, with the extra exposure that involved.

'Darren, surely I don't need to worry about walking around here in Athens?' Diane asked, perhaps picking up on my cautiousness. 'Well, that depends. Does Nick have any relatives here?' I asked. 'No,' she replied. 'Then it should be fine. We'll only be going between the shopping centre and the hotel, and we're pretty out of the way here anyway.' We looked like a normal couple on holiday; not a new couple holding hands, just two people comfortable in each other's company. There was, realistically, nothing to make us stand out apart, perhaps, for my 6ft 4ins frame.

In the course of answering Diane I had managed to quell some of my own misgivings. That was until we found an internet cafe and I checked my emails. Nothing. Not a word from Stephen or Peter. I emailed Stephen and told him of our safe arrival, gave him the contact details and the location of our hotel and mentioned the fragile emotional state of our client. Most of our overseas communication was conducted via the internet, which remained a relatively secure means of communication, depending on the type of server and provider, though following 9/11 we were more aware of the degree to which email traffic was being monitored and how certain words were flagged up to trigger recording devices. We were always careful not to mention words such as 'kidnap', 'abduction', 'police', 'FBI', 'CIA', etc. Although we operate within the law, we work on the principle that the fewer people who know our business, the better.

With nothing to do but wait, Diane and I found a restaurant for lunch and she began asking me more questions. 'How long have you been doing this type of work?' she queried. I thought about it for a moment. 'A couple of years,' I said. 'Though I mainly specialize in surveillance and protection.' Diane gave a little laugh. 'Well, I feel safe, given the size of you! Are you married?' I blushed a little. 'No. It's difficult to live this type of lifestyle and be married. I don't want any distractions. I just want to focus on my job.' Her question had sounded flirtatious but I sensed she was just softening me up for the question that was really bothering her. 'Have you had success in recovering other children?' she asked at last. I wasn't about to pretend that jobs like this were easy, or that they had a high success rate. 'Yes,' I said. 'We have, but sometimes the parent doesn't want to proceed with the recovery.' Diane looked confused. 'Why wouldn't the parent want to continue?' she asked. 'People have different reasons,' I explained. 'I guess some of the common ones are that they see their child happy on the surveillance tapes, or they run out of money, or they fear for their child getting hurt in the recovery.'

The truth of the matter is that we have had many successful recoveries of a child. It is the successful escape that has sometimes eluded us. Diane looked perturbed so I didn't elaborate further and we finished our lunch. When we returned to the internet cafe to see if there were any emails for us it was my turn to look dismayed. There was still no email from Stephen and nothing from Peter. It was now Monday night and my sense of frustration was growing.

I slept more from exhaustion than comfort but woke on Tuesday morning feeling a bit brighter. When I checked on Diane to see if she was OK I found she was holding up well and eagerly awaiting the arrival of the rest of the team, whenever that might be. We walked back to the shopping centre, to the internet cafe, to check our emails and at last I had one from Stephen: 'Skippy, Glad to see you've made it safely. Peter has finally organized my flight. I shall be arriving Thursday on Delta Air Lines flight DA 751 at 1050 hours. I have passed your hotel details onto Peter. Will only have enough time for a coffee before moving on. Need to get to the island straight away. I don't know about Peter, will have to play it by ear. I have a contact in Greece – from a guy I once trained. He may be useful if we need him. My guy's contact is Mikali and his phone number is ***-****. Give him a ring and introduce yourself. I've spoken to his boss, my contact, and he'll be expecting your call. Memphis was good fun, mate. You would have liked it. Will be good to catch up with you again. See you then, Stephen.'

Great! At least now I knew when he was arriving, and Diane was equally relieved when I told her. Finally, after fourteen months of heartache, things were starting to fit into place, although we were still unsure when Peter would arrive, if at all. We grabbed some lunch and chatted. Diane told me how her life had changed completely because of her ordeal, how much this job was costing her and how repaying the loan was going to impact on her life and the lives of her family for the next fifteen years. This was not the first time she had told me this and it wouldn't be the last. Because I didn't usually escort the parent I was not used to this kind of emotional pressure but my focus had to be on the recovery of the child. I did my best to appear to be listening, but at the same time I was trying to let it go over my head. It wasn't easy.

When we returned to the hotel, Diane went for a rest while I started planning for the operation. I needed a good description of the house, and even a floor plan should we need to enter the house, so I had asked Diane if she could draw me a sketch of what the house looked like from the front and if she could draw a floor plan complete with the location of furniture, from memory. I knew it was asking a lot, several years after she had last been there, but anything she could provide would help. While she put any architectural skills she had to use, I went back to the shopping centre, and the internet cafe, to organize transport from Athens to Kos. The flights departed at 7 am, 11 am and 5 pm. Since Stephen was due to arrive at 10.50 am, I knew we wouldn't make the 11 am flight and would have to wait for the later one so I booked four tickets on the 5 pm, presuming that Peter would have arrived some time on the Wednesday. I also got information from a travel agent on all the possible modes of transport to and from Kos and Kalymnos, their timings and costs. Next, I set my mind to finding a location for a briefing during the six hours' downtime we would have between Stephen's arrival and our flight to Kos.

I waited until I got back to the hotel and rang our Greek contact Mikali who, I gathered from Stephen, was an Athens police officer in the anti-terrorism unit and was working on the protection detail for the US Embassy in the Greek capital. I went through a few security questions to check I was talking to the right person and that he was expecting my call and then asked if he could help us with a secure location for a team briefing, for four people. I kept the details vague, telling him we were there to protect a client who would be flying in on Thursday, and he seemed surprised that one of our team was a woman. 'She's one of our best female operatives and is bilingual,' I said. Next, I knocked on Diane's door to see if she wanted to eat dinner.

We agreed to meet in the hotel lobby in an hour and she handed me a sketch and floor plan of the father's house which was admirably detailed. 'It's a double-storey, white cement house with a workshop cellar,' she explained, pointing to her drawings. 'It has a small patio at the front with a small table and chair and stairs going up to the front door. Nick parks his motorcycle, here, on the left-hand side of the stairs and there is a very small balcony on the second floor, only 2 feet wide. The windows have shutters on the outside and they are a reddish-brown colour, as well as the main door... at least they were, unless they've been repainted. There is no garden or yard. When you step off the stairs you are on the road. The bottom floor is open space with a kitchen, laundry and living room. Upstairs there are three bedrooms. Nick is here in the front right corner, Theo will be here in the rear right corner, I think, and Nick's mother is here in the rear left.'

I now had a good description of the house and was pretty sure I could recognize it on sight. I wanted to start laying out the case information, maps and drawings without making the room look like a security operations centre to any domestic staff who might walk in. Fortunately, there was a large framed painting of a bowl of fruit hanging on the wall. I turned it round and pinned the planning material to the back, then turned it back and left the room.

We ate at a nearby Italian restaurant, al fresco, and the food was great. The area might have been run down but I had one of the best spaghetti carbonara dishes I have ever had. Maybe things were looking up. I told Diane that I had bought the airline tickets for Kos, to let her know that things were happening. 'What about Peter? We don't know when he'll be here,' she said. 'Well, he has our contact details and we haven't heard from him,' I said. 'There's a plane ticket for him if he arrives but we can't wait for him for ever. We need to get going and start the operation.' I could sense Diane's frustration. I was equally frustrated. 'If he said he will be here tomorrow then I guess he will be here', I said. 'I will move out of my room tomorrow morning to get a room with two beds to cater for Peter. When he arrives he will hopefully either ring us or get a taxi straight to the hotel.' At this, Diane relaxed a little. 'How can you be so calm and sure of yourself?' she asked. I smiled. 'Because I know what has to be done and when it gets done things will fall into place.'

I could have added that it was from years of experience and from being in much more dangerous situations than this, but none of that seemed relevant. Yet. 'If it wasn't for you, Darren, I would be a nervous wreck,' she said. It was more a statement than a compliment. To me, she already looked like a nervous wreck. After waiting for fourteen months, full of anger and frustration, she realized the moment of truth had arrived. It was now or never; her last chance. Perhaps it was because of this stark reality that she was having doubts as to whether the operation would succeed and whether she would get her precious son back.

I kept changing the topic of conversation to try to get her mind off the problems and on to more positive thoughts. 'So, tell me, what's this island Kalymnos like?' I asked. 'It's a beautiful island, with clear waters and unspoilt beaches,' she started, with a smile, but whatever happy memory had filled her mind quickly faded. 'It's also a very close-knit community. They are all helping him to keep Theo there, you know. I really don't like the island anymore.' I tried again to steer her away from her darker thoughts. 'What activities are there on the island?' I asked, but Diane answered almost absent-mindedly: 'There's fishing, swimming, boating, hiking in the mountains, hunting.' The last one grabbed my attention. 'Hunting?' I interrupted. 'Yes, they hunt hares on the island. Actually, it's the hunting season now.' She must have seen the frown on my face because she added: 'Oh, not to worry Darren, the court suspended his weapons licence.'

But I did worry. This was a significant new piece of information and an alarming one. He might no longer have his licence but did he still have a gun? This was someone who hadn't shown too much regard for the law in respect of his son. Come to think of it, those who were meant to enforce the law hadn't exactly covered themselves in glory, so who was going to check whether his gun was safely under lock and key? 'Do you know what type of weapon he had?' I probed, trying not to sound too anxious. 'I don't know,' she said. 'It was just over a metre long and had red bullets.' In all likelihood it was a shotgun and one we certainly didn't know about before. If Stephen had known I'm sure he would have told me. So now we were going to try to rescue an abducted child from an island where everyone was aware of the situation and out to protect the child and where many of them might be armed because it was the middle of the hunting season! Diane realized I wasn't happy with the news but seemed oblivious to the danger that I perceived, not only to us but to the whole operation and, if it all got messy, to her child's life.

After dinner we walked back to the hotel in an awkward silence. 'By the way, good job on the house drawing, I'm very impressed,' I said, trying to relax the mood. 'Really? Thanks,' she said with a smile. At the hotel I said goodnight and when I got back in my room I was startled by the phone ringing. Only three people knew of my location. Four, I guess, if Diane had thought of something that couldn't wait until the morning. If not Diane, then it could only really be Stephen, Peter or Mikali. I was hoping it was Peter. Or Stephen. It was Mikali. He was calling to say he had been unable to get us a room anywhere official at short notice but he had another suggestion. 'You can use my house. Is not far from the airport, only fifteen minutes. Is very secure,' he said. 'That's fine mate,' I told him. 'I will have to check with our team leader first but I'll give you a ring on Thursday just after 11 am to let you know.'

You'll have gathered that I like to be thorough, professional and well-organized. Stephen, my employer, and Peter, our paymaster for this operation, would be arriving soon and I wanted them to know I had already been working hard on the case. I had put together all the information I needed to brief both of them and I now had an option for somewhere secure to deliver the briefing. I should have felt satisfied and yet... I tried to sleep but I couldn't. Thoughts about the operation kept spinning around in my head. Had I covered everything? What could go wrong? Had I accounted for any threats to the operation? I went over it again and again. What were the risks to a successful outcome? What were the personal risks to our safety? This was what was really nagging at me. What Diane had told me about the hunting season was reverberating inside my head. What if it does get messy? What are the dangers of one of us getting injured? Or even killed? What about the child? What if we get arrested? Or captured by the locals who we are told are hostile to any intervention in this Greek family's life? What would they do to us? Why had Nick's weapons licence been suspended? I would have to ask Diane more about that.

The more I drifted towards sleep, the more outlandish my thoughts became. I pictured being dragged off the streets by an angry mob, with grinning police watching and doing nothing. The locals could kill me and bury me on the island and no one would know. I had told my parents I was going on holiday to Italy. Only Stephen knew I was there, and if they killed him too...

Chapter Ten

I woke with sunlight streaming into my room. I must have slept, but I didn't exactly feel refreshed. At least in the cold light of day my imagination wasn't running riot. The father might or might not be armed but we would just have to manage that situation. Meanwhile, there were other factors over which we were more able to exert control.

I met Diane for breakfast in the hotel restaurant and I told her it would be a good idea to buy a hat to disguise her a little when she was on the islands. Our plan was to take her to Kalymnos only at the last moment but there were people on Kos, where we would set up our base of operations, who might recognize her, and if any of them forewarned Nick then the whole operation would be burned. The simple process of addressing that risk made me feel like I was back on track and thoughts of shotguns were pushed to the back of my mind. I was feeling much better. Then Diane derailed me again. She told me she had rung her Greek lawyer and informed him that she was in the country, which was a revelation to me. I didn't know she had a lawyer here. That was another potential source of a leak but Diane assured me that he was not only trustworthy but that he had got very close to the case and wanted Nick to suffer for what he had done.

Her lawyer's name was Nikolas and he had an office on Kos. As well as updating him on plans for an operation to recover Theo, she said she had got him to organize two hotel rooms for the four of us on Kos. Apparently, he was not just a lawyer but the local president of the Greek Hotel Association so had been able to book the rooms at a good rate. Obviously a man with lots of local contacts. I just hoped his contacts would be on the right side if things got tricky. Much as I was impressed with Diane for conjuring up yet another useful travel contact, Nikolas, it turned out, had booked a room for us three males in one hotel and a room for Diane across the road in a different hotel. This didn't work from a security point of view, as far as I was concerned, but I let it go for the time being and made a mental note to sort it out later.

I learned from Diane that Nikolas had been involved in this case from the start and had been extremely helpful to her. They not only had a business relationship, but had created a strong friendship over the past fourteen months. Diane trusted him implicitly. Apparently, he and a court clerk had gone to Kalymnos to serve some court documents for the apprehension of the child but their presence was not welcomed and they'd been escorted off the island by the local police. I began to understand why this proud man had a personal reason for wanting this operation to succeed and for Nick to be punished.

After breakfast, Diane and I went shopping for a hat and found a straw one with a large brim that, when pulled down, disguised her perfectly. We went to the internet cafe to see if Peter had emailed us with his flight details. He hadn't. Checking emails was now becoming a hassle since the cafe was a couple of kilometres from the hotel. It was even more frustrating when we made the long walk in the heat only to find there were no emails. I busied myself searching the shopping centre for maps of the islands, so that our trip would not have been a complete waste of time, and I found a bookshop which stocked road maps of Kos, so I bought two. They had no maps of Kalymnos but, luckily, I found another shop which did, so I bought two.

It was now approaching 11 am. This was the day that Peter was supposed to arrive at '11.50' but was it this morning or tonight? I thought it would be best to get back to the hotel and get myself moved to a larger room and wait for Peter to call while I prepared my briefing for the rest of the team. I returned to the hotel, changed rooms, remembering to retrieve my documents pinned to the back of the fruit bowl painting, and left a message at reception for any calls to my old room to be redirected to my new room. But as I waited for Peter to call I felt like a prisoner, unable to go anywhere. I occupied myself with preparation of the briefing, placing the maps of the islands on my hotel room wall and spreading all the necessary information about transportation on my bed. There wasn't a painting in the room big enough for all the material I had now gathered, but I turned the key in the door lock to make sure no one came in unannounced.

The distance between Kos island and Kalymnos was approximately 15 kilometres and the distance between Kalymnos and Turkey was approximately 24 kilometres. Kalymnos did not have an airport so the only mode of transportation on and off the island was boat. Our accommodation was booked in Kos Town with that unusual arrangement of two hotels across the road from each other. Now, as I studied the maps, I could see that Kos Town was approximately 30 kilometres from Kalymnos and not exactly convenient for us. I found there was a smaller town called Mastichari on the north coast of Kos which was 15 kilometres directly across the water from the main town of Pothia on Kalymnos where the child was reportedly staying. The map indicated that a ferry route went directly to Kalymnos from Mastichari. That seemed much better. I called Diane and got her to contact Nikolas to change the hotel arrangements and to book us two rooms, next to each other, in a hotel in Mastichari.

I continued compiling the briefing and wrote a fact sheet with all the details of boats on and off Kalymnos and Kos from Pothia and Mastichari, with timings, duration and costs. It was all well and good making a plan involving the most convenient transport, but plans often go wrong in the heat of an operation and we needed to know all the options available. I put all of this information into my briefing and recorded everything on to my small voice recorder, including references to the maps, just in case Stephen didn't want to use Mikali's house for the briefing. Then he could listen to the briefing via the earpiece in some small corner of the airport or on the aircraft to Kos. That way we weren't all sitting around pointing at maps in the airport with airport surveillance cameras, and who knows who else, watching our every move.

The recording lasted fifty minutes and I gathered together all the maps and documents and packed them away ready to illustrate my briefing or to give them directly to Stephen. It was now approximately 6.30 pm. Diane had already called by my room as I was working to see how things were coming along but I was now hungry and sick of waiting for Peter so I checked on Diane and we made our way out again for something to eat. Over another Italian meal, she expressed her amazement at how my room appeared while I was compiling the briefing. This was the first time I'd had an outsider observe my behind-the-scenes preparations. In a way, it was good for her to see just how much planning goes on prior to a recovery attempt, despite the fact she only saw a fraction of the larger picture. I explained that the more work we do in preparation, the easier the operation... or so it generally goes.

She was clearly feeling a little more at ease because she was joking more. She told me that she didn't usually smoke but that she had been smoking like a chimney while I was busy in my room and she was left alone with her thoughts about Theo and about how the operation might go. She asked about Peter and I told her it was now up to him to contact us. That snag aside, it was beginning to feel like we were about to put a plan into motion and there was a spring in our step as we returned to the hotel to turn in. It was now Wednesday night. Stephen would arrive tomorrow morning and we would fly out to Kos in the afternoon with or without Peter. The last time I had seen Stephen had been on a protection contract in South America the previous March and I was looking forward to seeing him again. I lay down on my bed going over the briefing in my mind to ensure I hadn't forgotten anything and fell into a deep sleep.

Ring, ring, ring. The urgency of the phone woke me with a start. 'Hello,' I answered, sleepily. 'Oh, Darren, it's only me. Did Peter ring you last night?' I recognized Diane's voice and realized that it must be morning. Unlike my previous room, this one didn't let in any sunlight. 'No, he didn't,' I replied, my senses slowly awakening. 'Bloody hell. What's going on?' she asked. 'I don't know, but he knows when Stephen is arriving because he booked the tickets, so we go to the airport to meet Stephen and Peter should be there,' I explained calmly. 'Yeah, ok,' she agreed reluctantly. 'I'll meet you downstairs for breakfast.'

It occurred to me how eating together in the dining room each morning made us look like a married couple. If that was our cover then all well and good, but I smiled as I thought about the hotel manager wondering why we were in separate rooms. We finished our breakfast and checked out of our rooms. It annoyed me, knowing the constraints on Diane's budget, that an additional charge had been added to our bill because I'd had to change rooms to cater for Peter, and he hadn't shown up to use it. I hadn't even met the guy and he was getting on my nerves. We gathered our bags and crossed the busy road to wait for the public bus which would take us to Athens International Airport. Not many tourists stayed in this part of the city and even fewer used the public buses so Diane and I were stared at throughout the slightly unnerving journey. I reached into a side pocket of my backpack and pulled out a *What to do in Kos* pamphlet and handed it to Diane to read.

It was 10.45 am when we made our way to the arrivals hall to wait for Stephen. I went through my counter-surveillance drills just in case

Diane was seen by someone she knew or a relative of Nick's, however unlikely that seemed in Athens. The irony was that the one stranger we did want to see, but who I felt sure would not recognize Diane, was conspicuous by his absence, though I presumed Peter must be in the airport somewhere waiting for Stephen just like us. Across from the arrivals hall was an information booth so I went over to have a word and minutes later an announcement boomed over the airport's PA system. 'MR PETER GONZALEZ, PETER GONZALEZ, PLEASE ATTEND THE INFORMATION BOOTH AT THE ARRIVALS HALL.'

Now, here was a funny situation. I knew what Diane and Stephen looked like but not what Peter looked like; Diane knew what I looked like, but not Stephen or Peter; Stephen knew what I looked like but had only seen photos of Diane and did not know what Peter looked like; and Peter did not know what any of us looked like and, on the evidence so far, I reckoned he'd struggle to find himself in a mirror.

We stood off to the side of the booth, but within listening distance of the attendant, and waited. I was scanning the area looking for any suspicious persons or a man who looked like he might work for a child abduction charity, if there is such an appearance. Judging from his surname, I presumed Peter might be Hispanic and it didn't take long before I saw a Mexican-looking male approach the information booth and ask about the announcement for Peter Gonzalez. The woman behind the counter pointed in our direction and the man approached us. At last, here was the elusive Peter. He wore black dress shoes, baggy white trousers and a large black shirt worn outside his trousers. 'Hi, you must be Stephen,' he said in a thick American accent. 'No, I'm Darren,' I said, hiding my amusement at being mistaken for my boss who, apart from being British, was a lot shorter than me, though stockier and muscular. Peter extended his hand and as I shook it I asked, 'Do you mind if I look at your passport, Peter?' He looked puzzled but agreed. 'It's just that I've never met you before and I want to make sure you are who you say you are,' I explained. 'Oh, sure, no problem. I understand,' he said, then turned to Diane and added, 'You must be Diane,' as he handed me his passport. 'Yes, I am. Nice to meet you, finally,' she said, with only a trace of rancour which in no way accurately reflected how she must have really felt.

'When did you get in?' I asked him as I handed back his passport which confirmed his identity but which, I noticed, had only been issued the previous week. 'Yesterday,' he said, nonchalantly. 'It's just that I had catered for a spare bed for you last night,' I said. 'Did you not get our hotel details?' Peter looked untroubled. 'Oh, I just stayed down the road in another hotel,' he said. My question wasn't answered and he clearly didn't appreciate how much confusion he had caused. I let it go. Obviously there had been a breakdown in communication somewhere. The important thing was that he was finally there. I also now knew that Diane and I did not stand out like an international security operative and a mother planning to recover her abducted child. Well, not to Peter, anyway, since he had passed us to get to the information booth.

At that moment I saw Stephen enter the arrivals hall and I alerted the other two. 'The one with the red backpack?' Diane asked. 'Yes, that's him,' I replied. At least Diane had a keen eye for observing people. Stephen cast a glance around the arrivals hall, easily picked out the 6ft 4ins blond bloke and promptly headed towards us. 'How are you going, mate?' he said, shaking my hand. 'G'day mate. Good. How are ya?' I replied. 'This is Diane, and this is Peter.' Pleasantries completed, Stephen turned to me. 'So, tell me the plan,' he said.

Typical Stephen: he'd just got off a thirteen-hour flight and was immediately ready to get on with the job. 'The next flight out to Kos is at 5 pm so I've organized a briefing to bring you up to speed,' I said. 'We can either go to our Greek contact's house, which is fifteen minutes away, or I have compiled the briefing on a tape recorder and you can listen to it with the maps via an earpiece here in the airport or on the flight.' Stephen nodded. 'Let's go to the house,' he said. 'Right,' I replied. 'I just need to ring him and let him know we're coming.' Diane couldn't stop smiling. Finally, her team was assembled and what had been keeping her up at night for fourteen months was drawing to a close. At least, that's what she must have hoped. I rang Mikali and let him know that we would take him up on his offer and that we were just leaving the airport.

The heat was unbearable in the taxi with the four of us crammed in. I sat in the front with the other three in the back getting to know each other as much as they could without any talk about the operation. I could hardly hear anything because I had my window down in a desperate bid to get some cooling air in the car and because the taxi driver was travelling in excess of 120 kilometres an hour, which seemed to be the norm for Greek taxi drivers. In spite of the speed, we had been sweltering in the taxi for thirty minutes by the time we hit the heavy traffic on the outskirts of Athens. So much for fifteen minutes from the airport! The heat was now making everyone uncomfortable and I was beginning to doubt that the taxi driver knew the directions. Diane asked him for a third time, in Greek, how much further we had to go. It seemed like each time she asked him he said 'three miles' and this time was no different.

Fifty minutes after we left the airport we eventually pulled up outside the house to be greeted by Mikali. '*Kaliméra. Ti kánis?*' I asked in my best phrasebook greeting. 'Good morning to you too my friend,' he replied with a smile. I ditched my pigeon Greek and continued in English. 'My name is Darren. We spoke on the phone. This is our team leader, Stephen; this is Peter; and this is, er, Jessica,' I said. 'Good, my name Mikali. Er, my home your home. Please excuse my English. Come,' he said.

His house was nice and well-kept and his wife was working from an office on the second floor where he would soon join her. The kitchen was laid out with a range of refreshments, including biscuits, orange juice, water and coffee. 'Please, be comfortable,' said Mikali. 'I am upstairs if you need me. This level is all yours. It is very secure.' As a trusted employee of Stephen's friend I had no reason to doubt him and, confident that we could not be overheard from other parts of the house, I started to set up the briefing as Diane poured coffees, water and juice for everyone.

'OK, this is the briefing for the operation,' I started. 'If you firstly observe the Kos map you can see in the centre of the island is an aircraft symbol. This is the main international airport of Kos near the township of Antimachia and the airport at which we will be arriving this afternoon. We are leaving Athens at 1700 hours arriving Kos at 1740 hours. Duration of the flight is forty minutes. I have arranged for accommodation at Mastichari which is located here, 7 kilometres north of the airport. We originally had accommodation booked in Kos Town but that is 30 kilometres from the airport, as you can see, in the top north east of the island, which would make our eventual recovery a little time-consuming. Plus, the father has relatives living in Kos. Also, the rooms were booked across the road from each other in different hotels. Mastichari has the second largest port after Kos and has a ferry service to Kalymnos and is a much smaller and quieter town. The hotel we have booked is called Mindu Hotel. The ferry from Mastichari departs for Kalymnos at 0900 hours, 1730 hours and 2130 hours. The duration is forty-five minutes and costs 3 euros. The ferry is a car-transportable ferry and has the capacity to transport twelve small cars. The ferry is located on the wharf which is approximately 500 metres from our hotel in Mastichari. The ferry from Kalymnos departs for Mastichari at 0700 hours, 1530 hours and 1930 hours each day.

'If you now look at the Kalymnos map, you can observe the town of Pothia in the south. This is the town where we understand the child is staying. You will also observe the locations of all the monasteries as indicated by the crosses. We know that a priest has assisted the father in hiding the child in one of these monasteries, as well as a monastery in Kos. Diane and I think that this monastery is located here, approximately 6 kilometres from the town, in the hills. If you turn the left side of the map over, you will observe a road map of Pothia. Diane thinks the road that the house is on is at this fork in the road *here,* alongside the harbour. The distance between the house and the esplanade is approximately 500 metres. I have a tourist brochure with a photo of Pothia taken from atop the mountain overlooking the town. As you can see, the wharf is situated here, the house is over here to the right of the photo and this area here is the esplanade with restaurants and bars. The port authority and coastguard building is situated here and the local police station is here. We can hire motorbikes on the island for approximately 15 euros per day and we can hire or charter a boat from Mastichari or Kos wharves. The prices for boats are negotiable with the owners. The national airline carrier, Olympic, has flights departing from Kos at 0900 hours, 1530 hours and 2245 hours Monday to Friday and additional services at 0700 hours, 1215 hours and 2000 hours on Saturday and Sunday.'

I paused for just a moment, then carried on. 'There is one small problem. I have recently learned that it is hunting season on the island and the father owns a firearm. They mainly hunt hares. The court has suspended his licence. However, he is probably still in possession of the firearm. I asked Diane for a description of the rifle and she said it was approximately 1 metre in length with red bullets. Stephen, she is unsure of the calibre but the only firearm I can think of with red bullets is a shotgun with 12 gauge shot. I don't fancy the chances of the poor hares.

'The father owns a small motorcycle and the grandmother may also own a scooter and transport the child on her lap. She is 58 years of age, short height with short brown hair. She does not speak or understand English. The father is 35 years of age, medium height and build, with short curly hair. His name is Nick. It is not sure whether or not he is working. Previously, he had worked under the house in the cellar as a carpenter making kitchens for friends. He may also be working for his uncle doing carpentry somewhere on the island. They own a property, here, in the hills approximately 6 kilometres from the town, where they are constructing a new house. They started construction eleven years ago, so it may be finished now. This is the reason the father and his father left Greece, for Australia, to earn money for the project. The father may be working in the house using it as a workshop. In any case, the child likes to be around his father while he is working.

'The child, as we know, is 5 years of age with short curly black hair. He has been abducted now for fourteen months and we are certain that his father and grandmother have brainwashed him into thinking that his mother doesn't love him and no longer wants him. Here are the photos of the child and the father to refresh your memories. In the late afternoon, around 1700 hours, after work, the father enjoys visiting a cafe drinking coffee while watching passers-by. He will normally return to the house for dinner around 1800 hours, then visit the clubs at around 2100 hours. He drinks straight vodka with a twist of lemon and smokes Marlboro Red cigarettes.

'According to the guide books, the Greek island culture is very religious. They are ordinary people who are not used to change. They are creatures of habit and their daily routine never changes much. The men will go out at night and drink and socialize. However, the wives are expected to stay home and are forbidden to be seen without their husbands. Their lifestyle is all about image and how others will perceive them. Diane has gone through the correct procedures, keeping within the law, and has even hired a local team to attempt a recovery. They failed. A court secretary tipped the father off before they even arrived. The Ministry of Justice is on our side but seemingly cannot get the Kalymnos police to do their job and, subsequently, the local police are under investigation. Diane's lawyer Nikolas and a court-appointed clerk from Kos visited the island to serve some documents but were escorted off the island by the police without being able to serve the papers.

'When we arrive on Kos this afternoon, it is my suggestion that Stephen and I travel directly to the island and start conducting surveillance. We will videotape the house and any possible sightings of the family and have them confirmed by the mother on our return in the morning, to ensure we have the right location. Obviously, the child will not be attending school since school does not start until 9 September. They cannot keep him locked up all day so the opportune time to recover him may be when he is playing but, as I said previously, he will not be far from the watchful eye of his grandmother. It would be better to recover him while he is in the presence of his grandmother, as opposed to his father. I see there being less trouble here, due to her age, and I expect she will be too emotionally distraught to do anything.

'If we can have a chartered or hire boat from Kos waiting in the harbour on the day of the recovery, we can get off the island quickly. We go directly to Mastichari which, in a speedboat doing 30 knots, should take around twenty minutes. We should have our luggage pre-packed on the boat. This will give us some flexibility should we run into trouble and have to travel to Turkey, some thirty minutes away. We cannot rely on any help from the locals as we have to assume they are all in on it. Diane's lawyer Nikolas said he is more than willing to help us out and can be standing at the harbour in Mastichari to create a diversion should we be chased. We also have Mikali on standby should we need him. Now, psychologically, the family may be feeling comfortable and relaxed about the current situation. It has been five months since any contact regarding the case and since Diane is remarried and has a baby daughter, they may think she has given up the fight. Are there any questions?'

Stephen and Peter studied the maps, photos and fact sheets, with me pointing out extra pieces of information where necessary. Stephen liked what he saw, considering no one had yet been on the ground, and then he asked Diane some questions. 'Do you have all the legal paperwork?' he queried, starting with the most important piece of the jigsaw. 'Yes, I do. I have the custody papers, the Australian court order and documents from the Attorney General's department,' she said. 'Nikolas also has everything on file in his office in Kos. Linda Hiddins also has documents on the case.' Stephen looked quizzical. 'Who is Linda Hiddins?' he asked. 'She is a consular official at the Australian Embassy in Athens,' replied Diane.

We will never do a child recovery unless we have the legal paperwork. Our office gets many enquiries from mothers and fathers but when they are asked to forward copies of the paperwork showing they are the legal custodian, some of them never contact us again. Did they want us to kidnap their children in defiance of the law courts? Perhaps. In one case in Curacao, the mother did have the legal paperwork so we agreed to do the job, but she kept stressing that the recovery had to be completed before 12 December and she did a mighty fine job of disguising herself without any help from the team. As it turned out, the father had appealed the court order and the case was pending a further hearing. On 12 December. If we had got caught recovering the child we would have faced jail for kidnapping.

There were no such doubts in Diane's case and Stephen was keen to get going. 'Right,' he said. 'Darren and I will get over there and conduct surveillance for a few days and find out where they are and if, in fact, the child is still there. If we can confirm that, we will talk to your lawyer, Diane, and arrange for support from the police and take it from there.'

'But Stephen, you cannot use the police,' Diane said with a look of anguish I recognized only too well. 'I have already tried that and it doesn't work. You cannot trust them.' Stephen adopted a reassuring tone: 'If you have paperwork stating you are the legal custodian, and the Ministry of Justice is on our side, then the police cannot refuse to cooperate. The Ministry of Justice is who the police work for. If they have an order for us, then the police have to cooperate and do their job.' Diane was unconvinced. 'I don't know, Stephen. I just don't know.' The frown lines above the bridge of her nose were more pronounced than ever. 'When they see international involvement, they will become nervous and be pressured into doing their job,' said Stephen, confidently.

We sat around for a little longer, drinking coffee and going over details, while Diane told Stephen many of the things she had already told me. Peter sat quietly listening. 'You have worked on international cases before, haven't you?' Stephen asked Peter. 'Yes, I have,' he replied. 'Have you done surveillance work before?' pressed Stephen. 'Yes, mainly in the US,' said Peter. 'Well, that's good. The three of us will be able to do the surveillance operation,' concluded Stephen.

Two hours had now passed and we agreed to pack up and make our way back to the airport. I went upstairs to get Mikali and he showed me around his office. 'You need to go pick up the client from the airport today?' he asked. I nodded. 'Yes, he arrives soon.' I was grateful for Mikali's help and hospitality, but he didn't need to know the truth. Lying is an occupational hazard in our game as you make sure people only get the specifics of an operation on a need-to-know basis. This minimizes the possibility of a leak and can assist in identifying any leaks. When working with people I haven't worked with before I will often make up some little nugget to tell them and only them. If that information leaks then I know the source. 'Then you are flying out, yes?' Mikali said. 'Yes, we are going to the island of Corfu,' I said, embellishing my little white lie. 'Well, if you need help with anything, please, contact me and I will assist you,' he said, generously.

I asked if he had any involvement in the security for the Olympic Games due to be held in Athens in 2004. He said he was part of the planning. Since I was always looking for possible contracts for the company, I voiced our interest should they require any specialized training or operations and we exchanged contact details. He said the Greek Government would be feeling uncomfortable soon as nothing had been built to cater for the games. I was beginning to think that the boy scouts were more prepared than the Greek authorities.

Mikali and I went downstairs to meet the rest of the team and to wait for a taxi. In the stairwell I shook his hand, thanked him again and placed 100 euros in his hand for his troubles, for which he was very grateful. Downstairs, he chatted with Diane, looking at her with amazement as she conversed with him in Greek. When the taxi horn sounded we made our way out to the front, said our goodbyes to Mikali and made the hot, uncomfortable taxi journey back to Athens International Airport.

In spite of the heat, it was the calmest I had seen Diane since our introduction five days before in Melbourne. She could presumably see an end to her months of trauma and the possibility of a reunion with Theo. A smile lit up her face and she leaned forward from the back seat so I could hear her in the front. 'Darren, what did you tell that guy?' she said. 'What do you mean,' I asked. 'Mikali,' she said. 'He kept looking at me funny and asking all these questions about how I got involved with you guys.' 'Ah,' I said with a grin. 'I told him you were our bilingual special operations agent!' Diane laughed out loud. 'God, that's hilarious. He thinks I'm Jane Bond or something.' Little did Mikali know that she *was* the client.

Chapter Eleven

'This is the part I hate,' said Peter as the aircraft taxied towards the runway. I stopped flicking through the in-flight magazine. 'What?' I asked, as if I hadn't guessed. Peter was sitting between Stephen and me and was shrinking into his seat. 'Flying,' he said, with a terrified look on his face. 'Personally, I'd rather crash over land than water,' volunteered Stephen, mischievously, with a perfectly straight face. Peter took a sharp intake of breath. 'Oh, great,' he whimpered. 'When your number's up, your number's up,' I said, fatalistically. 'We have no control over this aircraft or the pilot's actions,' I added for good measure. I could see the beads of sweat on Peter's forehead and his hands were gripping the arm rests. The aircraft turned on to the runway and paused for a while, then the engines roared, the thrust pushed us all back in our seats and Peter's knuckles turned white as his fingers dug into the toughened plastic. 'Ah, gee!' he said with a gulp before doing a quick Hail Mary.

Spanish-speaking Catholics doing a Hail Mary before take-off had become a common sight for me working in South America and I always thought it must be disturbing for first-time flyers. Stephen and I glanced at each other and smiled. Peter was certainly a character. I reflected on the date his passport was issued and wondered if he had ever left the United States before. On the other side of the aisle from me, Diane appeared oblivious to Peter's discomfort which eased only slightly once we were airborne before returning with a vengeance for a bumpy landing at Kos just fifty minutes later. I looked past Stephen in the window seat and saw a KLM 747-400 on the airport apron as we taxied towards the terminal. 'Direct international flights. That could be useful,' I thought to myself.

'Me and Darren will get the luggage. You take Diane outside, get her into a taxi and wait for us,' Stephen told Peter as soon as we disembarked from the aircraft and were walking into the main terminal building. 'You bet,' he replied. Stephen and I approached the baggage claim area paying close attention to who was there. It was full of European tourists so we blended in with our backpacks and casual clothes. I noted that many of them had come in on the KLM aircraft I had seen and they were mainly young and predominantly female. 'Steady, boy,' I told myself. 'You're not really on holiday. Concentrate on your job.' Nothing appeared to be suspicious in the terminal so we grabbed all our bags and made our way outside where Peter stood across the pavement waving at us.

If anything, it was even hotter than Athens and the sun felt particularly strong on my exposed neck, which was slightly sunburnt from all the walking around we'd done in Athens, thanks to Peter's dubious communication skills. We jumped into the taxi which Diane already occupied – a typical Mercedes Benz beloved of taxi drivers the world over – and sped off, and I mean sped. Four minutes and forty-seven seconds later we were in Mastichari.

'Good. Our hotel is situated in an ideal location,' I noted, giving myself a mental pat on the back. After checking in to our hotel we found our rooms and settled in. Both were on the top floor, with balconies overlooking a beautiful beach, and were quite private and secure. Diane's was next to our room which had two beds and a foldaway camp bed. I guessed I would rarely be spending any nights here in Mastichari but, nevertheless, I threw my gear down on the centre bed. Peter placed his suitcase on the other bed, close to the bathroom, which left Stephen with the camp bed.

At that moment Diane knocked and, without waiting for an answer, came straight in, looking concerned. 'Darren,' she said, anxiously. 'Yes, Diane,' I replied. 'The people running this hotel have Australian accents. You don't think they know about Nick and Theo, do you?' In spite of my own natural wariness I dismissed her fears. 'It's the height of the holiday season. I would think they have been too busy to know much about what might have been happening on another island, but don't worry. I'll throw them off the scent, just in case.'

It was now past 6.30 pm and the next ferry to Kalymnos was at 9.30 pm. Stephen and I packed our backpacks for the night's surveillance: maps, camera, tape recorder, video camera, notebook, binoculars, compass and GPS. I needed some black tape to mask the camcorder's red light which indicated when it was recording and which might be a dead giveaway if we were trying to surreptitiously film people without them knowing. I'd normally have some electrical insulation tape in my bag of tricks but

I'd left much of my stuff behind. Never mind, it was a good excuse to visit reception and lay a false trail in case any of the owners had, by any chance, heard about Nick and Theo.

'Good evening. You wouldn't happen to have any black insulation tape, by any chance?' I asked in my best British accent. 'Um, I don't know. Let me see,' said the young Greek receptionist in his Australian accent – more evidence of the close links between the Greek islands and Australia and reason enough to have aroused Diane's suspicions. 'What do you need it for?' he asked. 'I'm making some repairs to my binoculars case. Doing a spot of twitching,' I said. 'Birdwatching,' I explained when the young guy looked confused. He disappeared down some stairs and reappeared a few minutes later, brandishing a shiny black roll. 'Here you go. How much do you need?' he asked with a look of triumph. 'Terrific. Thank you,' I said. 'I'm not sure yet. Let me take the whole roll and I'll bring it back when I've finished.' I returned to the room, cut off a small piece and informed Stephen, Peter and Diane that we were now here on a birdwatching holiday. After taping the camera light I returned the tape to reception. 'Ta very much,' I said. 'No worries, mate,' replied the young man.

The four of us, including Diane disguised under her straw hat, walked around the area to check out what the town had to offer and then made our way to a seaside restaurant. After a day full of introductions and people getting to know one another, everyone was slightly subdued over dinner. Eventually Diane broke the silence with a new disclosure. 'You know this ordeal is costing me a lot of money.' She looked around to check we were all listening. 'Well, I have agreed to sell my story to *60 Minutes*,' she said, referring to Australia's Channel Nine current affairs programme. She let that little nugget sink in and then explained how the TV channel had given her a camcorder and they wanted Stephen and I to tape ourselves doing surveillance and, hopefully, capture some footage of the actual recovery, if and when it happened. 'Well that's a bit of a bombshell,' I thought. 'Are we meant to be recovering a child or making a documentary? There was I thinking our job was covert surveillance not TV broadcasts. Is this about to become some kind of media circus?' I had been worrying about the slightest leak betraying details of our mission and all the time the whole plan was being fed back to a TV station.

I wondered what Stephen made of all this but held off from saying anything as he may have already been informed. He seemed fairly sanguine about it. Diane was, after all, the client and we were being paid to do her bidding. He seemed to appreciate she had to do something to offset the cost of this operation. 'How much will you make on the story?' he asked. 'Oh, I don't know,' she said. 'Maybe $10,000. Look, if I don't do this my son is going to be 21 before I finish paying off the loan I took out for this. It has financially ruined us. But it's not just about the money. This whole thing has been a nightmare because there are so many loopholes in the legal system and I think it needs to be publicized so that something is done about it. I don't want anyone else to have to go through what I have gone through. It's not right.'

Stephen nodded and we got on with our meal. We all understood the dilemma Diane faced and we really felt for her. At least, I thought we all did, but then the bill arrived and Peter signalled to the waiter to give it to him. 'Let me get this,' he said magnanimously to the rest of us. 'Does anyone want anything else?' It sounded like a nice gesture but, in fact, he had the credit card which contained all the money Diane had sent him to cover the cost of the operation, so it was Diane's money he was being generous with.

It was nearly time for the ferry so Stephen and I scoffed down the last of our food and said our goodbyes. Diane had a worried look on her face as we made our way to the wharf. We were now just an hour away from our area of operation, and that much closer to bringing her news of her young son. It was my first time on the Aegean Sea but I could pick out which islands were which and which was the mainland of Turkey from the research I had done weeks before in my hometown library.

To the left of us I could see the passage my Australian forefathers had sailed through on their way to fight the Turks at Gallipoli in the First World War. It was a sobering thought, but everything else about the crossing was pleasant. The night was warm and the sky was studded with stars. The scene was beautiful, but the ferry journey would be the only time we would have a chance to enjoy the view. The rest of the time we would be preoccupied. We knew we would be making this journey regularly before the operation was over so we made it a standard operating procedure (SOP) that we enter the vessel early, walk through the lounge observing anyone there, and make our way to the deck beside the bridge to observe all the other passengers boarding the ferry. The ferry had vehicles on the lower deck and a lot of locals upstairs, along with a few tourists who blended in with us.

We sat on the top deck, outside the bridge and above the majority of the passengers who were sitting in an enclosed lounge complete with a kiosk and television screens. In the distance we could see the lights of Kalymnos though, for a long time, they didn't seem to get any closer and the journey seemed to take forever. Stephen and I didn't say much. As with the start of any operation, we were going over in our heads what had to be done and thinking of our counter-action drills should our counter-surveillance drills fail us and we encounter any unexpected problems. There is always an air of apprehension before going into hostile territory because you have no idea what surprises might be waiting for you, and though this was a holiday island to most people, it was definitely hostile territory to us because of what we were there to do.

At last we approached Kalymnos and Stephen and I made our way to the port side to get an early glimpse of the house which we were told should be visible from the harbour. I reached into my day pack for the video camera and began filming the area. 'See that one there, mate? That looks like the description of the house,' I said. 'No, I think it's the one next to it, with the shutters open,' Stephen countered. With a sudden gunning of the engines and the violent churn of water, the ferry turned and was backed towards the quayside and we could see people standing on the jetty waiting to board. Were they family, friends… or foe waiting for us?

The skipper completed his reversing manoeuvre, the crew moored up and the vehicle ramp was lowered. One of the ferry hands released a chain and the twenty or so passengers began to disembark. Motorcycles roared off the ramp like they'd done it countless times before; cars and vans followed while foot passengers were greeted by family members. Stephen and I were only too happy there was no one there to meet us. We scanned the area, disembarked and made our way towards the house. I recalled what Diane had told us: 'It's on a road next to the water, at the top of a hill where the road forks. The road then veers sharply to the side and up a hill. There is a vacant block next to it, and the neighbours who help them are next to that. It's only a two-minute walk from the water.'

We walked along the road that matched that description. And walked, and walked until we were now beyond the outskirts of the town, in the middle of nowhere, in a dark forest. The 'road next to the water', it turned out, was the main road around the island and we were now approximately 2 kilometres out of town with the road ahead continuing down a steep incline towards a valley. Clearly, if the house was on this road, we had missed it. There were no streetlights and the whole area was quiet and dark and not the sort of place genuine tourists would be wandering around at that time without arousing suspicion. 'Shh,' said Stephen. 'Get down!'

I saw the headlights before I could hear the vehicle and we both dived into the grass at the side of the road. The car passed and we could hear youths laughing as it carried them down the steep hill and into the distance. I climbed out from underneath the grass and rocks. 'You ok?' Stephen asked. 'Yeah, I'm fine mate. And you?' I replied. 'Yeah, I'm OK. That was close,' said Stephen, and he wasn't talking about the car. We both looked at the undergrowth where we had dived and just a few feet away was a steep cliff and a long drop into the ocean below. No wonder I had felt like my feet were dangling.

Stephen and I made our way back to the wharf to start the search anew. We headed towards the Hellenic Coastguard building near the esplanade and by the side of the building was a paved area with concrete barriers to stop vehicles passing through. Directly on the other side was a bike store with around fifteen motorcycles and scooters parked at the front. Beyond this, the road continued up past a large church on the right-hand side. This road ran parallel to the one we had just walked up, yet was up higher. We decided this looked more like what we were looking for and started to walk up it.

Just when it appeared as though we had walked into a dead end, with a house directly in front of us, we saw that the road veered off slightly to the right and then left again, running back parallel to itself as it climbed the hill. With sparse street lighting to illuminate the darkness, I gave a second look at the house that appeared to be blocking our path. It was a two-storey, white cement house with a cellar and a small patio with a small table and chair. The shutters and the front door appeared to be a reddish-brown colour, though it was hard to tell in the dark, and a small Yamaha motorcycle was parked to the left-hand side of the outside stairs. 'This is it!' I whispered to Stephen. 'Are you sure?' he queried in a whisper of his own. 'Yes, 100 per cent.'

We carried on walking up past the house on the road which eventually joined the main road we had previously travelled. 'It didn't look like the drawing,' Stephen remarked. 'Nah, it was definitely the one, mate. It's exactly how she explained it to me,' I said. 'She also said it was beside the water, that there was a vacant lot next to it and that the road forked sharply around the house,' added Stephen. 'No,' I insisted, 'It's exactly how she described it to me, mate. I'm sure that's the one.' Stephen gave a thumbs up. 'OK, we'll go back around and film the house and get Diane to confirm it,' he said.

It was now 10.50 pm and the town seemed strangely quiet. It was too early for the bars and restaurants around the esplanade to be shut up for the night so they must have had some very well-behaved customers. There was no loud music and not even the noise of well-refreshed holidaymakers making their unsteady way back to their hotels. The house was definitely shut up tight with no sign of life. The likelihood was that they were all asleep but were they even in there? Did they know we were coming? Had they gone off the island to hide the child? You can't help but be paranoid while conducting surveillance operations. Not to be paranoid is to drop your guard and potentially compromise the operation and endanger your life, or the lives of others.

After getting the camcorder out of the bag we made our way back to the coastguard building to begin filming. We could see a duty guard through the window, leaning back in his chair in his white uniform, his feet crossed on the table, watching television. I could hear the base radio monitor crackle with carrier wave but the coastguard was oblivious to our presence. We carried on up the road past the church with Stephen holding the camcorder down by his side with the viewing monitor facing up towards him so he could see what he was filming. As we approached the house he zoomed in on the motorcycle, paying attention to the license plate number. He then zoomed out again to view the whole house. With good shots of the front, we continued around the bend in the road and up past the side of the house, giving us plenty of footage for Diane to view and to confirm whether it was the right place or not.

It struck me that the neighbourhood was claustrophobic in its design. Most of the houses were two or more storeys tall with side walls which backed directly onto the neighbouring houses. There were no gardens, grassed or otherwise; no front or back yards. They just fronted on to the roads which were approximately 6 metres wide. This section of town was built on the side of a steep hill and the streets and houses were tiered up to the top. Balconies overlooked the houses and streets below and families seemed to use these balconies as their main area for entertaining. Since it was late, and most people were in bed, we decided that conducting further surveillance on the house would prove nothing, even if it was the right property, so we headed back along the esplanade, past the nightclubs, cafes and restaurants, to find a hotel for the night.

Halfway along the esplanade we saw a small door between two restaurants and above the restaurants was a three-storey hotel with a large sign – Hotel Therme. The lights were on and it looked to both of us like a good place to base ourselves as the view from the balconies overlooked the harbour and the chairs and tables of the outdoor restaurants and bars. We made our way wearily up the staircase to the reception and rang the bell. After a long wait, an old man who looked like he hadn't shaved for a week approached the desk and stared at us. To be fair, I don't suppose many of his customers checked in after 11 pm, but he wasn't exactly rolling out the welcome mat.

'*Kalispera*,' I said, trying out my popular Greek phrases again. 'One room please,' I added in English. I reckoned I'd got the Greek 'good evening' bit right, but I held up one finger to make sure he understood the number of rooms we wanted. The old man stood staring at us for a while, but then turned his back to look at the pigeon holes behind him, and reached in and grabbed the key to room eleven which he handed to us. 'How much?' I asked. He gave a shrug of incomprehension so I placed two 20 euro notes, one 10 and one 5 on the counter for him to choose from. He picked up a 20 and a 5. 'Identification,' he rasped. Stephen handed the old man his British passport and the hotelier took it and walked slowly around the corner of the reception. We waited for him to reappear, and waited, and waited until it was clear he had gone back to his room for the night. Friendly chap!

We climbed the stairs to our room which looked comfortable enough and I opened the balcony doors to survey the view. It was excellent, despite being only two floors up. I could hear the drunken conversations of some local men below me and could see waiters sweeping the pavements as they closed up for the night. It was now close to midnight. As Stephen had just flown in from the US that day, and must have been exhausted, he went to bed. I stayed on the balcony checking landmarks against my maps before retiring fifteen minutes later. The occasional motorcycle buzzed past below us, the noise of the tinny exhausts penetrating the open balcony doors and echoing around me as I lay on the bed trying to sleep. The room was stuffily hot. There was no air conditioner, just the whoomp, whoomp, whoomp of a ceiling fan which whirled rhythmically as it cut through the thick warm air. Whoomp, whoomp, whoomp, whoomp, it continued, as I drifted out of consciousness.

Chapter Twelve

Whoomp, whoomp, whoomp, whoomp. A rhythmic pounding echoes in my head as I take in the messed-up scene unfolding in front of me. A young Japanese mother has stepped out from her apartment on to the streets of Yokohama holding the hand of her 4-year-old son. It is the boy we have been conducting surveillance on for nearly two weeks; the boy we are about to snatch. But something is wrong. The woman has a young man walking with her. Japanese, like her, medium height and build, but this is the first time we have seen him. Is she on to us? Is this a bodyguard? As the tension mounts I realize that the whooping in my head is the sound of my own heartbeat.

The mother, child and mystery male leave the residential compound, turn left and walk down the side street towards the main road. What do we do? This is the day it was all planned to go down as she walked her son to school but the snatch was meant to happen in the quiet spur road and the man is not supposed to be there. This changes everything. The boy's father, who is with us, will be panicking. He had prepared to leave for home tomorrow, with his son. He won't want to delay. Half way down the road, the mystery male turns right and the mother and child go straight on as we follow a short distance behind. We're back in business, but the mum has now reached the busy main street. Stephen looks at the father and gives him a nod. The father nods back. He's ready.

We move forward. I push myself between the mother and the child. Stephen makes sure the boy doesn't run away, and his father grabs him. All hell breaks loose. The mother screams. The child screams. It's 8.30 am on a bustling city street and hundreds of Japanese pedestrians watch as three white men abduct a small boy from his Japanese mother who is collapsed on the pavement. Cars slow down as drivers stare at the mayhem. Dozens of people punch the emergency number into their mobile phones. We have got to get the hell out of here, and fast.

It makes no difference that the child is a US citizen; that the father has legal custody of the child through the US courts; that the boy was taken illegally to Japan by his mother or that the FBI has a warrant for her arrest. Japan, at this moment in time, is not yet a signatory to the Hague Convention and if we are caught the authorities will regard this as kidnap, plain and simple.

We beckon furiously to the taxi that fellow team member Glenn has had waiting for us on the main road and when it pulls up the four of us jump in: team leader Stephen, the American father Henry, his traumatized son, and me. I almost squash the screaming child as I jump into the taxi over the top of him and his dad. The driver looks bewildered. 'Go! Go!' I yell. 'Where to?' he asks. 'JUST FUCKING GO!' shouts Glenn in the front passenger seat and the taxi speeds off. 'Where to go?' asks the very nervous driver again. 'Four Seasons Hotel,' I say, raising my voice to make myself heard above the wails of the child.

This is the escape plan: taxi to the Four Seasons as a decoy; then another taxi to our real hotel where we've already checked out and our bags are ready for collection; then separate taxis to our respective train stations. By the time we are in the third taxi the child, Connor, has realized it is his father who has grabbed him and has calmed down, and so has my heart rate, a little. Stephen and Glenn are already headed for the train that will take them to Narita International Airport, Tokyo. At Yokohama train station Henry, his son and I make our way to the ticketing booth. Our tickets should have been bought in advance, with cash, but the father was reluctant to shell out so much money before knowing the snatch had worked. Now, while I wait with our bags, he happily buys tickets for the three of us. We are on the bullet train to Shimonoseki, 820 kilometres away while the authorities, if they are looking for the child, will hopefully expect us to head for the airport. At the end of the three-hour rail journey we'll jump on to a boat to Seoul, South Korea, where an American official will be waiting to escort us to the US Embassy which has a new passport waiting for Connor. The US Embassy in Tokyo has already given the father documents to explain that his son's original passport has been 'lost' and he already has his legal custody documentation. This should get him through immigration at the port and, from Seoul, flights will be arranged to get Henry and Connor back to the US and me back to Australia.

We wouldn't normally consider a recovery from a country that is not a signatory to the Hague Convention but with the US authorities behind us on this one, unofficially at least, we feel emboldened. As the train rockets through the Japanese countryside, putting valuable distance between us and the all-too-public 'kidnapping', Connor is playing with his father, his big cartoon-like eyes beaming with joy to be reunited with his dad after nearly twelve months. My hands, however, are still shaking from the adrenaline overload. I can feel my legs shaking too. It is two hours into the train ride before I feel my body start to calm down, but this recovery is not over yet.

As we get closer to our destination I go through the plan with the father. 'Henry, remember, let's not walk together,' I explain. 'If you can't see me, don't panic. I can see you. Just continue walking out of the train station to the port.' He acknowledges what he has to do and I conduct a final check of our belongings. I have a knapsack with basic clothing; my surveillance equipment, consisting of binoculars, monocular Night Vision Goggle (NVG), video camera, stills camera and tape recorder; and the case file. The father has a suitcase with an overnight carry-on bag and, of course, he has Connor.

He is full of excitement and optimism. The operation he spent so much money on has paid off and he and Connor are laughing and hugging each other. The boy is the apple of his eye and, for this wealthy financier, the completion of his happiness for the first three years of the child's life. Then acrimony clouded his world. The father and his Japanese wife were divorced. With his financial resources, and his extended family close by to help look after the child, he won custody, but the mother wanted to take the boy on a two-week holiday to see her only surviving relative, her mother, and the father agreed. That was nearly twelve months ago and all attempts to persuade the mother to return with the boy had fallen on deaf ears.

The high-speed train starts to slow down. Shimonoseki is the end of the line where the train will load up with more passengers for the return journey to Tokyo. As we get off the train the father hands me his overnight carry-on bag. 'Could you take this please, Darren? I've got too much with Connor as well,' he asks, struggling with his suitcase and his small son. I take it, not knowing what is in the bag. Once on the platform, I go on ahead to put some distance between us. I follow the signs to the port and, at the bottom of a set of stairs, I see a small arcade of shops on the left-hand side, just before the station entrance. I slip into one of the stores, pretending to look at the items on display, while I wait for Henry and Connor to pass me before I fall in a safe distance behind to watch them on the last stretch to the port. Henry is pulling his wheeled suitcase by the handle and carrying Connor as they approach the front entrance to the train station. I am willing them on. Just a little further. Cross the road then walk down to the ticketing booth at the port. It's only 400 metres away.

Suddenly I see three Japanese men come out from the right-hand side of the station entrance. They make a beeline for Henry and Connor then push them against the wall on the other side of the station. Connor begins to cry. Henry looks around desperately for me to come to the rescue. Who are these men? I see the fear in Henry's eyes and am ready to intervene. Maybe others will help me when they realize I am stopping an attack. I take a step out from the shop display and then freeze. One of the men talking with Henry has lifted his arm and in raising his jacket has exposed a sidearm and a pair of handcuffs. Plain-clothed Japanese police! I jump back behind the display, watching helplessly, not knowing what to do.

The man now shouting at Henry still has his arm raised but he is motioning with his hand, held level at approximately 6ft 4ins above the ground, and there is only one thing around here of that height… me! I know that the operation is blown and I have to run for it, but I can't risk going out of the front entrance of the shop from where I am watching. A crowd of bystanders is gathering to see why the officials have stopped this Westerner and his small boy. The shopkeeper comes out from behind her counter and moves to the shop entrance to see what the commotion is about and I seize my opportunity.

To the left of the counter is a door and I slip through it. It opens into a delivery room which has another door. I push that one ajar and peer through the crack. No people. I open the door, go through it and close it behind me. I'm now in an alleyway and I have to think fast. How did they know we were on that train? If 'they' are looking for me now and they know how tall I am, they must also know what I am wearing. I can't change my height but I can change my clothes, my look, my walk, my gait. I find a large waste bin and hide behind it, out of view from people walking past the end of the alley. I change my shirt and trousers, replace my boots with trainers and take off my cap. I wonder what is in the small bag Henry gave me and I open it in the hope there is something of Henry's I can wear that will change my appearance. It is full of clothes… for a 4-year-old boy! I dump the contents of the bag into the bin and try to condense my backpack to fit in the overnight bag but it is just slightly too big. Whoomp, whoomp, whoomp. My heart is pounding again and I'm sweating profusely. I realize my surveillance equipment is taking up too much room and if I am caught and questioned I definitely don't need them to find this stuff.

Reluctantly I throw my NVG monocular into the bin with the binoculars, tape recorder and memory cards from both the video recorder and the camera. Now my backpack fits the overnight bag. I look up the alley, see an opening and cautiously make my way there. From the opening, I can see the station platform high above a concrete wall and behind a fence. Heaving myself up on a concrete pillar I am now level with the station. There are a few people around but I don't see anyone paying attention to me so I pull myself up and over the 8 foot fence after throwing my bag over. I am now in the station and can see the train I just came in on. I look down towards the stairs which lead to where Henry and Connor were captured. I want to go down and sneak a peek to see if they are still there but I know I can't afford to.

I buy a ticket to Tokyo and take my seat on the train. I am desperate for it to start rolling and for us to get out of here. Adrenaline is coursing through my veins once more as I scan the platform just outside my window for any sign of police, uniformed or plain-clothed. The minutes tick by. It seems like forever but finally the train gives a jolt and begins to roll out of the station, then gathers speed. My mobile rings and I almost jump out of my skin. 'Skippy, where are you?' says a voice full of urgency. It's Stephen. 'I'm on the bullet train, coming back to…' I begin to explain, but he interrupts me. 'ABORT! ABORT! ABORT!' he shouts. 'I have done. I'm on the bullet train going back to Tokyo,' I start, but he interrupts again. 'They have set up road blocks on the highway to the airport. They are searching vehicles and opening up car boots looking for the kid!'

This is a big deal. I am in serious trouble and I need to get out of the country fast. 'Oh my God! Where are you guys? Are you safe?' I ask. 'We're OK, but where are you?' replies Stephen. 'What's happening?' I check no one is listening to my conversation and then I tell him. 'Three plain-clothes police grabbed the father and child. I didn't hang around.

I'm now heading for Tokyo, but they're after me, Stephen. They have a description of me!' Now Stephen's voice is calm. 'OK mate, settle down,' he says. 'You need to lie low until this whole thing blows over. Stay in Tokyo for a few days and then get the hell out of there. Better get off the phones now. Good luck, brother.' I know he's right. 'I will,' I say. 'Good luck to you too, mate.' It's the last time I will speak to Stephen for the remainder of this operation.

I am alone and worried. The train back to Tokyo seems to take a lot longer than the earlier journey in the opposite direction but the time is filled by the thoughts racing through my head. I'm not about to hand myself in but where do I go? What do I need to do? What is happening right now to Henry and his son? How did the operation get so fucked up? Did I do something wrong? Then it occurs to me. Did Henry pay for the train tickets with his credit card, against all our advice? That would be how they traced him, and how they knew where he was going. What about me? Unless he has told them my name, they only have a description of me. My best bet is to check into a low-profile hotel under an assumed name and, if I get asked for a passport, tell them I have lost it and am in Tokyo to arrange a new one.

Outside the window I see Mount Fuji in all its majesty. It will help my cover as a tourist to take photos of it in case I am questioned but, after fumbling through my bag for the camera, I remember throwing the memory card in the bin. I grab the spare one I keep in the side pocket of my bag, load it into the camera and snap away. As we approach Tokyo, I wonder if the police will be waiting. Do they have photos of me? I am grateful that Stephen had us stick close to the walls when we walked through any subways during the surveillance phase of the operation. He noticed the CCTV cameras were 'fish eye' – perfect vision in the middle but distorted at the sides – so we always split up and walked up against the walls. Hopefully there aren't any clear CCTV images of me.

We pitch into darkness as we enter a tunnel before emerging into Tokyo station. I scan the platform for any police or officials who may be waiting, but the coast seems clear. I get off the train, put my head down and make my way up the escalator on to the teeming streets of Tokyo where I'm happy to be swallowed by the crowds. I walk for forty minutes searching for a mid-range hotel and find one in a side street, near an alley crowded with food vendors. I give my name as Nathan Phillips-Ross, from Sheffield in the UK and blame my lack of passport, or any other ID, on their loss during a visit to Mount Fuji. Fortunately, the hotel is happy to take cash.

I check into my room and search it extensively for bugs – force of habit – then go over my actions of the last several hours and try to think if there is anything that can link me to the 'kidnap'. Of course! In the outside pocket of my backpack is the case file! The file contains court documentation, photos of the child, photos of the mother, photos of the apartment, our company information and contact details, US Embassy documentation and FBI documentation. Thank God I have not yet been stopped for questioning. Any bogus cover story I came up with would have been instantly unravelled by the discovery of this treasure trove of incriminating evidence. I need to get rid of it fast, but I can't just dump it in a bin. The contents could be very damaging to me, the team, the father and probably the US Government.

I need to destroy it, but how? The room has a sprinkler system and, in any case, I don't have a lighter or a match, so burning it is out of the question. I decide to run a bath and make papier-mâché. I tear all the papers into quarters and anything with logos denoting courts, US Government/Embassy or our company I tear off, chew and swallow. I feel sick. While I wait for the paper to soak I turn on the television and flick through the channels for any clue to what has happened to poor Henry and his son. Virtually all the programmes are in Japanese and many are news bulletins. I am about to switch to the next channel when on the screen there is an interview with a police officer, which I can't understand, and film of the street where we snatched Connor. There is an interview with a witness, which might well be where the description of me came from. There is no word that I can understand on what has happened to Henry.

I switch the TV off feeling hounded. I can't talk to anyone and there is no one to call for help. Stephen and Glenn are hopefully in the air and the father, sadly, is probably in prison by now with his son in foster care awaiting the arrival of his mother, and these are the only people who know I am even in Japan. I told my parents I was off to Bali on holiday. I am a one-man team, on a failed mission, on the run. I am also hungry, in spite of the paper now sitting like a lead weight in my stomach. Satisfied that the documents in the bath are well and truly soaked, and that the ink has run, I mash the paper into twelve cricket ball-sized blobs which I put into a laundry bag. I put on a hat and slip out of the front entrance of the hotel.

Steering clear of any CCTV cameras on lamp posts, on buildings or at road intersections, I walk the streets in search of a suitable restaurant and each time I pass a rubbish bin, I throw in one of the papier-mâché balls. By the time I've found a back-street restaurant I have seven paper balls left. Over a sushi meal I now have time to think. I feel desperately sorry for Henry. If only he had listened and not used that credit card, but I have my own worries. I am a fugitive and I still don't know how I'm going to get out of this mess. I set off on a different route back to my hotel, seeking out new bins, watching out for CCTV. About 100 metres from the sanctuary of my hotel I adjust my hat to make sure the staff, and any cameras in the foyer, don't get too good a look at me. At least I've survived the day and tomorrow I will mostly stay in my room. I throw the last of the papier-mâché balls in a waste bin. As I step towards the road crossing a strong hand grips my shoulder and pulls me back.

Chapter Thirteen

'Hey, Skippy! You awake, mate?' It was Stephen shaking me by the shoulder. I rolled over to find the room full of sunlight, and a noisy motorcycle passing below the window told me I was in the Greek islands, not in Tokyo. It was 6.30 am. Fuck! The ferry leaves in thirty minutes. I quickly conducted my morning routine then we grabbed our bags and made our way downstairs. No one was around at reception so I left the key on the counter and headed for the stairs to the ground floor. 'Wait! My passport,' whispered Stephen. We looked at each other and paused before Stephen jumped the counter and quickly opened drawers and cupboards until he found the drawer which contained his and other passports. He grabbed his and we made a hasty exit.

'Sorry if I overslept a bit,' I said as we walked down to the quayside. 'I was having a nightmare about the Japan job.' Stephen gave me a sympathetic glance. 'Whoa! Don't even go there,' he said. 'Bad memories.' They certainly were. After three days lying low I had managed to catch a flight out of Japan but Henry was sentenced to three years in jail for kidnapping before he was allowed to return to California and, to my knowledge, he was never allowed to see his son again. It was a dreadful outcome and a harsh lesson for all of us; a salutary reminder of how these jobs can go bad.

The ferry was relatively busy when we got to the jetty. Passengers were saying goodbye to their families, motorcycles and cars were being driven on to the vessel and a variety of workers in different uniforms and overalls were walking on board ready for their daily commute to work on Kos, or further afield. A fish wholesaler, whose van was among the first loaded on to the ferry for the crossing, was already trying to attract customers for his crates of ice-packed fresh fish.

Stephen and I followed our routine of entering the ferry, making our way through the lounge while observing passengers, turning up the stairs and sitting down in front of the bridge, observing the passengers still boarding. It was now 7.10 am and the ferry eased off its mooring and made its way out of the harbour. Just then two young men wearing work boots, dirty shorts and T-shirts walked on to the bridge deck, leant on the railings and started talking to one another. 'Oh shit!' I whispered to Stephen and pointed to one of the guys who had the words 'A&C PLUMBING, DARWIN' in bold letters on the back of his T-shirt. 'I know that company from three years working in Darwin,' I said. 'Well, do you know him?' Stephen asked. I shook my head. 'I don't think so, but I just hope he doesn't know me.' The young guy ignored me throughout the ferry trip so it seemed I was safe, but I was starting to give everybody a second glance.

'So, what do you think of Peter?' asked Stephen who was less jumpy than I was this morning, but then he hadn't spent his night's sleep on the run in Tokyo. 'I'm definitely unimpressed with his communication but I haven't seen his child recovery skills yet,' I said. 'He has done this type of work before, hasn't he?' Stephen latched on to the note of scepticism in my voice. 'Apparently so. You heard him at Mikali's place. Why do you ask?'

I *had* heard him but I wasn't convinced. 'Because,' I explained, 'when I met him at the airport I noticed he had a brand-new passport, issued only last week. He's not dressed for this type of work and he does seem to be rather young and quiet. Plus, you don't know this, but he spent the night in Athens by himself the night before you arrived.' Stephen frowned. 'Interesting!' he said. 'We'll just have to play it by ear. He is the one who put Diane in touch with us, so we are effectively sub-contracted to him.'

It wasn't long before the ferry arrived in the small harbour at Mastichari and moored up. Stephen and I made our way ashore and strolled the five-minute walk to the hotel where Peter and Diane were preparing coffee, juice and toast in the communal kitchen beside the empty reception. 'How did it go?' Diane asked the moment she saw us. 'Well the house is not quite where you told us it was so we spent a long time trying to find it,' said Stephen. 'We don't know if it's the right one, but take a look.' He handed her the camcorder and pressed play.

Diane's face was a mask of concentration as she gripped the camera and the footage of the harbour and then the coastguard station, filled the monitor. She could hardly hold the camcorder with her shaking hands – and then the house appeared on screen. 'Oh, that fucking asshole!' she exclaimed. I guessed we'd found the right house. It was a place she knew well and it clearly reminded her of her ex-husband, the abductor. I placed my arm around her. 'Are you alright?' I asked. She nodded and I could feel she was shaking. 'That is definitely the house,' she said.

After breakfast which Diane and Peter had prepared, and which she picked at absent-mindedly, I headed to the room and saw on the way that the receptionist was at his counter. 'Excuse me, but can you recommend a good place for birdwatching?' I asked in my best British accent. 'Umm, there's the marshes at Psalidi and the Tigaki saltpans,' he said. 'Or, if you fancy a boat trip, I believe Telendos is quite good. It's an island just off Kalymnos,' he replied, knowledgeably. 'Kalymnos? Is that the island to the east of here?' I asked. 'No,' he said. 'That's Rhodes. Kalymnos is just to the north of us.' I thought that ought to be enough to put him off the scent and with that I carried on up to the room and lay on the bed.

The other three came in and we discussed the operation. 'Right,' Stephen said. 'This is what we'll do. Darren and Peter can go over this afternoon, do surveillance up until tonight, then check on the house in the morning before coming back over. Now that we have the right house, we need to find out if the kid is on the island.' It looked like I was about to get the chance to work with Peter, the child recovery expert, but I wasn't the only one who wanted to know a bit more about him before we went into action. 'How old are you Peter?' Stephen enquired casually. 'Twenty-nine,' he replied. It confirmed my impression that he seemed to be rather young for his position. 'And how long have you been doing this?' 'About five years,' Peter said. 'Do you have a degree in anything?' continued Stephen. If Peter felt he was being interrogated he didn't show it. 'I have a degree in criminal justice,' he said. 'I've also been through the police academy.' It was my turn to pitch in. 'You were a police officer?' 'No. I just went through the academy.' Stephen and I looked baffled. 'How can you go through the academy and not be a police officer?' Stephen asked. 'I know it sounds funny, but I just did the training,' said Peter with a shrug. 'But you'll be up to speed enough to do surveillance with Darren, right?' pressed Stephen. 'Yeah, sure,' said Peter. 'Because, if not,' added Stephen, 'Darren will bring you up to speed before you both go.'

The time was now 9 am on Friday, 30 August. Peter and I were going to board the ferry at 5.30 pm. Diane and Stephen went to check their emails while Peter and I went over the details of the surveillance operation. I could tell, in spite of his assurances, that this was new to him because he was asking me some pretty rudimentary questions. 'How are we going to do this?' he asked, first off, which wasn't necessarily one of the stupid questions. All teams work slightly differently, but I started my explanation with the absolute basics so I knew we were both on the same page.

'Firstly, we need to establish whether the child is on the island,' I said. 'We know where the house is so we'll start by walking past the house so you recognize it, then we need to find out if any of the players are there.' I was met with a blank expression. 'Players?' Peter asked. 'The father. The son. The grandmother,' I replied. 'Obviously, if the father and the grandmother are there, the likelihood is that the child is too. We need to get some footage of the package to put Diane's mind at ease.' More blank looks from Peter. 'What package?' he said. 'The child!' I replied. 'It's a code word we use in case communications are intercepted or conversations overheard. "Package" also has connotations of "handle with care" and "delivery",' I continued. 'Once we've checked out the house, we'll look around the bars and clubs tonight to see if we can locate the father and see what he is up to. Since it will be Friday night there is a good chance he will be out drinking at the bars. We'll use the camcorder where possible but we won't overuse it.'

I paused to check he was following what I was saying. 'I don't know how you work,' I said. 'But Stephen and I don't use radios; we use body language. Obviously holding a radio to your mouth sort of gives the game away and the only way round that is to use an earpiece, but they stick out to the trained eye. Military field signals also look too "Hollywood", so we developed natural body movements to communicate while we are conducting surveillance on a target.' No matter how expert Peter was, he wouldn't know our personal communication system so I went through our signals and what they meant, went over them again, and then had Peter go through and demonstrate them, describing what each one meant. Some of the signals we used when following someone were: taps on the thigh – come forward; hat worn backwards – stay back and keep your distance; hat return to the front – maintain distance; looking in the next shop window up from the target – target entered a shop; tying shoelace – take over the lead.

The trick when following someone is to have a lead team member with eyes on the target and the second team member keeping eyes on the lead team member. It is important not to get in front of the target or within 45 degrees either side of the target's front otherwise you risk being exposed and 'burned'. If there is a danger of straying into the target's sight line you rejoin the team at the rear. Using reflections in shop windows is an effective method of maintaining a visual on the target without obviously looking at them. You don't have to follow on the same side of the road as the target, either. The most important thing is for the lead member to act naturally while maintaining the visual.

I remember conducting surveillance on a hostile threat in South America and I was keeping an eye on the team member in front of me, some 20 metres away. I saw him stop to look in a shop window which meant that the target had done the same, or had entered a shop, further down the road. In order not to overtake them, I entered the first shop on my right to keep my profile to a minimum and realized I had walked into a lingerie shop. I then had to pretend I was buying for a girlfriend but I knew I would have to exit the store the moment I saw the team member behind me pass (we often swapped positions). As I glanced over the bras and knickers, with half an eye on what was happening outside the front window, the attendant asked if I needed any help. I said I was just looking – which I was – but if she caught me peering past the mannequins at the pavement outside she must have thought I was some kind of pervert.

On another job, Stephen was the rear team member, behind me. I stopped to look in a shop window and checked to see he was still in contact but I could not find him. He had been wearing a red North Face jacket all morning and he should have been easy to locate, so now I was concerned. The target was stationary so rather than stand too long on the pavement looking in the same shop front and attract attention to myself, I spotted a telephone box nearby, went in, motioned as if putting some coins in and dialled a random number. As I was moving my mouth, talking gibberish to a non-existent person on the other end of a dead phone, I was also watching the target and scanning behind me for Stephen. I was beginning to fear we had been burned; that Stephen had been dragged off into an alleyway and disposed of and that I was next, when I saw a movement behind a green rubbish bin; a hand moving through a head of hair. It was Stephen. He was sitting on a concrete wall in front of a tree. He had reversed his jacket which had a green lining and he was perfectly camouflaged. He knew what he was doing.

When I was satisfied that Peter knew the signals, I went through some basic surveillance skills, just in case they were different from those in which he'd apparently been trained. 'If I start to talk in a strange accent, don't laugh, just go with the flow. There will be a reason why I act the way I do,' I told him. 'As I said, try not to get in the line of sight of any of the players, but if you are spotted by one of them, do not look at them, just calmly leave the area. If we end up at a bar, order a coke with ice in a spirit glass. Do not leave your drink unattended. It could be drugged by the time you return to it. If you are approached by a female do not pass her off, use her to your advantage to make things look normal, yet maintain surveillance.'

It's an occupational hazard of our employment: females hitting on you in bars while conducting surveillance. It sounds corny but you'd be surprised how often it happens. You can't just say, 'Piss off, I'm working.' And you can't direct all your attention to them, however flattered you might be. It might be your perfect future wife but you can't do anything about it except try to conduct a natural conversation. You can't even leave a phone number, to follow up on the interest later when you're not working, because it could be a set-up.

I explained to Peter: 'Do not look at your target while conversing with someone. Use your peripheral vision. If we are together, we can't just sit there drinking coke looking out the corner of our eye and not saying anything. Just have a normal conversation with each other but be aware of your surroundings and what your target is doing. Whatever you do, make it look natural.'

Until this point, I had never seen a Mexican turn white, but he looked like he was suffering from information overload and was probably thinking it would be pretty hard to look natural while trying to remember that lot. But it's a skill that's developed over time. My concern was that I was with someone who appeared to have little experience in international surveillance and we were not on a training exercise. This was for real. A number of things could – and were likely to – happen if the mission were compromised: they could move the child elsewhere where we wouldn't find him and the mother would have wasted all her money. Also, depending on how hostile the father was, we could get caught doing surveillance and end up injured, or worse.

'Do we sit together if we are at a bar, or do we sit separately?' Peter asked. It was a fair question. 'We sit together. It looks more natural.

We need to sit where we can observe the whole bar and the front entrance. If not, we need to sit directly in front of each other like over a table and watch each other's six,' I explained. 'Six?' queried Peter. 'Yes. Imagine you are at the centre of a clock face. Directly in front of you is twelve o'clock; to your left is nine o'clock; to your right is three o'clock; and directly behind you... is your six.'

I went on: 'We may be separated with, for example, one of us following the father and one following the grandmother with the child. If this happens, we will each stay with our different target until they return home tonight. If we decide to go different ways we will have rendezvous (RV) points pre-arranged, along with times to check in with each other. We will discuss those exact times when we get to Kalymnos, have taken a look and decided what we are doing. You got any questions?' I asked. I felt sure he would have.

'What clothes do I wear?' he asked. I hadn't expected that one. 'Not what you've got on now,' I said firmly, feeling as though I was working in a child care centre. 'You need to get rid of those black slip-on sneakers. No one wears them over here. Just wear a shirt and trousers that look casual,' I said. 'And don't wear any aftershave or spray deodorant. Use a stick or roll-on.' 'Oh, OK, why is that?' he asked. 'We don't want to smell like a perfume shop. Familiar scents will attract the attention of the wary.' I felt like the head teacher of a grooming school with a brand new student. I needed this Californian Mexican to look like just another European holidaymaker enjoying the Greek islands, but he looked like a Mexican from California on his office lunchbreak.

It was approaching midday and I was anxious to get going on the surveillance operation, but we still had another five hours until the ferry. Diane wanted to get something to eat so we all made our way to a restaurant for lunch. It felt like all I was doing was eating, but I nearly choked on my food with the next bombshell. 'So, what's the plan of attack?' Stephen asked Peter over lunch. Peter looked nonplussed. 'Um, I don't know,' he said. 'Well, *you're* from the child recovery company,' countered Stephen. Peter was like a rabbit in the headlights. 'No, I'm happy for you to run things,' he said. 'I'm just here to learn.' Jaws dropped around the table. Here to learn! What the hell was he saying? The client who had paid him a very large sum of money to do this job, to contract us, was sitting at the same table. Stephen laughed sardonically; Diane looked stunned and I sat there in disbelief. I was going to do hostile surveillance with someone who was just there to learn! That would be a great help if the father happened to turn psycho with that 1.2m object with red bullets.

The rest of lunch was subdued but we let Peter's revelation pass. As far as Diane was concerned, I guess, Peter's company was just the go-between which had sub-contracted the job to professional recovery specialists – us – and we were there and ready to go, so not much had changed. But I couldn't help but reflect on the fact Stephen and I had come to recover an abducted child and we seemed to have taken on the added duties of filming a documentary, and babysitting a child recovery novice.

After lunch Peter announced he was going to another cafe – the only place in town that had internet access – to check his emails. Diane went back to the hotel and Stephen and I went window shopping. We often look around small stores, not searching for anything in particular but seeing if there is anything which can be of use to the operation. I picked up a pamphlet on local birds to help our cover story and to tell me a little bit about bee-eaters, long-legged buzzards, Eleonora's falcons and the like, and then we headed back to the hotel. As we passed the internet cafe, we noticed Peter still inside on a computer, typing away madly. Stephen motioned his head towards Peter, indicating he wanted me to go in and do surveillance on him.

The cafe had booths and Peter was in a booth against the wall, not where I would have been situated because it didn't allow him to see much of the rest of the cafe. It meant I was able to walk in unseen by Peter and sit in a booth in the aisle two back from him, over his left shoulder but facing him. The attendant walked over and without saying anything I handed him 5 euros and indicated I didn't want any change for fear of getting into a conversation which would attract Peter's attention. I sat upright in order to look over Peter's shoulder at his computer monitor and I realized that if he was to blur his vision and use the reflection of his screen he would see a large head looking at him – mine – but I felt pretty confident he wouldn't be that savvy. As far as I could tell, it was a very long email, with many paragraphs. Unfortunately, I was too far away to read who he was sending it to and the longer I craned my neck, the sooner I felt I would raise the suspicions of the attendant, so I snuck out the front entrance.

Back at our hotel room, Stephen was on our balcony chatting with Diane on hers. I sat on the bed and studied the maps and photos again until the door opened and Peter entered. 'All done?' I asked, innocently. 'Yeah, I got another case in Hawaii. The FBI are working on it right now,' he said. I was intrigued. 'Hawaii? What's the FBI's involvement?' I asked. 'The father abducted the child and since the child is an American citizen there is a warrant out for the father's arrest,' he explained. Visions of Japan flashed through my head again. 'You ever been to Hawaii?' Peter enquired. 'No, I haven't.' He smiled. 'I can see if it's alright for you to get involved, if you want.' 'Um, well, we'll talk about it later,' I said. 'We need to focus on this case first.'

Peter and I went over our plan of action again, including the communication signals. I wanted to make sure he understood every little detail before we arrived on Kalymnos. As fate usually has it, nothing goes to plan anyway and I have been on very few jobs where it does, but if you've got a plan, and a back-up, you're generally in better shape to react to the unexpected. I had begun to think about our counter-actions drills – the secondary plan we needed in case things didn't go according to the original plan so we weren't left wondering what to do next. I explained to Peter I was going to go through the 'actions on' drills. 'Right,' he said, preparing a notebook and pen. 'Don't write any of this down, mate,' I snapped. 'You're going to have to memorize it. We don't want to take anything that will give the game away should we be searched.' It can be hard at times, but you really do have to memorize every detail. I'd learned that lesson in Japan.

I explained to Peter that we couldn't carry photos of the father and the child, or make any notes about the operation, on surveillance. I had posted the pictures on the wall of our hotel room and had sat staring at them, looking at the features until they were etched into my memory, and I urged him to do the same. Should we look suspicious and have the local police search us – and we had an indication they were sympathetic to the father – I did not want them finding anything associated with the case. It would blow our cover as tourists.

I told him what to do if we lost communication, came up against any hostility, had problems with the authorities, needed medical treatment and evacuation or had to abort the mission for any other reason. I realized it was probably too much for him to take in and things could still turn to shit even if we both knew exactly what we were doing, but I did the best I could and he seemed to listen. That was one good thing about Peter. He did seem keen and willing to learn. After all, he did say he was there to learn. I just hoped, for both our sakes, he wasn't about to learn the hard way.

The contingency plans were to either meet up at the Kalymnos ferry wharf – Staging Area 1; or the wharf at Mastichari – Staging Area 2; or our hotel on Kos – Staging Area 3. I told him: *Lost Comms (communications) – wait for an hour and meet at Staging Area 1; *Medical Emergency – go to the local hospital. The other team member adopts Lost Comms protocol and if no one is at Staging Area 1 after an hour, goes to the hospital; *Hostile Surveillance – go to Staging Area 1 immediately. The other team member adopts Lost Comms drill; *Problems with authorities – keep to the cover story, try to talk your way out of it. If detained, say nothing about the operation and sit tight. The other team member adopts Lost Comms drill, then Medical Emergency drill. If he finds you are not in hospital he will assume detention, get off the island and meet up with other team members at Staging Area 3; *Abort Mission – shirts worn inside out. Get off the island by any means possible and meet up at Staging Area 2.

By the time I had gone through all of this, Stephen had finished chatting to Diane and entered the room. 'How's it going?' he asked. 'Good,' I replied. 'We've covered a lot of stuff and he's up to speed with everything.' Stephen turned to Peter. 'Just listen to what Darren has to say and follow his lead. He's good at surveillance.' Then he added: 'So, how much is Kid Find making out of this?' Peter looked embarrassed. 'Nothing. It's a non-profit organization.' 'Fair enough,' said Stephen. 'But how do you get paid?' Peter clearly wasn't sure what Stephen was getting at. 'I get an hourly fee,' he replied. 'Yes,' added Stephen. 'But where do they get their money from to pay you?' Finally, Peter twigged. 'Ah, I see. We get money from donations. Corporate America will make donations regularly and parents give us donations out of any money left over from the cost of recoveries.' Stephen nodded. 'So, whatever is left over from the cost of this job, Diane can choose to give to Kid Find, as a thank you?' Peter shuffled awkwardly. 'No, n-not exactly,' he stuttered. 'What do you mean?' asked Stephen. 'I don't work for Kid Find,' said Peter.

I could sense Stephen was about to blow a gasket at this. We had been contracted to Kid Find to conduct this operation and now we found Peter didn't work for them. 'What?' barked Stephen. 'Who are you? Who the hell DO you work for?' Peter stiffened. 'No one. Kid Find was contacted by Diane about the case and I worked on it, but then they said they didn't want to go ahead because they didn't want to be held liable. They thought the chances of success were minimal and the risk of it going wrong was too high. They said if I continued with it I would no longer work for them. I couldn't very well turn the mother away, so I carried on working on the case.' The room went silent. 'So you no longer work for Kid Find?' said Stephen. 'No,' replied Peter. 'But depending on the result of this case, I may get my job back.'

This was getting more and more bizarre and now Peter's future employment was resting on our shoulders. I had to admire his courage for not turning his back on Diane; for getting someone prepared to carry out the recovery – us – and for having the balls to come on the job himself, as ill-suited to it as he seemed. But he should have put us in the picture a lot earlier and I hoped Diane didn't find out too soon. She had enough on her plate without having to get her head around this. We would just have to make it work. In the meantime, we had an operation to get on with.

It was now approaching 5 pm and Peter and I started packing our things for the night's surveillance ready to catch the 5.30 pm ferry. 'How many shirts shall I pack?' asked Peter. 'For God's sake, we're only going overnight!' I replied, flabbergasted by his lack of common sense. We gathered our stuff and I checked over Peter and his equipment in the way I had done so many times before with my soldiers in the military. Thankfully he looked more like a tourist and his daysack carried just the bare essentials. I told Stephen we were ready to go and he reiterated the plan for tonight: 'You guys go over, check out the house and see if the kid is on the island. Play it by ear, Darren, and come back tomorrow whenever you want.' I signalled my agreement and told him that if we got what we wanted tonight, we'd be on the 7 am ferry.

Diane came into the room and wished us luck before Peter, Stephen and I made our way to the wharf. Stephen told Peter to get the tickets as we walked on past the ticket booth. 'Did you get anything on Peter?' asked Stephen referring to my little surveillance mission earlier. 'He was sending a very large email to someone, but I couldn't see who,' I said. I repeated what Peter had told me about the job in Hawaii. 'But his level of experience doesn't suggest he would be involved in any operation to that extent,' I said. 'Besides, he's just told us he's no longer working for the company.' Stephen nodded. 'Something's not right,' he said. 'I think he's telling someone what we're doing. Keep a close eye on him, will you?' I didn't need telling. 'Don't worry,' I said, 'I certainly will.'

Chapter Thirteen

Stephen wished us luck and left us to board the ferry. Peter and I went through the boarding routine I had explained to him, ending up on the deck by the bridge. He was quiet and I sensed he was nervous. I was too, because I was about to enter a hostile environment with Peter as my wingman and it didn't fill me with much confidence. Something else that made me uneasy was the last-minute appearance of a uniformed man who arrived late on the boat on a noisy motorcycle just after we had settled on the viewing platform by the bridge. The officer waved at the ferry hand as the ramp was raised. He looked like a coastguard but he could have been some kind of law enforcement. Was it a routine journey for him or was he there looking for someone? I kept an eye on him as the ferry slowly moved out of the harbour and we set sail for Kalymnos.

Chapter Fourteen

Diane paced the room like a caged tiger. She couldn't sit down; couldn't stand still; couldn't sleep. She couldn't easily go outside, because of the need to disguise herself, but there was nothing for her to do trapped in her hotel 'prison', and so she paced, backwards and forwards, picking things up only to put them down again without any idea why she had picked them up in the first place. She stared at the clock on the wall, willing the hands to move faster but they wouldn't. It was 6.12 pm. Too late to call her husband in Melbourne where it was now gone 1 am; too late to ask him how her daughter was doing, though she longed to do so; too late to hear his comforting voice.

She felt such an aching in her bosom. Was it just the empty feeling that being without her baby gave her, or the knowledge that, if life had not been so cruel, she would still be at home breastfeeding her wee one? Being away from her baby and her husband was tearing her apart, but it would have torn her apart not to be here, doing what she could to get her beloved son back. She couldn't win. She pictured her daughter's tiny features; recalled the softness of her skin; her sweet smell. And then her mind leapt back, remembering breastfeeding Theo, his cherubic face as he suckled, his little fingers stroking her involuntarily as he did so, his tiny toes twitching.

She looked at the clock again. It was 6.13 pm. The boys would be going ashore in Pothia about now. She pictured them walking up the jetty and walking along the quayside in the early evening sunshine, the sun glinting off the crystal-clear waters making wavy patterns of light on the curved hulls of the boats. The harbour had seemed so idyllic when she had first set eyes on it as a carefree 21 year old. She had grown to love the town and the island and had been happy to call it home for a while, smugly watching each new arrival of holidaymakers knowing that after a week, or perhaps two, they would have to return home while she would still be there, in paradise. She recalled the kindness and hospitality of the cafe owners just down the road from Nick's family home who had found her a room to stay, and their smiles of delight as she had learned her first words of Greek. They were wonderful moments at the time. Now the memories made her shudder. She hated that island, hated the people. How could they have been so kind before and now conspire with Nick to deprive her of her son? How could they do that to her?

Her holiday romance, once so exciting, had turned into a nightmare, she had long since acknowledged. She could never again watch the movie Shirley Valentine *without shrivelling inside with embarrassment at the memories it evoked. She couldn't even eat a Greek salad without feeling sick. And now here she was back on Kos, watching out over the approach to Mastichari harbour that she had grown so familiar with all those years ago, afraid to go out lest she be spotted by the very people she had once practised her Greek language on.*

Diane paced some more and looked at the clock again. It was 6.14 pm. This was such agony. She didn't know what to do with herself and all the time her thoughts ran wild. Would Darren and Peter find Theo? Would he be playing with his toys in the house; the toys she had lovingly packed in his bag to take on holiday? Did he still have them, or had they been casually and callously jettisoned and replaced by toys of his father's choosing? Would her little boy be missing her? Would he even know her? It had been so long. 'You bastard, Nick!' she cursed under her breath, thinking for the umpteenth time about what he had done to her and what he had done to their son. Then a new thought barged its way in. What if Theo wasn't there? What if the family had hidden him again? They might all be wasting their time there. Diane couldn't stand the helpless waiting to find out. Darren, Stephen and Peter had all been so kind; had made all the right sympathetic noises, but they couldn't possibly begin to know what she was going through, missing Theo, missing her daughter, longing for a hug from her husband to make everything better.

A voice from the balcony pulled her up sharply. It was Stephen on his balcony, enquiring if she was there and if she wanted to go for a meal, but she didn't. She couldn't face eating. She thanked Stephen but explained that she would just take a little walk on her own. She had to get out of the room, if only for a while but she would take care to wear her floppy hat and sunglasses, she assured him. Five minutes later, suitably disguised, she stepped out of the front of the hotel, turned left and walked along the palm-lined street, past the statue of Neptune; past the low-rise tavernas starting to fill with young families. It was Friday night. Many of them, healthily tanned, full of smiles, would be heading home tomorrow and were enjoying a last meal out as their excited children played together in front of the restaurant, enjoying the freedom that was the dividend of their parents' relaxation.

Diane's heart skipped a beat as a curly-haired boy, aged about 4, was chased into the street by his elder sister amid whelps of joy. How like Theo he looked from behind but did her son even look like that now? She only had her memories, and her treasured photographs, to call on.

Further up the street, a few locals were looking to extend into the weekend the religious festival they had missed the night before because they had needed to be up early for work. They raised their glasses to the Prophet Elijah, to John the Baptist, and to St Fanourios – the first drinks of what had all the makings of a long night. Diane sat alone at a table in a small neighbouring cafe, her hat pulled down to her brow, and ordered a coffee. She might as well enjoy the caffeine as she knew she wasn't going to get much sleep tonight. She might even have joined the locals in something stronger to toast St Fanourios had she realized his significance as the persecuted martyr to whom Greek tradition dictates you are meant to turn for help in recovering lost things. Instead, she remained lost in her own thoughts until it was time to make the short walk back around the corner to her hotel for a night tortured by uncertainty over what was happening across the water on Kalymnos.

Chapter Fifteen

The sun was sinking behind the monastery of Agioi Pantes, perched high on the hilltop overlooking Pothia, as we walked towards the Hellenic Coastguard building, turned left and started to walk up the road. The evening air was still warm and in other circumstances it might have been a pleasant stroll, but I was too anxious about what we might find or, more worryingly, not find and Peter must have been equally nervous because he was walking in silence. I had pointed out the house to him as the ferry had entered the harbour. Now we would hopefully discover if anyone was at home.

As we passed the motorcycle hire shop near the barricades, I saw a small boy playing with a much younger girl by the corner of the church, approximately 30 metres ahead of us. It could easily have been Theo as he was not very different from the boy whose photo I had been staring at for days on end, but your mind can play tricks and every boy of that age can start to resemble the picture in your mind. This lad, in any case, was much taller than the boy in the photo. He didn't have the same chubby cheeks and his arms and legs were longer. Still, there remained something about him that nagged at me. I didn't want to alert Peter to my thinking for fear of getting him excited but it occurred to me that Theo might have grown up quickly in the past fourteen months. The photo was, after all, taken when he was just 4.

'Peter,' I said, calmly. 'Stand in front of me and smile, would you?' Peter did as requested. Maybe he was learning. I scanned the area to make sure we weren't attracting attention and, satisfied that we weren't being watched, I reached into my bag, pulled out the camcorder and pointed it in Peter's direction. As he stood there grinning, I zoomed in on the boy over his left shoulder and began to record. The lad could not have been a better subject. Perhaps thinking he was hijacking my footage of my friend, he danced cheekily in the background for approximately seven seconds before disappearing behind the church.

'What's up?' asked Peter as I lowered the camcorder and walked towards him. The look on my face must have betrayed my excitement. 'I think I got the kid,' I replied in a whisper. 'Where?' exclaimed Peter, turning around. 'Don't look! He disappeared behind the church. I'll play the video back to you later but he may still be there,' I said. 'We'll walk on and I'll look straight ahead as we pass the church but you take a glance.'

We continued up the road and as we walked by the church Peter looked towards the steps which lead to the road above us. 'The boy's playing with a small girl,' he said, quietly. I glanced out of the corner of my eye towards the house and saw that the front door was open. Yes! Whether that's the boy or not, we know at least one of the players is at home. It would be the icing on the cake if the boy I had just filmed was Theo, but we would have to wait and see. We were, by now, only about 10 metres from the house and my heart was beating faster as we tried to appear as disinterested as possible in that particular property.

I heard a motorcycle approaching from behind. This was good. Stepping to the right-hand side of the road to allow the motorcycle to pass us would give us a valid reason to stop and have a longer look at the house without arousing suspicion. I made a point of ushering Peter to the side of the road, as if he hadn't heard the noise behind us, but no sooner had the motorcycle passed us, it decelerated rapidly and came to a stop on the left-hand side of the stairs to the house, just a short distance in front of us. I couldn't see the face of the rider but it was a man in his thirties, I judged, with greying curly black hair. 'Shit!' I thought. 'It's him!'

The man cut the bike engine and the narrow street went quiet. We were just 8 metres from the abductor. Standing still was no longer natural and I felt suddenly exposed. The silence was equally uncomfortable and I needed to turn Peter's attention away from the house so that the father did not see our faces, but I didn't want to say anything that would give away my Australian accent. Trying to lower my heartbeat and keep calm as we began to walk again, I looked ahead to where the street dog-legged and saw a kitten in the road. 'Aww! Look at that,' I said to Peter in my best British accent, pointing at the tiny cat. 'They look so cute at that age.'

We carried on past the house, not daring to look back in case the father was watching us. Peter caught on, luckily, and started to point at various interesting features until we were out of the father's earshot. Around 300 metres from the house we neared an intersection in the road and were able to stop walking. 'Phew! That was close. It was him, the father!' I said. 'Yeah, it definitely was,' said Peter. 'Although his hair really isn't black like in the photos. It's more of a grey.' I nodded. 'Yeah, well, if I was in his shoes I'd be going grey too,' I said. 'Anyway, that worked well. He didn't see our faces, which is a good thing, and I don't think he had any reason to suspect anything from the way we acted so well done. Good work, mate.' Peter smiled like a kid who'd been given a gold star for his homework.

The problem with international child recoveries is that you don't know if the players know of the operation even before you get there. The danger is that the parent trying to recover the child might have indicated in the course of a fraught conversation, or correspondence, that something was about to 'happen'. It might have been the tiniest detail but it could have been enough to put the abductor on his or her guard. It might be something they said over the phone to the child; it could be that they are seen in the country upon arrival; or someone close to both parties, and privileged to the plan, might have leaked some or all of it to the abductor.

I took the mere fact of the father being at home as a good indication that the operation had not been compromised. Paranoia is an occupational hazard or, at least, it is for me. You get to a state where, with every person who gives you a second look, you automatically think the operation must have been blown. In some cases, paranoia is a good thing, as it keeps you on your toes, but the real skill is to act naturally even when your every sense is telling you things have gone wrong.

Back in Arkansas, Stephen and I would use a local shopping centre for our students to conduct surveillance training. Stephen or I would pick out random people getting out of their vehicles or entering the shopping centre and we would instruct the students to follow them and gain information on them – how much money they take out of an ATM; who they talk to; what they buy or eat; right down to what brand of toothpaste they might buy or what size trousers they were looking at in the clothes shop. Even the brightest government or military students find it challenging to act naturally when conducting surveillance to the point that, in some cases, it was obvious what they were doing and complaints were made to the shopping centre's security officers. Luckily, we had an agreement with the security department which was aware of what we were doing.

Peter and I walked back along the road towards the harbour and Hotel Therme. The wide esplanade that separated the harbour waters from the main town was a hive of activity with people setting up a small stage and sound equipment. It looked like Friday night was party night on Kalymnos and there would be a concert later. We crossed the road to the hotel and entered the small door, but not before I had looked back in the direction from which we had walked in case we had been followed. Everything appeared to be normal so we carried on up to the reception and checked in. The same old man looked us over but if he recognized me and noticed that I was with a different bloke from the night before he didn't appear in the least bit bothered. Without a word he handed me the key to room number eleven. 'Oh shit,' I thought. 'The helicopter room.' I paid the old boy 25 euros and he didn't even ask for identification this time.

Ordinarily, it would not be ideal to use the same hotel again but I was concerned that, in such a small town, using a different hotel each night might increase the chances that someone would think our activities suspicious and the wagging tongues might alert the players. Having found a hotel where the owner was obviously disinterested in us seemed like a good thing and the fact that he now asked no questions and no longer required any identification just reinforced that view. Besides, the hotel seemed to be nearly empty and the view from the balcony of the entire esplanade and the water's edge made it perfect for us. Going against standard operating procedures (SOPs) we might have been, but we were adhering to another well-known security procedure – adapt and overcome.

We made our way upstairs and I replayed the footage of the boy. I was certain that this was Theo, even though he had changed considerably since the case photos that we had been studying. After watching the footage, Peter agreed. We would know for sure when we got Diane to confirm it the next day. I wondered how she would be coping with the agonizing wait for information and how she would react to the video if it was Theo.

After settling in, we changed our clothes for the evening and wandered out on to the balcony to watch the esplanade. Most of the harbourside restaurants were filling up with locals and tourists. 'Right,' I said to Peter. 'It's now 1900 hours. I'll go back and check out the house; you go and check out the restaurants and the clubs. We'll rendezvous at the restaurant downstairs at 2100 hours, OK? Be careful, and don't get caught.' We went downstairs, out the front of the hotel and I headed straight across the road in the direction of the house. Glancing back, I saw Peter sit down in the outdoor seating of a fish restaurant, which seemed natural enough. I wanted to approach the house from a different angle this time and check out a good location for an observation post (OP) so, instead of carrying on up the road, I turned right before the church and walked up a long set of steps to the road above the house and walked along that for a short way.

Adjacent to the front entrance of the house was a small, narrow set of steps leading up to this road. I walked back down these steps to a small pedestrian alleyway very near to the house and then along the alley, away from it. The sun had disappeared behind the hills and the long, sharp shadows of late afternoon had given way to the less distinct shading of dusk. I stood in the protective gloom cast by a crumbling brick wall, just off the alley, and observed the front of the house. The motorcycle wasn't there. I glanced over my shoulder and up above me to see the balconies of the houses. All was quiet apart from the occasional clinking of dinner plates and metallic clatter of pots and pans.

I could hear footsteps approaching. They were coming from the alleyway behind me. I froze and clung as flat to the wall as I could, cloaked by the evening shadows. An elderly lady and a young woman walked past carrying shopping bags and slowly turned and made their way up the narrow steps that I had come down. My heart was beating fast but, so long as I was not compromised, this was what I loved about my occupation... the rush of adrenaline. I didn't have time to enjoy the buzz before a streetlight flickered on and stole away the gloom that hid me, illuminating my position with a weak orange light that was growing stronger and whiter.

I approached the alleyway and looked left, then right. The coast was clear so I made my way down the alley, further away from the house. I had only gone a few paces when I came across a large window opening in the brick wall that adjoined the wall I had been standing against. I peered inside and saw a large tree growing in the middle of the rubble within. It was a derelict house without a roof. This might well be a good location for an OP but I would need to check it out some more. I looked up the alleyway once more, to the left and to the right, then heaved my way up to the window ledge and lowered myself into the rubble. Moving quietly was difficult because of the loose debris under my feet, which threatened to betray every footstep with the loud crunching of broken brick and concrete, so it took me about fifteen minutes of painstakingly careful steps to reach the other side of the building, some 10 metres away. From there, I was rewarded with a direct view down onto the side and the front entrance of the house. Bingo!

The derelict building I was in had all of its four walls shielding me from any outside view. Two were the adjoining walls of neighbouring houses which, naturally, did not have windows. The window I had just clambered through could not be seen from my new position due to an internal brick wall. It now appeared that I was standing in an old bedroom and the wall facing the house now directly in front of me was broken in the middle, giving me an escape route. There was also a small triangular-shaped hole in the corner of the wall which was big enough for the camcorder to film through, enabling me to conduct surveillance without being in direct sight. The distance from the OP to the front door of the target house was about 15 metres. I had the perfect OP.

A perfect OP is one which has two exits so that if someone were to enter the OP through one, you can escape out of the other. It was very dark as the walls shut out any street lighting. The window entrance was high and because of the length of time I estimated this building had been derelict, I doubted that anyone would make the effort to look inside. Though caution would be needed to enter during the day for fear of being seen, it could be used day and night and could not be overlooked by anyone standing on their balconies. This was a textbook OP.

Many OPs these days seem to be nothing more than the front seat of a vehicle parked near a target, which always looks suspicious, in my book. I was taught how to build OPs properly in the military although, as carefully as you choose them or construct them, they aren't always as perfect as you think. I once had a good OP well hidden in scrub bush across the road from a target in Russia. No one would see me in there, I thought, except that one particular day as I was watching the child and the abductor through binoculars I *was* detected, by a curious stray dog which came from nowhere and attacked me, biting into my left calf muscle. Thankfully, due to the thick scrub, I was able to make my escape unseen, though perhaps not unheard. I didn't foresee any such problems with this OP and the view onto the target house seemed ideal.

At that moment the front door of the house opened and I watched through the hole in the wall as a middle-aged woman came out of the door on to the patio, picked something up from the small table and went back into the house. The grandmother. We now knew that the father and the grandmother were both on the island and so, almost certainly, was Theo who, hopefully, was the boy I had filmed. Right now, the boy was either inside with his grandmother or out with his father. Since Diane had said the father would probably be out drinking tonight, I presumed the boy was inside with his grandmother.

It had been a productive night's work so far. It was now approaching 2015 hours and I needed to check out other areas for an alternative OP in case this one became inoperable for any reason. I carefully, and quietly, made my way back across the rubble, out of the window opening and back into the alleyway. I could see a house up the hill which had a large padlock on the front door indicating to me that it was vacant. I cautiously walked up the steps towards the front door and peered through the windows. It was dark and definitely looked unoccupied. Above me I could see that another stairway made its way up from my current level to the second floor so I climbed these stairs and peered through the second-floor windows. Again, it appeared to be vacant, although I could see furniture illuminated by the nearby streetlight. From beneath this stairway, near to the front door, the father's house could be seen clearly.

It wasn't an ideal location, because there was only one way in, but as an alternative to the main OP it would do and I could overcome the lack of an escape route if I used a cover man at the alleyway entrance to the house to give an early warning if anyone was coming. Then I had an idea for another counter-surveillance measure. I reached into my bag for some sunscreen which I had bought earlier. The shop assistant who sold it to me had put it into a paper bag which she had secured with a small piece of clear sticky tape – a bit unnecessary, maybe, but a nice touch. Now I had a use for that tape. I peeled it off carefully, tore a small piece of it and stuck it over the keyhole to the large padlock on the front door. That way I'd know in future if someone was using the house.

It was now approximately 2045 hours and I needed to rendezvous with Peter to see if he had seen the father and to let him know what I had found out. I walked casually back down the road towards the harbour and as I made my way towards the RV point something caught my attention. At the front of a restaurant, watching the activities on the esplanade, was a lone man sitting at a table. A quick glance told me it was the same man who had driven past us earlier that evening and parked his motorcycle at the front of our target house. The father.

The restaurant he was sitting at was on the side of the esplanade facing up the road and towards our hotel. I approached the RV point and could see Peter sitting at a table drinking coca cola out of a spirit glass. 'I found him!' he said, excitedly. 'Is he sitting at the front of the restaurant down there?' I asked, with a slight nod of my head in the direction I had just come from. The realization that I had also seen him did not deflate Peter. 'Yes, that's the one. He's sitting by himself. He's been there for some time,' he replied, excitedly. 'Right,' I said. 'Let's go upstairs to the room and watch him from the balcony.'

Upstairs, I asked Peter to check out the balcony next to ours to make sure there was no one on the other side of the small chipboard wall that divided us, then I got out the camcorder and zoomed in as close as possible on the father, something I would not have been able to do from the restaurant downstairs. He was about 200 metres from our balcony and I watched and filmed him for about ten minutes. Even at that distance I could see he was drinking a clear liquid on ice and smoking Malboro Reds. As soon as he finished one cigarette he lit another and the drinks came almost as often. No one spoke to him apart from the waiter as he sat watching passers-by. His face was expressionless and he looked like a man with a lot on his mind, frequently staring into space. We had found our abductor.

'I want to get a closer shot of him,' I said to Peter. Since our man seemed to be fully occupied watching the traffic go past, both vehicles and pedestrians, I decided to take a gamble and position myself across the road from him, near to the boats in the harbour, and to film him from there. That way I could get a front-on shot. The best surveillance photos are those taken at an angle of 45 degrees. That way you are getting some frontal and some profile.

I walked along the esplanade and sat on a bollard in an area unlit by the streetlights or by the bright lights of the harbour front. Blending into the darkness, approximately 80 metres from the father, and appearing to be listening to the concert on the esplanade, I set the camera up on full zoom and started filming the stage, occasionally re-aiming the camera towards the father. He regularly glanced at the passing traffic but was oblivious to my presence.

Confident I had some good footage, I made my way back to the hotel where Peter was waiting in our room and I showed him the film. He suggested that he go down and sit in the concert crowd and film the father front-on. Peter seemed to be growing in confidence and I thought it was a good idea so I agreed and he headed out to mingle with the concert crowd as I watched from the balcony. He returned thirty minutes later and I viewed the footage he had shot. It wasn't too bad, despite the father's face being occasionally obscured by a pole in the foreground, which I pointed out to Peter. Most importantly, Peter had successfully blended into the crowd and filmed without drawing attention to himself.

It was now 2200 hours and we knew where all the players were. The grandmother, and presumably the child, were safely tucked up at home and I decided it was safer to conduct any further surveillance on the father from the hotel balcony, so we sat there and watched him from a distance. I could see him clearly through the binoculars so there was no reason to risk compromising ourselves. At approximately 2300 hours the concert finished and we saw the father pay his bill with two 50 euro notes and receive between 30 and 40 euros in change before he walked to his nearby motorcycle, mounted up and rode past our location in the direction of his house. There was nothing more for us to do so we decided to turn in for the night and leave on the 0700 hours ferry the next morning.

As I lay on my bed with the whoomp, whoomp, whoomp of the fan blades once more sounding like helicopter rotor blades, my feeling of satisfaction with a night's work well done gave way to an awful thought. Why were we given this room again? Was it bugged? Had the old man's indifference been a clever act and was someone setting us up? I quashed the growing wave of paranoia. The mere fact that the father was not only on the island but going out drinking reassured me that the operation had not been compromised. I relaxed but still I couldn't get to sleep. The problem this time wasn't the whoomp, whoomp, whoomp of the ceiling fan, but the deafening sound of Peter, snoring like an asthmatic wildebeest. It felt like his every breath made the room shake, but eventually I nodded off.

'Shit! Quick, Peter! We have thirty minutes,' I shouted. I had woken naturally at around 6.30 am and Peter was still snoring until my words brought the cacophony to an abrupt, spluttering halt. We hurriedly got dressed and made our way to the wharf with just a quick detour to the motorcycle rental shop. If you placed yourself up against the wall of the shop and looked up the hill you could just see the front of the father's house. The motorcycle was parked on the left-hand side of the stairs.

The father had evidently returned home after being out the previous night. We boarded the ferry and went through our usual routine, ending up on the bridge deck. I was satisfied with the night's surveillance and the footage we had obtained.

The ferry horn sounded and we made our way out of the harbour once more en route for Kos island. I was beginning to wonder whether the deck hands might be getting suspicious of my regular comings and goings but they rarely glanced at us. The ferry had at least a handful of tourists on each trip to date and the fact that it was the summer holidays was perfect cover for our movements, but I was acutely aware that the season was about to end. We needed to do the recovery before the holidays were over and the tourists went home leaving us sticking out like sore thumbs. Time was against us.

The early morning sun rose into the deep azure Mediterranean sky, burning down on us as the ferry ploughed its gentle furrow through the benign sea on the way to Mastichari. With no one within earshot, Peter and I debriefed the previous night's operation, discussing how it had gone and what we might have done better. To be on top of this type of work you need to be able to continually find ways of improving. I had developed a method of 'self-debrief' going over every aspect of an operation and I did it now, going over the night's work in my head.

I was beginning to worry that we would compromise the operation because of the claustrophobic layout of the town – or the harbour side of it, at least, which had so far been our only area of operation. We'd had no need to use vehicles because everything was within walking distance. The distance between the house and the hotel was approximately 800 metres; the hotel to the wharf, 400 metres; the house to the esplanade, 400 metres; the house to the wharf, 300 metres. It was the most challenging surveillance I had encountered due to everything being so close and tight. We were told the whole island knew of the father's illegal action and was helping him, and here we were running around taking pictures of his house. The danger of someone spotting us and questioning what we were doing was high, but I really couldn't think of anything I could have done better with the equipment we had and the environment we were working in, so my self-debrief was complete.

The ferry pulled into the harbour at Mastichari and we made our way towards the hotel, with me looking back occasionally to see if anyone was following us. The last thing we needed was hostile surveillance knowing our base of operations, especially with the mother there. I satisfied myself that no one was paying us any attention. However, as we neared the hotel, a figure in front stepped out from the shadow of a large olive tree. It was Stephen. 'How did you go?' he asked, startling Peter who hadn't spotted him. 'Good,' I replied. 'We have some good shots. We saw the father, the grandmother and, we think, we saw the kid.' Stephen looked pleased but he knew better than to get too excited. 'That sounds good,' he said. 'Let's go and show Diane. She's making us some breakfast in the hotel. Anything to keep herself busy, I think. She managed to speak to her husband this morning, which calmed her down, but it will be great to put her out of her misery with some information. It can't be easy for her.'

Despite the fact I knew Stephen was checking our six as he spoke to us, I glanced back over my shoulder as we walked to the hotel then went into the communal kitchen where Diane had indeed prepared some breakfast. Her face lit up with a mixture of excitement and anxiety. 'Did you see him?' she demanded, without waiting for us to take a seat. 'We think so, but I need you to see some footage to confirm it,' I explained. 'Come and sit down outside and watch it. It's a bit more private.'

Diane was shaking like a leaf as I sat her down on the patio, opened the camcorder monitor, pressed play and handed the camera to her. I wanted her sitting down, and not overheard, as I didn't know how she would react to seeing her son for the first time in such a long time, if it was Theo we had filmed. I didn't have to wait long to find out. The first shot was of the small boy dancing for me outside the church. The camera was shaking in Diane's hands and tears welled in her eyes, overflowing in rivulets down her cheeks. 'Oh my God! Oh my God! That's him!' she said. 'That's him!' Her eyes never left the monitor as she spoke, transfixed by the images which she rewound and replayed. 'I wasn't sure if it was him because he has changed quite a lot from the photo, but I thought I would film him for you to verify,' I said. 'No, that's definitely him,' said Diane, still mesmerized by the footage. 'My, hasn't he changed? He's got so much taller. Oh, my God,' she sobbed.

I tried to remain dispassionate but had to walk over to the balcony edge with my back towards Diane so she could not see my own tears which I was struggling to contain. Her reaction and the joy on her face at seeing her son was priceless. Having not been married, and having no children of my own, I could only imagine what she was experiencing.

The video continued to play, moving on to the footage of the father sat at the table outside the restaurant. 'Oh, that fucking arsehole!' she spluttered. 'Look at him, out drinking while my son is home without him!' Her anger seemed to help her to refocus and stem the flow of tears. 'I saw the grandmother as well,' I told her. 'Where?' Diane asked. 'She came outside to get something off the table, then went back into the house.' 'Does she still have short hair?' 'Yeah, it was very short, and brown,' I replied.

'Now, Nick, as you can see, is alone,' I explained. 'He was alone the whole time we watched him, speaking only to the waiter to order drinks. He was drinking a straight, clear liquor on the rocks and smoking Marlboro Red cigarettes. He would sometimes stare into space and, Diane, he looked like a man with a lot of problems on his shoulders.' Diane grimaced. 'I told you he would be by himself,' she said. I thought she told me he would be leaning against a bar with his mates with his shirt unbuttoned, enticing females to join him for a drink, but I let it ride.

The good news was we had a confirmed sighting of the father, the boy and the grandmother. It had been a very successful night of surveillance. Stephen had joined us by now and he gently took the camcorder from Diane, rewound the tape and viewed it for himself. 'Good shot!' he said as he watched the boy dance. After watching the video, he handed the camera back to me. 'Right,' he said. 'We now know that the kid, the father and the grandmother are all on the island. We'll all go into Kos Town to meet Diane's lawyer and organize for local law enforcement to help us recover the boy. Darren, you and Peter go and clean up while I organize a taxi.' Everything was falling into place. Everything was how we were hoping it would be. We now needed to continue the surveillance operation while we started to plan the recovery. Finally, some progress. It all seemed too good to be true. It almost certainly was.

Chapter Sixteen

The spectre of the failed Japanese recovery loomed large in my mind as Stephen briefed Peter on our money requirements. We knew only too well the dangers of an operation being compromised by penny-pinching and for a want of cash. 'Peter, when we get to Kos, you will need to go and draw out some more money for the operation and give some to Diane,' Stephen explained. 'Darren, you will come with me and Diane.' Peter's face had that blank look again. 'How much money should I get?' he asked. 'Just as much as you can,' Stephen snapped.

Peter and I had got back to the room earlier, to unpack and hide our surveillance equipment. We'd then had a quick wash and now we were downstairs with Stephen and Diane waiting for the taxi that Stephen had ordered. 'What's this lawyer like?' Stephen asked Diane as we sat in the reception area. 'Oh, Stephen, he's a lovely man,' Diane said. 'He has been tremendously helpful and will do anything for me. He has made this case personal because he wants to see Nick suffer for what he has done. Nikolas is a legal aid lawyer and everyone uses his services because he is the best. A local judge was very impressed by his work too. He's just a wonderful man.'

The taxi pulled up and we began the 23-kilometre trip to Kos Town. It was a ride from hell. The driver threw the Mercedes around as if it was a Formula One car. Sat in the front passenger seat I dared only once to look across at the speedometer and it read 140 kilometres per hour! I glanced periodically into the side view mirror to check if we had any tails. I don't know why, other than force of habit, because I can't believe any tail would have kept up with us anyway with Greece's version of Stirling Moss at the wheel. The taxi driver wasn't the only thing making me nervous.

One of my reasons for booking a hotel in Mastichari instead of Kos Town had been to minimize the possibility of Diane being seen by a member of the father's family and there were apparently some of them in Kos. Now, as we sped towards the island capital, I felt uncomfortable that Diane was with us on the journey, but she needed to be with us to talk to her lawyer. At least she had brought her hat to disguise herself a little, but would it be enough? The taxi came to an abrupt halt at the front of Nikolas' building and we all climbed out slightly shakily, grateful to have arrived in one piece, and traipsed upstairs to the office. It was modern with a waiting area and a receptionist's desk. Nikolas greeted us and we sat down to discuss the case.

My first impression of Diane's lawyer was that he was an unusually-dressed, overconfident, smooth-talker. He wore a lemon-coloured shirt, lemon trousers, lemon socks and lemon shoes. As I looked around his office, I noticed a diploma in international law from the University of Essex hanging on the wall, but I didn't see any degree certificates. It's safe to say I didn't immediately share the rapport Diane had with this lawyer. They embraced each other and Diane looked the happiest I had seen since I met her. Nikolas had been involved with the case a lot longer than we had and I guess it was a comfort for Diane being with someone who had been on her side from the start. Seeing her so relaxed with Nikolas meant I was less concerned than usual about whether the office might be bugged. Diane and Nikolas conversed cheerfully in Greek and English and occasionally Nikolas would break out of their chat to talk to Stephen.

'Diane tells me you know they are on the island,' he said, as if to translate some of their Greek conversation. 'Yes, we have video footage of both the child and the father,' Stephen confirmed. 'Well there is not much I can do today, Saturday, but I will contact the Department of Justice on Monday morning and inform them,' said Nikolas. 'I did not even know Diane was coming to Greece until the other day and did not know anything about you guys. You have all surprised me.' His smile was friendly but his words contained a hint of suspicion. Peter excused himself and left the office but I didn't pay much attention. My eyes were drawn to a table to the side of the office with about fifty named files on it and, in particular, one file five times the size of all the others. It was this file that Nikolas grabbed and placed on his desk, shuffling through it and reading some of the papers within, and it was Diane's name on the front of the file. Clearly he had been extensively involved in the case.

He left the office and my attention wandered. It was stuffy and warm and because there was little I could add to the process right at that moment, I was getting bored. I stood up to look out the window and I could see Peter in a phone box at the side of the street below us. Our position on the third floor gave me a bird's eye view of the scene and I watched as Peter fumbled through his wallet, apparently looking for something. I moved closer to the window and saw him extract a piece of paper from the wallet. I watched his left index finger as he dialled the number – zero, zero, one. At that point Peter moved his body, blocking my view of the dial, but he was clearly calling the USA.

Nikolas came back into the office and Stephen spoke. 'OK then,' he said in his no-nonsense way. 'We will continue to do surveillance and come in and see you on Monday morning and take it from there.' Nikolas nodded approvingly. 'Yes, that will be fine. I can then ring the relevant authorities.'

We left the office just as Peter was returning and we all found an outdoor restaurant overlooking Kos harbour for some lunch. Diane was more relaxed than she had been for days and she took off her hat and shook out her hair as she prepared to choose her meal. 'Do you know, for the first time I think I actually feel hungry,' she said with a little laugh. 'Er, I'm sorry Diane, but I think you should keep that on,' I said. She smiled before putting the hat back on, her face disappearing beneath its wide brim. After a light lunch, Peter went to the bank to get some money and we sauntered after him, waiting outside until he emerged ten minutes later. 'Um, I need my passport and it's back at the hotel,' he said. If looks could kill, Stephen would have been facing a manslaughter charge. 'What?' he demanded. 'You knew you were going to the bank. Why didn't you bring your passport?' Peter clearly wasn't accustomed to drawing out money internationally. 'I didn't think I would need it,' he said, apologetically. We had enough money between us to last until Monday, but only just.

It was now 2 pm on Saturday, 31 August. The four of us walked to a nearby taxi rank and jumped into a waiting Mercedes to make another hair-raising journey back to Mastichari. When we got there, Diane went to check her emails while Peter, Stephen and I went to a supermarket to look for some camera film and a cap for me. 'Do you guys need any gifts to take back home?' asked Peter. It seemed an odd request until I realized Peter was buying himself a hat and a souvenir shirt, on the card charged with Diane's money. Incredible! As it happens, I did pop into a souvenir shop as the three of us, having left the shopping centre, were walking back to the hotel. I wanted an artist's sketch book and a pencil. It would give me a reasonable cover story while sitting on top of the steep steps which led to the front of the father's house on Kalymnos. I found what I was looking for and we continued back to the hotel.

'We won't go over tonight to do surveillance,' Stephen said. 'We know they're there so we'll give it a break tonight and go over tomorrow, yeah?' I agreed. It made sense to me. 'So, just chill out and get a good night's sleep,' added Stephen. 'I'll let Diane know.' He didn't have to go far to do so. Diane returned from checking her emails and came straight to our room. 'Zoe asked how we are all doing,' she remarked. 'Who's Zoe?' asked Stephen. 'She's the reporter for *60 Minutes*,' Diane explained. Great. We had the media wanting to know our every move and neither Stephen nor I could do anything about it.

Stephen updated Diane on our plans while Peter went to check his own emails and make some phone calls. Again. When Diane returned to her room, she and Stephen carried on their conversation on their respective balconies. Stephen was good at keeping the client fully informed. He was also regularly monitoring her mental state, particularly in times of high stress, and was always ready to offer comfort and support if necessary. That should really have been Peter's job. I work for Stephen, Stephen was working for Peter and Peter was working for Diane. At least that's the way it was meant to be, but Peter had abdicated all leadership responsibilities to Stephen.

I decided to take advantage of the downtime to do some exercise. It was now about 4 pm and I was keen to take a swim in the warm Aegean Sea but it was still very hot and I decided to wait a couple of hours until the sun had lost its sting. As I lay on my bed I could hear Stephen and Diane talking and I began to doze. By 6 pm the sun was lower on the horizon and not so burning so I put on some football shorts and made my way down to the beach. I swam and ran on the sand, free from any concerns about the operation; just enjoying the balmy early evening weather and the feeling of salt drying on my forehead and sand between my toes. I've been in many oceans and seas around the world and I found the Aegean to be particularly salty, but just chilling out for an hour in the fresh air was cleansing my mind of any worries. I jogged back to the hotel and went for a shower, the lukewarm water washing away the salt from my skin. Peter had been lying on his bed when I went into the bathroom but as I came out, wrapped in a towel, I walked in on a heated conversation he was having with Stephen.

Above: Personal protection team, Ecuador, 2000. The author is back row, third from right. Stephen Mastalerz is back row, first on left.

Below left: Explorer, Rear Admiral Sir John Franklin, the author's great, great, great, great, great uncle.

Below right: John Nuttall (the author's grandfather), on the right.

Left: Former US President J. F. Kennedy behind the Resolute Desk with his son, John Junior, playing inside it. The desk was made with timbers from HMS *Resolute*, the ship that was sent to rescue Sir John Franklin. You can see the brass plaque, which has Franklin's name on it.

Below: John Nuttall (the author's grandfather), on the right.

Above: John Nuttall (the author's grandfather), second from right.

Below left: Harriet and Elsie Hopwood (the author's great grandmother and grandmother), Toowoomba, Australia.

Below right: Harriet Hopwood (the author's great grandmother), Toowoomba, Australia.

Above left: The author at basic training, Australian Army, 1989.

Above right: The author doing bayonet assault training, Australian Army, 1989.

Below left: The author at the Royal Australian Air Force Base sergeants' mess, Sale, 1996.

Below right: The author with his parents at training graduation, 1996.

Above: Pothia harbour, Kalymnos, 2002.

Below: Pothia, Kalymnos.

Above: The hotel at Mastichari, Kos. The recovery team booked the top two rooms on the right hand side.

Below: Mastichari harbour, with the island of Kalmynos in the background.

Right: The target house where Theo was living with his father and grandmother.

Below: The church near the target house, which the team briefly considered using as an observation post (OP).

Left: A steep staircase, typical of those near the target house. This one led from the pedestrian lane to the OPs.

Below: The steep cliff the author's legs were left dangling over on the second night of surveillance.

Above: OP1, in a derelict building, with the target house in the background.

Below left: Pathway from the church leading to OP1, with the balcony of the alternative OP2 to the left.

Below right: OP1, now overgrown with weeds, and with a collapsed front wall.

Above left: OP2, used for night surveillance.

Above right: Narrow pedestrian lane leading to the OPs.

Below: Author's diagram of the OPs and the target house.

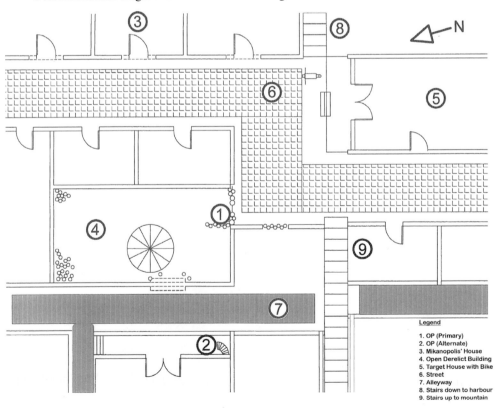

Legend

1. OP (Primary)
2. OP (Alternate)
3. Mikanopolis' House
4. Open Derelict Building
5. Target House with Bike
6. Street
7. Alleyway
8. Stairs down to harbour
9. Stairs up to mountain

Above: Pothia harbour showing the esplanade and piazza.

Right: The Pothia dock, and the ferry, used daily by the recovery team.

Hotel Therme, Pothia, used by the surveillance team. Room eleven is on the left, below the top floor, with the balcony door open.

The view of the piazza from the balcony of the room in Hotel Therme.

The father's view of the piazza from his favourite bar. Hotel Therme can be seen in the centre background, past the trees.

Diane's lawyer's office in Kos Town.

Kos courthouse, where a court order ruling the child should be released into Diane's custody was issued. It was not enforced.

The author on the ferry on the day of the recovery, 2002.

The alleyway at the end of the piazza where the surveillance team lost sight of the grandmother and the child.

Above: The site where the child was recovered.

Below: The Hellenic Coastguard HQ, Kalymnos. The cell where the recovery team was held is on the middle floor, on the left, without windows.

Above: The gate to Pothia port, which was closed to the public to expedite the recovery team's escape from the island.

Below: Antimachia police station.

Above: Diane and Theo in Athens after the recovery, 2002.

Below: The author in Yemen, 2015.

'We don't want people to know what we are doing, that's all,' Stephen was explaining patiently, as if to a child. 'OK, sure, I understand. I didn't tell him exactly how we are doing it, though,' Peter said. Stephen looked at me. 'He told that private eye in Chicago what we're doing,' he said with a roll of his eyes. 'What?' I exclaimed. 'Peter! We don't want other people or companies knowing what we are doing.' Peter looked crestfallen. 'OK, no problem,' he said quietly, but Stephen reinforced his point: 'We don't want people to know what we're up to, Peter.'

There was a knock on the door and I went into the bathroom to get dressed. I could hear Diane's voice and a conversation about going to a restaurant for dinner. The afternoon off had been relaxing but now it was time to get our game heads back on and the meal would be a good opportunity to discuss the operation as a team. We found a restaurant, sat down and ordered. 'How are we going to do this?' asked Diane immediately. 'Well,' said Stephen, 'We need Nikolas' help to know who to talk to on the law enforcement side. Then we will organize for their help and go and do it. The father won't do anything, I reckon, if we are standing there and have police officers with us, though we may have to use police officers from another island. We can't enter the house of our own accord, but if the police choose to do so, we can follow. You, Diane, are the one who has to grab Theo, yeah, because the police officers can't and we won't either. As soon as you grab him, you walk right out and one of us will escort you to a boat and get you off the island.'

Diane's brow furrowed. 'But what if the police don't want to help?' she asked. 'They will have to help. They are there to keep the peace,' Stephen insisted. I threw in my own view to back him up. 'As soon as the police know there is a recovery team comprising of a Brit, an Australian and an American they will help because they will want to avoid an international incident.' Diane didn't look convinced. 'We'll play it by ear and find out what the locals can do for us and how they can assist,' Stephen told her.

He turned to Peter. 'Did you bring your ID?' he asked. 'Um, I've got my Californian driver's licence and my passport,' he said. Stephen laughed. 'No, not your licence. Your ID to say that you're a child recovery agent.' I wasn't holding my breath and I doubt Stephen was either. 'I haven't got anything like that,' replied Peter, surprising none of us. Stephen sighed. 'OK. Just bring the paperwork.' Peter gave us that increasingly-familiar blank look. 'What paperwork?' 'The paperwork with reference to this case!' said Stephen, exasperated. 'I didn't bring any,' Peter confessed.

Oh, boy, here we go again. I knew Stephen well enough to know he was going to blow a gasket soon. 'How the bloody hell do you expect to sort out any trouble with a California driver's licence?' he asked Peter. There was no reply and I could see that Peter felt bad that he had stuffed up yet again. It didn't help that Diane was present to witness it, once again, and I could see that she was not impressed. I had seen a Mexican turn white and now I had seen him blush red, but Stephen cooled down and started to explain things to Peter in a rational manner. 'You need to bring identification and paperwork you have on the case in the event that you need to justify why such an action is taking place,' he said. 'You are the one who may need to explain our actions after we have grabbed the child. I guess we can work around it for now, but you need to be prepared next time you do this type of thing.'

Peter nodded and things settled down, but it was another potential time bomb ticking away in the background. Without paperwork, any operation can go belly-up. Thankfully, in this situation, Nikolas would have all the necessary documentation with him.

We finished our dinner and Diane wanted a drink so we left for a small bar which had a big screen showing an English football game. Diane ordered a vodka, lemon and lime in a tall glass, Stephen and Peter had a Greek bottled beer, Mythos, and I had a Corona. It was my first alcohol since the beer I'd had with my father as a send-off for my 'Italian holiday' the previous Saturday. It tasted good and went down quickly, but we ordered one more round before returning to the hotel and retiring for the night. The temptation to stay and make a night of it and watch the football, was strong but we were there to work, not have a holiday. While Diane went to her room, Stephen, Peter and I settled in for the night and Peter drifted off to sleep almost immediately. That's when it started.

'Fucking hell,' whispered Stephen. 'What the hell is that? It isn't normal.' I couldn't stop snickering. I'd forgotten to tell Stephen about Peter's intense snoring. It was the strangest noise I had ever heard. It started deep and low and built to a high-pitched crescendo. The sound reminded me of an old cow stuck in a rabbit trap. I guess I'm lucky. Once I'm used to a repetitive noise, however loud, I can sleep anywhere. I had been known to sleep on top of cargo crates in the back of a military C-130 Hercules transport plane without hearing protection. Stephen wasn't so lucky and I could hear him tossing and turning before I drifted off to sleep.

Chapter Seventeen

I awoke to find no sign of Stephen. He'd gone. His bed was gone too. I jumped out of bed to look out of the window for any sign of him but I didn't need to look down the street. There he was on his stretcher bed on the balcony. 'What the hell are you doing out here?' I asked, giving the stretcher a kick. 'That fucking snoring!' he mumbled. I laughed and started my morning routine. The first ferry from Mastichari would be at 9 am and we wanted to be on it. Stephen wanted Peter to stay behind and the two of us would go to Kalymnos again, this time just for the day, returning in the afternoon.

Diane was making breakfast and we packed our gear and went down to eat. 'Do you think they'll be at church today?' I asked Diane. It was Sunday after all. 'Oh, yes, definitely,' she replied without hesitation. I asked which church they went to but this time Diane wasn't quite so certain. 'Um, they would probably go to Saint Nikolas because they all go to the church in their neighbourhood,' she explained. 'Sunday is a family day and all the families will be out walking together around the harbour and the esplanade.' This was good as maybe we could see all three of them together. I needed to check out Theo's well-being by studying his actions and body language and seeing how he acted in the company of his father and grandmother. This would give me an indication of how he might react during the recovery.

At 8.30 am, Stephen and I said our goodbyes and left for the ferry, going through our standard operating procedure. There was an influx of passengers on this trip, with more tourists than usual. The horn sounded and the ferry made its way out of the harbour. 'So, what do you think of Peter now?' asked Stephen. 'Well, he's an interesting character,' I replied, charitably. 'He's not what I expected, but at least he is willing to learn and he listens. I can't help anyone who is not willing to listen, but I do have some serious reservations about him.' Stephen chewed his lip.

117

'Yeah, he does listen. I guess that is a good thing,' he conceded, but his own reservations were clear. 'We can work with him in the future, so long as he passes on everything to us – and doesn't come along! He can be a point of contact in the US. We will do everything else – contacting the parent, arranging the flights, etc.' I nodded. 'I've already told him he'll need to do a surveillance course and he wants to come down to our October course,' I said. 'OK,' replied Stephen. 'We can do something with him there, no probs.'

The heat was intense and it was still only 9.30 am. Passengers around us were laughing, enjoying the magnificent view and taking the occasional photograph. I stared at the mountainous coast of Turkey on my right and thought, once more, about my countrymen fighting the Turks almost ninety years before. Stephen's voice jolted me out of my daydreams. 'When we get there, we'll walk around and check out the house and see if we can locate them,' he said. 'We won't overdo it on the camera, but if we can take the shot we will take it.'

That sounded fair enough. 'OK mate,' I replied. 'And I need to point out to you an OP location I found. It has a great view of the front of the house and you can remain undetected both day and night. Mate, this is one of the best urban OPs I have ever seen,' I added with a satisfied grin. 'OK, good. Show me after we do a walk past of the house,' said Stephen with his usual quiet efficiency. I described where it was and explained that it was visible from the front of the house. Stephen wasn't about to get over-excited – it wasn't his style – but he smiled in acknowledgement that I might have found a good spot.

The ferry made its way into the harbour and we both glanced towards the house which was now becoming all too familiar. The upstairs, left-hand shuttered opening, which led into the main stairway between the two floors, was always open, we noted. Something else we clocked, as the ferry docked, was a Greek Navy patrol boat which we hadn't seen before. Was there a good reason for that to be there, and was it anything to do with us?

The ferry ramp dropped and the passengers, cars and motorcycles disgorged onto the quayside. Stephen and I walked amid a group of tourists as far as the coastguard building, then peeled off up the road towards the house. As we passed the church all was quiet. Maybe the church had already had its service earlier in the morning. We walked on up the road and saw the house in front of us. The front door was open and a line of washing was strung out on the small second-floor balcony. The father's motorcycle was parked out the front. We walked past and Stephen glanced up to his right to observe the front of the OP as I had described it to him. As we passed the window to the house's lounge we could see a television with cartoons on the screen.

All the signs were good. The motorcycle was there, washing had been recently put out and there were cartoons on the television. That told me we probably had all the players inside the house. We continued to the end of the road and stopped to sit down. I reached for my map and placed it on my lap to make it look as if we were tourists finding our bearings. 'Did you see the television, mate?' asked Stephen. 'Yeah, cartoons,' I replied. 'Right, that's a good sign,' he said. He suggested we go and look at the OP and then head to the cafe for coffee. I agreed, but I also wanted to film the washing line to see if there were any of the father's work clothes on it. It was still unclear whether the father went off to work in the week. It would obviously be better if he did because that would mean he would be out of the way if we were to recover the child during the day.

I led Stephen up to the entrance to the OP and glanced up and down the alleyway before giving him the 'all clear'. He leapt up into the window void and lowered himself down the other side. I forgot how steep it was on the inside and while looking up the alleyway I held out the camcorder for Stephen to take, thinking he was already on the ground. He wasn't and as he tried to find the ground with his feet a brick he had been hanging on to dislodged and fell on to the camera. Shit. We'd broken the camera.

I followed Stephen through the window until we were both inside the derelict building, then I checked out the camera. It had a small dent on the side but appeared to be in good working order. Relieved, I took Stephen around the large tree growing in the centre of the building and led him to the OP. 'Here it is,' I whispered. 'There's a hole here which the camera can film through. We're protected from the window entrance by this wall, should anyone walking down the alleyway look in, and we have an alternative escape route here in this break in the wall. We can then utilize the alleyway, the stairway, or the road to escape. The house to the rear and to the left of us has solid, windowless walls, and we are out of view from any balconies.' Stephen looked impressed. 'Perfect,' he whispered.

After making our way back to the window entrance, we heard footsteps and pressed ourselves against either side of the window to hide. Whoever was in the alleyway took their time to pass and the footsteps seemed close together – it was either a small child or an elderly person. Eventually, they passed from left to right and I peered through the window. It was an elderly woman with a scarf on her head carrying a plastic shopping bag. Had we been in the middle of the derelict building I doubt she would have looked inside. I glanced to my left again and up towards a balcony, then leapt out of the window into the alley. I placed my hand inside for Stephen to give me the camcorder and walked off as quickly as possible as Stephen followed me out. As I passed the possible alternative OP, I glanced at the front door and noticed that it was still padlocked. Stephen joined me and walked up the steps.

'This is the alternative OP,' I whispered. 'We just need a cover man here on look-out. From up there, under the stairway, you can see the front of the house perfectly.' Cautiously, we entered the balcony of the property and Stephen made his way towards the stairway and glanced down towards the front of the house. He then joined me at the base of the steps leading to the balcony. 'It looks OK, mate. Good view,' he whispered. As Stephen stood aside, I made my own way onto the balcony and stood beneath the stairway. With the camcorder in my hand I looked at Stephen who indicated 'all clear' and I began filming the washing on the clothes line in front of the house, zooming in and out on every piece. It looked like there were large shirts, dresses, kids' socks, shorts and shirts, male singlets and male work shorts with stains, but we would be able to study them at length later.

Satisfied I had filmed enough, I exited the vantage point, stopping to look under the padlock on the property's front door. The tape was still there. Considering I had placed it there on Friday night and it was now Sunday, there seemed to be a good chance that the occupants were not currently on the island. Stephen and I checked out a few other alleys and vantage points. On one occasion, we had to walk sideways as the alley was so narrow, ducking as we passed by windows. Eventually we came out of an alleyway onto another stairway which we walked up and came out on a road. We were by now quite high up and the view was spectacular. I took a moment to enjoy the vista but Stephen was yearning for coffee so we headed back down towards the esplanade to a cafe at the bottom of the road which the father's house was on, and near to the coastguard building overlooking the harbour. Stephen loves his coffee. Me, I'm a water or orange juice man and at that moment I needed plenty of water as I was beginning to feel the heat.

'I filmed the clothes on the line,' I said to Stephen after the waiter had placed our drinks on the table and walked away. 'Was there anything obvious?' he asked. 'I'll double-check but it looked like there were clothes for all three of the players, including work shorts with paint stains.' Stephen nodded. This meant it was likely the father was working.

Everything seemed to be going in our favour. We just needed the assistance of the local law enforcement to make this an easy gig, except I knew from experience there were never any easy gigs, and the involvement of the local law enforcement was certainly no guarantee of success. 'Looks like the church service has either finished or hasn't started yet,' I remarked.

We continued sipping our drinks and watching the world go by, when a squad of Greek soldiers, marching in formation with rifles on their shoulders, came heading up from the wharf towards us. 'What the hell is this?' asked Stephen. 'I don't know,' I said. 'But I hope they're not coming for us.' The soldiers came closer, and closer and just before they reached the cafe, their leader barked an order and they executed a swift right turn and marched off towards the esplanade. I ordered another water and asked the waiter what the soldiers were doing there. In broken English he explained that they were there for a memorial parade. 'Great,' said Stephen. 'That should be a big event here and maybe we'll see all three of the players watching the parade.' I hoped so too. 'They have to let the kid out some time,' I replied.

Stephen finished his coffee and put enough money to cover the cost of the drinks and a tip on the table. 'It's now 1100 hours,' he said. 'We'll split up and do some more surveillance and meet back here at 1300 hours, OK?' He was already getting up and ready to go as I signalled my agreement by swallowing the last of my water. I bought another bottle of water for my bag then made my way up towards the top of the hill. I wanted to see if I could get a good view of the house from long distance. I had all the short-range locations I needed, which was fine, but they were no good if the players started to move, because all the buildings would mask their route from my sight. If I could find a long-range OP, I could track them from a distance if they left the house.

I continued up the mountain, via stairways and alleys, passing locals on the way. It's always a good thing to acknowledge anyone you pass in close-knit communities like this one. A smile and polite nod of your head does the trick. To ignore them and do nothing can be more suspicious, especially if you are headed in the direction of their house. Occasionally I would pause to sit down on a step, as if taking a rest from the steep climb, in order to look back in case anyone was following me but no one was.

Eventually I reached a point where there were no more houses. I walked a little further up the mountain, turned to my left and headed along a line of trees to mask my movement rather than walk in the open ground between the houses and the trees. When I was satisfied I was perpendicular to the house, I exited the brush and walked down the hillside, across the open ground, to join the maze of houses again. I could see the roof of the father's house and the top floor balcony, but the rest of the house was obscured by the many houses below me and I was too far away and too far up on the mountain. I was reaching for my binoculars for a better look when I was interrupted. I heard it before I could see it… an army helicopter, virtually on top of me!

The sound of the rotors was almost deafening, but not enough to drown out the cacophony of dog barking and chicken squawking from the houses near me. I watched the helicopter swoop down towards the harbour then veer off to the left into the next valley. Considering there was a military parade today, it occurred to me that the helicopter might be bringing dignitaries for the event and, if that was the case, the ceremony must be close to starting. I checked my watch. 1220 hours. Stephen would be waiting for me at the RV in forty minutes.

I made my way as casually as I could down the mountain towards the alleyway that was just up from the house. All was quiet with no sign of the players. Perhaps they had left the house to watch the parade. I went back up to the top of the stairway, sat down, pulled out my sketch book and pencil and started drawing the scene in front of me. I quickly sketched the side of the house to my left and the wall to my right, then the mountains in the background, to at least have something on paper visible for any casual observer. I started to draw the harbour and wharf, but stopped after drawing half a boat. I could see down the steps to the front entrance of the house. I was watching for any movement when I heard footsteps behind me and returned to drawing the boat. A small girl of about 10 looked over my shoulder, smiled and continued walking down the road. I was glad it was a child and not an artist appraising my work. I don't think they would have been too impressed.

There seemed to be no more to see so I gathered my stuff together and continued towards the esplanade. I noticed Stephen speaking on a public telephone across the road. We often pretended to be speaking on public telephones when observing someone nearby so I was not sure if he was conducting surveillance or actually speaking to someone. If the latter, it could only be Peter or Diane. I decided that if he was conducting surveillance I might as well stay put to minimize the risk of walking near any target, so I sat at a table to the rear of the restaurant RV and ordered a bottle of water. I checked to see if anyone else was paying any attention to Stephen. After a while, Stephen put the phone down and came over to join me. 'How did you go?' he asked. 'Nothing,' I replied. 'You?' Stephen shook his head. 'Nothing yet. I just spoke to Diane. Peter has gone to the airport to get some money from the bank. He went to the airport because it's closer than Kos,' he said. I asked if it was a bit risky, leaving Diane by herself but Stephen was unperturbed. 'She'll be alright,' he said. 'He won't be long.'

We could hear the beat of a bass drum in the distance and looked towards the other side of the harbour. The parade had begun and people had gathered along the side of the esplanade. Stephen and I decided to stand on the harbourside, with the sun behind us, and scan the faces of the crowd. Stephen looked for the child while I searched for the father and the grandmother. The end of the parade came into sight and we could see children following behind, mimicking the marching of the soldiers, but neither Theo, Nick nor the grandmother were anywhere to be seen. Considering the population of the town and the number of tourists on the island, the crowd was relatively small but maybe that was because we were coming to the end of the season.

After the parade had broken up, sailors, airmen and soldiers flocked to the bars and restaurants on the esplanade. Attractive local women were much in evidence but there were few local men. I doubted that Nick would be out today. I thought perhaps he and his mates might be out shooting on the other side of the island but then, reflecting on my observations of him the other night, I doubted if he had many mates.

The ferry was due to depart at 1530 hours and it was now 1400 hours. Stephen stayed around the esplanade, watching out for the players and, after agreeing to meet back at the cafe at 1500 hours, I made my way to the OP. I approached it from a different direction and went through my routine for gaining entry via the window void. Once inside, I reached into my bag for my camera and started filming the house through the small hole in the wall. That's when I discovered the camera automatically focused on the nearest object in the centre of the lens which happened to be a few long strands of grass directly in front of the OP. I would have to rip those strands out of the ground to get a good clear shot of the house, but I couldn't do that in the light of day.

I continued filming anyway and at that moment the front door opened. The grandmother, dressed in her Sunday best, came out of the house, locked the door behind her, placed the key underneath a pot plant and walked off down the street towards the esplanade. The motorcycle was still parked at the front of the house so it seemed like the father and child might still be inside but, if that was the case, why was the grandmother locking the door? Stephen was down at the esplanade and I reckoned he would pick up sight of the grandmother since she was headed in that direction, so I stayed in the OP to see if the father or the child would leave the house. I also noted that I now knew how to gain access to the house if necessary. Crack! A twig snapped behind me. Oh shit. I had been so engrossed in what was happening in front of me I had been unaware of my six. I glanced around and saw a kitten walking around the rubble and I breathed again.

It was fast approaching 1450 hours so I made my way out of the OP and headed towards the cafe to meet up with Stephen. 'Anything?' he asked. 'Yeah, the grandmother walked out of the house, locked it and hid the key under the pot plant. She headed off down your direction. Did you see her?' He nodded. 'She walked straight past me, then spoke to the lady owner of the souvenir shop up until I came here. Looks like she was going shopping. You didn't see the father or the child?' I shook my head. 'No. The motorcycle was still there, though, so they may be still in the house, and if not they haven't gone far.' Stephen reflected on my observations. 'OK mate,' he said. 'We know the operation isn't blown so we'll start organizing some local support and do this next week.' It sounded good to me.

The ferry was packed with passengers, once again allowing us to blend in with the throng of tourists. We docked forty-five minutes later in Mastichari and made our way to the hotel. There was no reply to my knock on Diane's door but no sooner had we entered our own room than she walked in. 'You haven't seen Peter, have you?' she asked with a note of worry in her voice. 'No, why?' asked Stephen. 'He left for the airport to go to the bank four hours ago and hasn't been back since,' she said. 'Four hours?' repeated Stephen. 'What is he doing?'

Well, here was a predicament. Diane was worried about Peter running off with her money and I was worried about the operation being compromised. We were conducting surveillance in a foreign country and one of our team members had disappeared. Could he have been identified and arrested? Been involved in an accident? Had problems getting any money? Or was he just plain lost? His suitcase was still in the room so Stephen and I felt confident he had not done a runner, but then we have seen stranger things. 'I'm sure he'll turn up,' said Stephen. 'His suitcase is still here so he won't have gone far.' Diane didn't look reassured. 'I hope so, Stephen. He has a lot of money of mine, and without that we can't get Theo.' I was looking at it differently. The chance of Peter having done something silly and compromised the operation was a far greater threat than him running off with Diane's money, and then she would never get her child back. I was also thoroughly pissed off with Peter for leaving the client alone for so long.

Poor Diane could not stand still for worry and when she went back to her room for a lie down I started going over the surveillance tape and looking at the maps again. Another hour passed before Diane came back into our room looking more worried than ever that there was no sign of Peter, but just at that moment we heard a key turn in the lock and Peter walked in.

'Where the fuck have you been?' demanded Diane as she pushed Peter in the chest. Shocked by the attack, Peter stuttered a reply. 'T-t-to get some money,' he said. 'What, for five hours?' asked Stephen. 'The airport ATMs were closed so I got a taxi to some other town and it was also closed,' he said. 'So I had to wait for a taxi from Kos to come out and take me into Kos. The ATMs there were closed when I got there, so I had to wait for them to open. While I was waiting, I went to an internet cafe and checked my emails and made some phone calls,' he explained. I told him he should have called Diane and updated her. 'She's been worried sick, and we're not exactly happy either,' I said. 'Understand the situation, mate. We're conducting an operation which, if we are caught, could lead to all sorts of bother from the authorities or from the father's relatives, and you go to get some money from a bank and are gone for five hours. We're thinking you're in trouble. Now what do we do? Does one of us go out looking for you and risk getting into the same trouble themselves?'

Peter looked shame-faced, and not for the first time. He apologised and said he understood why we were angry but did he really? How many more times would he stuff up, or was the naivety just an act? How could he be so thoughtless? 'You need to communicate and put people in the picture, yeah?' I said calmly but Stephen was still angry. 'How much money did you get?' he barked. Peter looked like a rabbit in the headlights. 'Around $2,000,' he said. 'Around, or exactly $2,000?' demanded Diane. '$2,000,' he said. Her eyes burned into him like lasers. All the stress and all the worry she had gone through was being focused into her fury at Peter, and I couldn't say I blamed her. 'We need to do a reconciliation of expenditure so far, for Diane's sake,' Stephen announced. 'Yes please!' proclaimed Diane, who mentioned yet again how she had to take out a bank loan to fund the operation. 'I can have that ready for you by the end of the day,' Peter promised.

There was nothing much else to be said, so Diane announced she was going to sit on the beach to try to calm down. It was now 1745 hours and the sun was still high and hot, but she was riding high on an emotional roller coaster and I wasn't about to suggest she stay cooped up in her room. 'Don't forget your hat,' was all I could offer as she walked out. Stephen sat down to go over the maps and view the surveillance footage again. I could sense Peter was suffering in the awkward silence so I suggested we get out. 'I'm going to take a walk. You want to come, Peter?' I said. 'Er, no thanks, I think I'll just stay here and sort out those figures for Diane,' he replied. The numbers wouldn't take him long and I felt Stephen needed some space. 'I think you'd better come for a walk,' I said and this time Peter agreed.

I had spotted a secluded resort nestled into a hill to the side of Mastichari as we had come into the harbour earlier, and I planned to check it out. It would also allow me to keep an eye on Diane from a distance as we walked past. 'I guess Diane is pissed at me,' sighed Peter as we walked. 'Yeah, well, don't worry too much about it. You know what you did, we told you how to fix it. Now we need to move on and concentrate on the operation, right?' I said. 'He nodded. 'I'm just sorry,' he said. I gave him a reassuring look. 'Don't dwell on it mate. We all make mistakes. I made one in 1984,' I joked. 'But it's an even bigger mistake not to learn from our errors. We are in a critical phase of our operation where it could easily be compromised. We must be at the top of our game, every one of us. We owe it to Diane and we owe it to little Theo.'

We arrived at the resort from the beach side and took a look around. It was a large complex with a swimming pool and a pool bar. We sat down and had a couple of sodas, casting an eye in the direction of Diane who was sitting alone on the beach. When we got back to the hotel, Stephen was going over the operation and Peter set to work reconciling the expenses for the operation so far. Diane returned from the beach soon after and went to her room for a shower before coming back to ours to go through the plan for the following day.

'Tomorrow we will go to see Nikolas and start organizing some local legal support for the recovery,' said Stephen. 'Then, depending on when we get back, Darren and I will go over to Kalymnos and do some more surveillance to check the players are all still in place.' Everyone signalled their agreement. 'What day do you think we can jump?' I asked. 'As soon as we have the support,' said Stephen. 'Darren, you can start looking for a boat to hire or charter. We'll need something very fast that can outrun any other boat on the island.' I gave him a thumbs up. 'We'll also buy a mobile phone tomorrow,' Stephen added. 'Peter, you need to make sure we have enough cash and calling cards to ring each other.' He paused before adding: 'Police, speedboat, comms.'

It was starting to come together. Diane had brought her Australian mobile phone with her, which worked in Greece, but up until now we hadn't had a need for mobile phones and it would have been burning up money. As the day of the recovery loomed, things were different and we would definitely need to be in immediate contact with each other. I would need to look around the harbour and marina at Kos to find out about hiring a speedboat faster than anything that might be on Kalymnos.

We had dinner nearby and went back to the hotel for an early night. Stephen shifted his stretcher bed from the room to the balcony in readiness for Peter's snoring. I lay awake trying to think what fast boats I had seen in the harbour at Pothia. I remembered the navy patrol boat I saw docked in the harbour that morning. Surely we wouldn't be chased by the Greek Navy.

Chapter Eighteen

The waves crashing on the shore woke me the next morning. It was Monday, 2 September and the operation had already taken longer than I had hoped it would. After breakfast it was back into a taxi to Kos and another high-speed Mercedes ride before we pulled up at the taxi rank around the corner from our destination. Diane put on her hat and sunglasses and we walked the short way to Nikolas' office. He was already on the phone, apparently organizing the legal authority for our operation. 'That was the Ministry of Justice,' he said after hanging up. 'The minister has given the authority for the use of police officers. She will contact the public prosecutor and get his authority and then we can organize the police.' Seeing the smiles on all our faces, Nikolas raised his hand to quell our enthusiasm. 'The public prosecutor is in court all day and I also need to go to court soon until four o'clock. I will try to speak to him at court but it won't be early. You can wait until I return or come back tomorrow.'

Neither seemed like a great option and it promised to be a long and frustrating day, but what else could we do? 'What do you think Stephen? Should we wait?' asked Diane. Stephen shrugged. 'Since we are in town we can wait and find out, I guess.' Diane agreed. She was desperate to see something happening. 'I think we should wait so that we can get an answer today,' she added. 'OK, then,' said Stephen. 'You wait here and us three will go to buy a mobile phone. We'll be back soon.'

We quickly found a mobile phone shop to buy a pre-paid device and some phone cards but I was still worried about Diane being spotted by anyone connected with the father, especially because her long blonde hair made her stand out, even with much of it hidden beneath a hat. With time on our hands and while we were near some shops, it made sense to try to find her a wig. Now, finding a wig shop in a major city might be difficult; finding one in sleepy Kos was mission impossible.

We did come across a couple of hairdressing salons but with three blokes pointing to their hair and trying to explain 'false' and 'long', in English, it was never going to be easy. Eventually Stephen decided we had wasted enough time and ought to get back to Diane, but there was one shop between where we had got to and Nikolas' office that I'd seen earlier, and which seemed to stock all sorts of things, so we agreed to have a look in on our way past.

Peter and Stephen waited outside while I went in and, like someone playing a game of charades, tried to explain 'wig' to the elderly shop assistant. She gave me a toothless smile and pointed to a corner display of fancy dress costumes. A minute later I joined Stephen and Peter triumphantly clutching a jet black, nylon Snow White-style wig. 'I can tell you now, she'll never wear that,' said Stephen. I had to agree it was more likely to attract attention than disguise her if we were out in a restaurant, but when we took her over to Kalymnos for the recovery it might be necessary.

We returned to Nikolas' office where we left Peter with Diane while Stephen and I made our way down to the harbour to look for a boat. It wasn't promising. There were tripper boats for bikini-clad tourists, small fishing boats, and a wide selection of craft which would struggle to match our walking speed. We decided to take a look at the marina where there were some nice vessels, including very expensive yachts and speedboats. With no one in sight near the pontoons, we walked into the marina shopping courtyard to ask about speedboat charter. There was a distinct lack of anybody to answer our query so we made our way upstairs to a shop that advertised chartered sailboats.

The shop attendant was busy sewing a sail when we walked in and didn't bother to look up until Stephen coughed loudly and said that we were interested in chartering a fast boat and asked whether he might be able to direct us to someone who could help. With just a cursory glance, the man said he didn't hire speedboats and went back to sewing his sail. I asked the top of his head if he knew of anyone who did hire speedboats and he got out of his chair and went into a backroom to get something, but if I thought he was going to help us with a name or a number I was mistaken. He simply found whatever it was that he needed for his sewing and returned to his task, completely ignoring us. So much for Greek hospitality.

After asking in nearly all of the nearby shops and without the slightest offer of help, we made the 3-kilometre journey back to Nikolas' office on foot, still no closer to finding a boat to hire. I was beginning to think it was impossible to get the attention of the average Greek man but as we walked back we passed a stretch of beach with many topless sunbathers and I noted that, under the trees nearby, a bunch of old Greek men were paying plenty of attention.

It was approximately 2 pm when we arrived back at Nikolas' office and filled in Diane and Peter on our lack of success. We headed back towards the harbour for a late lunch. Following our meal, we were sitting at the table talking about nothing in particular when I noticed Nikolas walk out of the court building across the road from our restaurant. He wore the same lemon shirt, lemon trousers and lemon shoes but his socks were brown and he had a brown sports jacket on. Maybe if he was finished at court he might have an answer for us about the public prosecutor. Peter paid for lunch with Diane's money and we all headed back to Nikolas' office.

'Did you talk to the public prosecutor?' asked Diane. 'No, I didn't see him today, but I shall try again tomorrow,' Nikolas replied. 'Have you had any luck today?' he countered. It wasn't the news we wanted to hear from Nikolas and we didn't have any better news for him. 'We've been looking for speedboats to hire but haven't found anything,' said Stephen. Nikolas didn't look surprised. 'The problem with hiring a speedboat is the owner will want to be with the boat so you will have to hire the boat and the driver,' he explained. 'That's OK,' Stephen told Nikolas. His face lit up. 'In that case, I have a client who has a water sports company and he has a speedboat,' he said. 'I will talk to him.' It was a glimmer of hope after a thoroughly frustrating day. 'Other than that, there really isn't much I can do now until tomorrow. I will contact the boat guy and the public prosecutor tomorrow.'

Just then, a new option emerged from an unlikely source – Peter. He told us he had a contact in Greece, a female judge. He said that maybe she would be able to help us, or at least direct us to someone who could help us with the case. We were all pleasantly surprised to find that Peter had any contacts, let alone abroad, and an influential one at that. 'That sounds promising. Do you want to give your contact a call?' asked Stephen, but Peter hesitated. 'Um... yeah... OK,' he agreed, at last. Nikolas handed him the phone and Peter fished around in his wallet to find the number for the woman in Athens. We were all on tenterhooks as he dialled the number and waited. 'Hello, Monica?' he said. 'This is Peter Gonzalez, how are you? I'm currently… yeah, Peter Gonzalez. From the Staminos case. Yeah, I was wondering if you could help me. I'm currently… Peter Gonzalez, from Kid Find in California.' After explaining what he looked like and the situation we were in, he hung up. 'She can't help,' he said. Ah, well. At least he wanted to show that he was contributing to the operation and he gave it a shot, even though it turned out his 'contact' didn't know him.

We said goodbye to Nikolas and found a taxi for the grand prix ride back to Mastichari. It was 4.30 pm. Stephen wanted me to go over with him to Kalymnos and the next ferry was due to leave in an hour so we needed to get ready quickly. The four of us went to the hotel and Stephen and I packed our bags for the night then made our way down to the ferry for the now all-too-familiar trip.

Our first job on arrival in Pothia was to search the harbour for speedboats, to gauge what we might be up against. I soon found the fastest one. It was 18 feet with a fibreglass hull and twin 200 horsepower Evinrude outboard motors. Thankfully, it had 'Hellenic Coastguard' written down the sides. The next fastest boat in the harbour was a wooden craft with a 12-foot canopy and a 90 horsepower Yamaha motor.

Next, we headed for the cafe at the end of the father's road and looked up towards the house. Bingo! The child was playing outside the church with the little girl. There was a very large blonde woman, dressed all in black, holding a baby and keeping an eye on the two children. From where they were playing, there was a clear view of the harbour. 'Excellent,' said Stephen. 'We'll go around the front, along the harbour, and watch them from there.' We made our way back towards the wharf then took a right-hand turn along the harbour's edge before sitting down with a clear view of the child. Stephen sat down on my left looking at an open map and I lay down with the camera set up on the ground at full zoom, filming the boy behind us. Stephen's body position shielded me and the camera from the people on the balcony of a property neighbouring the father's house; people who had apparently helped Nick to hide Theo from the authorities in the past.

I filmed for a good ten minutes and we sat there for another fifteen minutes observing the boy. At times he appeared bored, picking leaves off a tree and even throwing a stone at a passing motorcycle. The large blonde woman looked at us and looked away. The mere fact that the boy was still on the island, and not supervised by an immediate family member, indicated that no one was aware of our operation.

Stephen and I walked to the cafe and had a drink before checking into the Hotel Therme. Once again we were given room eleven – the helicopter room. After a short while we gathered our things and headed back to the cafe. This was the night I wanted to fix up the front of the OP by flattening down or removing the grass strands for an uninterrupted view of the house. As we neared the cafe we crossed the road to get a view up the street and saw Theo still playing at the front of the church but this time his grandmother was sitting on a concrete pillar talking to the large blonde woman.

We sat down in the cafe, ordered a bottle of water each and put the money on the table. While Stephen crossed the road to telephone Diane and reassure her that her son was still on the island, I watched a group of tourists with camcorders walking in our direction with a tour guide pointing out landmarks. I didn't have to explain my plan to Stephen. He was already thinking the same thing and I was up and walking as he got off the phone. We put our hats on and joined the back of the tour group as they looked round at the different sights. We gradually made our way forward into the centre of the crowd and as the tourists filmed with their camcorders, Stephen did the same, getting a brilliant shot of the kid, his grandmother and the blonde neighbour as the tour group turned in front of the church and made its way towards the harbour. Once we were out of sight of the players we broke off from the tourists and made our way back around to the cafe. We had close-up footage of the child and the grandmother without having exposed ourselves unnecessarily.

By now it was around 8.30 pm and getting dark. The streetlights flickered on and Stephen and I made our way to the highest street up on the hill. I decided to peel off early and head for the church and we arranged to meet up there in one hour. I made my way under cover of darkness around the church towards the stairway behind it and once there I glanced over the railing. The child and grandmother were still there, talking with the neighbour.

I could hear footsteps above me on the stairs and I pressed myself tightly against the brick wall which was part of the stairs as the person descended. I could see their shadow, cast on the church wall to my front. When the shadow had passed, I looked down and saw an old man, wearing a cap and steadying himself with a walking stick, acknowledging the women and the children before he tottered off towards the esplanade. The grandmother was sitting opposite the street looking directly towards the stairway where I was standing, a quarter of the way up, and about 10 metres from my position. I placed the lens of the camera between the railings, flipped the monitor open and started filming. I had turned the brightness of the monitor right down for night operations but to me the glare was still far too obvious, to the point that I had to place my hand over it and only peek occasionally. The grandmother kept facing away and then looking back towards the steps and I moved the camera in and out of the railings accordingly. This was no good. I was in a bad position and needed to get out fast.

Just when I was about to move, a female figure appeared at the base of the steps, greeting the players just as she was about to climb the steps. I froze. If I were to move she would see me directly in front of her and doubtless wonder why I was lurking there. Instead, I pressed myself face first against a concrete pillar to the side of the entrance gate to the church. The middle-aged woman passed me slowly, just 2 metres away, and continued on her way, all of her attention devoted to negotiating the steep steps.

As soon as I could, I left my position and made my way back around the side of the church and into the darkness to gather my thoughts. I still needed to fix up the OP so I walked around towards the top of the stairway that overlooked the house. Several vehicles passed me as they made their way through the narrow streets and the occasional pedestrian would pass and say '*Kalispéra*' – good evening – to which I replied in kind. When I reached the entrance to the steps I walked down them towards the house then peeled off towards the OP. My heart jumped up into my throat when I saw a figure standing still in the shadow before the entrance to the OP. There was no reason for anyone to be stood there, not moving, unless perhaps they knew about the OP. Had I been caught? Had we been compromised?

My eyes adjusted to the darkness and I could see it was Stephen. Sometimes we test each other out because, if a trained eye cannot easily detect you, then you know you have a good position, so I was pleased he was so well hidden, even if he had scared the shit out of me. 'I see the father's inside,' he whispered. 'He's just finished eating dinner and is now watching TV.' I was still trying to lower my heart rate. 'OK,' I whispered, somewhat hoarsely. 'The child and the grandmother are still near the church. There's a good vantage point from above, on the church level. I'll go into the OP for a while and meet you back there in thirty minutes,' I said. 'OK mate,' he said, and he stood watch as I entered the OP and melted away into the shadows.

I made my way through the derelict building, being careful not to disturb the rubble under my feet. It was pitch black and I needed to feel my way. Once I had turned around the interior wall, the streetlight near the house provided me with some illumination to help me move into position. Through the hole in the wall, I watched the scene at the front of the house for about five minutes to ensure that we had not disturbed anyone, or attracted any attention, and then I leopard-crawled out of the OP to the front of the building and patted down the few strands of grass. I didn't want to just tear them off. It had to look natural and undisturbed, which was hard to do in the semi-darkness. Then I froze. The front door opened and Nick was standing there, 10 metres from me, yelling out something in Greek. I was caught out in the open, albeit cloaked by the gloom, and dared not move. A female voice further down the street – perhaps the grandmother – answered Nick's call and he went back inside, closed the door and I saw his figure sink below the level of the lounge room window. I'd got away with it. Just.

I finished making the improvements to the OP then headed back towards the church, my heart pumping hard. Already on edge, I slowly and silently crept to the entrance to the churchyard only to make out a body lying near the corner, almost directly above where Theo and his grandmother were out and about. It was Stephen and he was just 5 metres from where the players were chatting. I stayed in the shadows of the stairway to give Stephen cover until he slid backwards away from his vantage point and made his way towards me. 'The kid seems happy enough,' he whispered. 'You see the father?' I gave him a thumbs up. 'Yeah. He opened the door, yelled out something to the grandmother, I think, then went back in to watch television.' 'Right,' said Stephen. 'I could see him from where I was and the grandmother did shout something back to him.' We arranged that I would go back to the OP, he would stay there and we would meet up when all the players were inside the house.

I made my way back. It was approaching 11 pm and all was quiet, apart from occasional laughter coming from a distant balcony. Inside the OP I watched the lounge window for any movement. It would be interesting to know if there was any pattern to when the father went to bed, his routine, any late phone calls, anyone leaving the house, any visitors, that sort of thing. Night time wasn't when we were likely to conduct the recovery, and we certainly weren't going to wait a few hours then let ourselves into the house, chloroform the sleeping occupants and make away with the drugged child, as some unscrupulous and dangerous outfits might, but anything that added to the intelligence picture could be useful.

It was 12.20 am before I saw the grandmother and the child enter the house. The light to the boy's bedroom went on and was soon turned off. Downstairs, the television was turned off and it appeared that all the players had gone to bed. The house was locked up and dark so it was time to head back to where I had left Stephen in the churchyard. I slipped out of the OP, checked the sticky tape under the padlock at the door of the alternate OP as I went past and, satisfied that it was still in place, proceeded to the churchyard. There was no sign of Stephen so I made my way around the side to the front.

'What are you doing?' demanded a voice from the shadows. 'Oh, shit!' I gasped. 'You bastard!' I added realizing it was Stephen. 'You scared the hell out of me, again.' We walked round the side of the church, made our way towards the hotel and were soon crashed out for the night. It was 12.45 am and I had no trouble falling off to sleep.

The next thing I heard was Stephen shuffling equipment in his bag. It was 6.30 am. I got out of bed and had a quick shower before we checked out and headed towards the motorcycle rental shop and looked up towards the house. The father's motorcycle had not moved since last night so we continued down to the wharf, paid for our tickets and went through the ferry routine. As we stood near the bridge and Stephen leant on the railings to observe the faces of the other passengers, I reached into my bag for the binoculars and focused them on the entrance to the street near the coastguard building. I used my right eye to look through the left-hand ocular at the enhanced view, leaving my left eye open to see the other end of the street with my peripheral vision.

We still weren't sure where the father worked but it occurred to me that he might be working in the family's second house, which we had been told about. If that were the case, he might leave the house and travel up the street towards the T-junction and join the main road. Fortunately for us, the ferry was running late, increasing the chances that we might see him leave for work and, sure enough, nearing 7.10 am, my right eye caught sight through the binoculars of a motorcycle with Nick on it.

I pointed him out to Stephen and watched as he rode along the esplanade and around the harbour before heading off towards the valley. He wore a buttoned shirt and work shorts. We agreed that he must be off to work, but clearly not in the family's second house which was in the opposite direction.

The fact that the father worked gave us some flexibility. The fewer parties present when we made the recovery, the better, particularly if the abductor was not there. It seemed that we now had a window of opportunity to recover the child. The emotions of a direct parent are always likely to be stronger and not necessarily something you want to contend with, and we suspected that Nick could be a fiery character. I was haunted not only by the screams of the mother in Japan, but by memories of another case we tackled.

We were in a suburb of Lusaka, Zambia, standing on the outskirts of a shanty town at the end of a dirt track, waiting to make a recovery before the scorching sun rose too high in the sky. The operation had gone well in spite of the difficulties which had been obvious even before we started the mission. It was never going to be easy for the only two white people in the area not to stand out like ghosts, but for two weeks we had successfully posed as missionaries while we conducted surveillance on a mother and her two young children, a 6-year-old boy and his 4-year-old sister. We had booked accommodation in a local monastery in order to authenticate our disguise and we'd had white T-shirts made up featuring a sky blue crucifix logo with rays of sunshine coming out of the top. Below the logo was printed the bogus 'International Missionary Foundation'. Stephen had even had large magnetic 'IMF' logos produced to stick on the side of the car, over the rental car logo, and whenever anyone looked into the vehicle, which we very successfully used as our mobile OP, they would see us each poring over a bible.

The operation was being funded to the tune of $2,000 a day by the father of the children, a New York-based African American who worked for the United Nations. Having discovered where the mother was keeping the children, whom she had abducted illegally, and having established their routine, all we needed was the help of the police to enforce the recovery. This, it seemed, was easily negotiable, at the right price. A high-ranking member of the Zambian police force was only too happy to authorize the use of two of his officers following a clandestine meeting in the back seat of a car in a golf club car park where he was handed a folded newspaper containing an envelope with $5,000. Such was the way of business in Africa and the way of many child recoveries there.

And so we found ourselves in the front yard of the mother's shanty town shack, behind the two very large policemen, as they banged on her door and demanded the mother hand over the children. The presence of such figures of authority did nothing to persuade the desperate mother who screamed at the top of her lungs at all four of us before slamming the door in the policemen's faces.

Within minutes our targets were barricaded inside the property by the wailing banshee and the scene was attracting an angry crowd of neighbours and passers-by who had no trouble picking out the two white men as the source of the trouble. We had lost the element of surprise and the two policemen, terrified by the mother's screams, were left rooted to the spot, too scared to try to force entry into the property in spite of the orders from their boss. All we could do was make our escape and break the dreadful news to the heartbroken father that his money could buy him cooperation; it could even buy him policemen; but it couldn't guarantee success.

I could hear that mother's screaming in my head when I was startled by a shrill whistle. The ferry pulled out of Pothia harbour and steamed through the sun-dappled Aegean towards Kos island and, hopefully, towards an appointment with more reliable members of the law.

Chapter Nineteen

The sun was already hot by 8.30 am but the hotel patio was nicely shaded and though the gentle breeze barely rustled the fronds on the nearby palms it brought with it the fresh smell of the sea. It was a timely reminder to me how lucky I was that my job was not your average nine-to-five, that my 'office' environment was rarely boring and that there were worse places to hold a morning conference. Diane and Peter had been waiting for us with breakfast when we arrived in Mastichari and since there was no one else on the communal patio we sat out there to eat it.

I was feeling confident about today. Finding out this morning that the father worked, away from the home, had been a bonus. Things surely had to be looking up. I gave Diane the camcorder and showed her the results of the night's activities. This time there was no shock for her, but I could sense her mixed emotions – the joy of seeing more footage of her son tinged with the sadness that he was still, for now, out of reach of the embrace in which she longed to hold him. 'We now know the father works,' Stephen said. 'We saw him depart this morning around seven o'clock and head towards the valley.' This chimed with Diane's knowledge of the island and the family. 'That means he's working for his uncle,' she offered. 'He owns a carpentry shop on the other side of town.'

As Stephen went to answer her, some movement caught my attention. A couple had stepped out onto their balcony and leaned over the edge on the floor above us and to our left, over Stephen's shoulder. I motioned with my knife near my throat, a left to right horizontal movement, signalling for him to cut what he was saying as I looked at the couple. Stephen cottoned on immediately, halting what he was about to say. I took up the narrative in a quieter tone which signalled to the others that we could be overheard.

'Theo was up until after midnight with his grandmother as she spoke to a large blonde lady, about 35 years old,' I told Diane. 'Why do they let a wee boy stay up that late?' she said, her anger clear in spite of its hushed level. 'That will be the busybody woman who lives down the road from them,' she went on. 'She must look after Theo occasionally,' I explained. 'Because we saw him playing with her daughter and she was the only parent in the vicinity.' Diane looked at the camcorder footage again. 'Oh, look at how bored he is, the poor thing,' she said. 'You cheeky monkey! He just threw a stone at that motorcycle.'

The extent to which her son was growing up without her and picking up what she called 'Greek qualities' was cutting her to the quick. Pools of liquid were welling in her eyes as she handed the camcorder back to me. The sooner we could get on with this recovery, the better for everyone, but especially for Diane.

After breakfast we cleaned up, got our things together for the day and got a taxi into Kos Town, hoping Nikolas might have made progress. As we entered his office we found him busy on the phone, with a mountain of paperwork and files on his desk. Eventually he wound up the call and put the phone down. 'That was the Ministry of Justice and they will issue an order for the use of police officers and an order requesting the public prosecutor's assistance,' he told us. It was what we wanted to hear but we also knew by now there could be a big gap between promises and action. 'When will this happen?' asked Stephen. 'Today,' said Nikolas, as if that had never been in doubt. 'My client with the speedboat has agreed to the use of his craft, also. He will come around here this afternoon to take you to look at it.' It all sounded too good to be true.

'Great. When do we speak to the police?' pressed Stephen. Nikolas smiled. 'As soon as I know that the public prosecutor has agreed.' Diane looked worried. 'I don't know about this, Nikolas,' she said. 'Someone will tip off Nick, I'm sure of it.' We all felt her anxiety but Nikolas went on to explain what we knew to be true. 'We need their assistance and we will explain the situation to them about the Kalymnos police,' he said. 'I should have court cases today but I will send someone else in my place because this is more important.' He was making the right noises but I had my doubts. I couldn't help be suspicious that, with all the work Nikolas had, he just happened to be on the phone to the Ministry of Justice about our case both mornings as we arrived. It was almost as if he'd been watching out the window for us and then made the call, or pretended to do so, as soon as he saw us coming.

We all waited in the office for notification of the public prosecutor's approval, and the time dragged. What was I saying about my life rarely being boring? I didn't understand the Greek system and I still don't to this day. The public prosecutor works for the Ministry of Justice, yet the Ministry of Justice was waiting for the public prosecutor's agreement? How can that be? As we waited, a trickle of clients came into the reception area but were all turned away because this case was taking all of Nikolas' time.

At approximately 11 am the phone rang. It was the call we had been waiting for. Nikolas spoke briefly and then hung up. 'That was the Ministry of Justice,' he said. 'The public prosecutor has given approval for this operation and the Ministry of Justice has suggested speaking to the commissioner of police for Rhodes and not Kos.' Yes! That was great news. But Rhodes? That was miles away. It seemed like the Ministry of Justice not only didn't trust the Kalymnos police but had doubts about the Kos police too. Then I remembered what I had read about the bungled Kos police investigation into the disappearance of the British youngster Ben Needham.

Stephen and Diane went with Nikolas to the Ministry of Justice office to receive some paperwork while Peter and I walked around the town to stretch our legs and soak up the sun. It was around 4 pm by the time Diane, Stephen and Nikolas returned to the office and updated us. The Ministry of Justice had organized the commissioner of police in Rhodes to compile an order for the commissioner of police in Kos to have plain-clothed police officers in attendance when we carried out the recovery. Their job was simply to keep the peace. They did not have a search warrant to enter the house, although the commissioner of police in Rhodes had apparently suggested that if they 'bent the rules' he would turn a blind eye.

The commissioner of police in Kos had been handed the order from his superior which informed him that three police officers from Kos were to be in attendance at the Kos police station tomorrow morning and were to travel to the wharf at Mastichari to be met by a court clerk by the name of Franco. The officers were not to be told of this until they arrived in the morning, in order to ensure confidentiality. The chosen officers would also be given an order from the commissioner of police in Rhodes to hand to the commissioner of police on Kalymnos requiring two local police officers to assist, so a total of five police officers would be present when we carried out the recovery.

Excellent. We now had local law enforcement support and it sounded as though the commissioner of police for Rhodes wasn't taking a chance on any leaks. Stephen looked pleased with the arrangement. 'It looks like this will happen tomorrow,' he said. I gave Diane a smile, turned to Stephen and asked, 'What would you like to happen tonight?' He said Peter and I should go over to Kalymnos and check all the players were still there and then conduct surveillance tomorrow morning. 'We need to know where they are to conduct the recovery,' he said. I agreed. 'Diane, are you alright?' I asked. She gave me a weak smile and nodded. I put a hand on her arm. 'If at any time you don't want this to go ahead, you just say so,' I said. She tried again to smile. 'No, no, no, I want this to happen. I'm just very nervous.' Stephen gave her a sympathetic look. 'Just take it easy and try not to think about it for now,' he said. 'Hopefully you'll have Theo in your arms very soon.'

Stephen stood up. 'Diane and I are going to check out this boat now,' he said. 'Darren, you stay here and, Peter, we need you to go to a travel agency to book flights for all of us from Kos to Athens any time tomorrow afternoon. That's four adults and one child. Right?' A smile lit up Diane's face. Now she knew the time was near.

With the three gone, I chatted with Nikolas about general stuff, but it wasn't long before Stephen and Diane returned. 'It's old, but it will do the trick,' he told me. I asked after the horsepower and he said 200, which was bigger than any other private boat we'd seen on the island. Suddenly Nikolas spoke up. 'You know, I was in the military,' he volunteered. We looked at him. 'What branch?' asked Stephen. 'Special Forces,' Nikolas replied, and both our jaws dropped. Stephen and I had to try hard not to laugh. This guy had the body of a 14 year old and I doubt he could walk 50 metres with a pack on his back. Besides, I'm not sure they do army fatigues in lemon.

Further examination of Nikolas' military career was put on hold by the return of Peter who had booked tickets on the 3.30 pm flight the next day. With the law enforcement assistance organized and a boat on standby, we headed back to Mastichari. It felt like we were within touching distance of the recovery.

Back at the hotel, Stephen, Diane and I headed for our rooms while Peter announced he needed to go to the shops. I don't know why but, when I got halfway up the stairs I decided to see what Peter was up to and I left the hotel to follow him. I caught sight of him just as he walked around the corner to a shop which had a phone box outside and, positioning myself out of his line of sight, I got close enough to see the number he dialled, which I recognized as a California number, though I couldn't hear the conversation. He was on the phone for about five minutes before he popped into the shop, bought more phone cards and headed back to the hotel. I ducked around the corner and sprinted to the hotel alleyway to get back before him.

'Where have you been?' Stephen asked me as I entered the room, slightly out of breath. 'I followed Peter,' I said, filling my lungs with a large gulp of air. 'Where did he go?' he asked. 'He went to make a phone call. It was a number in California but I couldn't hear what he was saying.' Stephen raised his eyebrows. 'I can't help but worry that he may be letting someone know of our progress,' I said. Just then the door opened and Peter walked in. 'Where did you go?' asked Stephen. 'I went to make a phone call,' Peter said. 'Who did you ring?' pressed Stephen. The interrogation had a feeling of deja-vu after Peter's previous indiscretions, but he insisted he had simply rung his brother to let him know he was alright. To my surprise, Stephen nodded his acceptance. 'OK. Darren, go and get Diane and we'll explain what's to happen.'

The four of us sat in our room as Stephen outlined the plan. 'Darren and Peter will go over this evening and conduct surveillance tonight and tomorrow morning. We need to know the exact location of Theo for the recovery. The speedboat driver is bringing the boat around to the harbour here. I will meet the police officers here in the morning and Diane and I will go over with them to Kalymnos in the boat. As soon as we get there, Diane and I will go to the local police station with the police officers with the order from the commissioner of police for Rhodes. Darren and Peter will locate Theo and await our arrival. The child and his grandmother should be in the house at that time, or nearby, judging by what we have seen so far. Diane, you may have to enter the house with the police officers and grab Theo. The police officers cannot touch him and we cannot either. It has to be you that grabs him.

'When you've got Theo, we will escort you to the boat and we all leave together and make the 1530 hours flight. The police can stay behind to sort out the mess. Franco is a court clerk working with Nikolas. He will travel over with Diane, me and the police and will have copies of all the legal documents. He will also stay behind with the police after we leave. Any questions?' I had one. 'Can you or I enter the house?,' I asked. Stephen's expression suggested it was not clear cut. 'The police have no warrant to enter but they may bend the rules. If that is the case then, yes, we will enter the house behind them. When we locate Theo we will call Diane in to pick him up.'

It sounded like a plan and a pretty good plan at that, but in our experience nothing ever really goes to plan. That is where the experienced operators can adapt and overcome any obstacles. Stephen and I have seen a lot of different scenarios which we can easily adapt no matter where in the world and we are still experiencing new scenarios. However, there was one issue with this plan that I was not comfortable with. Apart from Stephen, Diane and me, there were now six other individuals who would know of our operation, and that did not include the clerks for the public prosecutor, the Ministry of Justice, the various police commissioners, the TV station in Australia and whoever else Peter was informing, but this was out of my hands and I could only hope that no leaks would compromise the operation. Tomorrow was D-Day.

We packed up our belongings and Peter and I packed our day bags for our last trip to Kalymnos. We had plenty of time before the 9.30 pm ferry so we all had dinner together, having carefully chosen a restaurant we had not used before. It was an enjoyable three-course meal and one which was not as rushed as usual. Stephen checked that we had enough phone cards, which Peter handed out to everyone, then we finished our meal and made our way to the harbour.

'OK, guys, good luck,' Stephen said. 'Give me a ring tomorrow morning, first thing.' I said we'd update him that night as well. Stephen turned to Diane. 'This is going to go down tomorrow, Diane. Are you still sure you want to go ahead?' She nodded enthusiastically. 'Yes, of course,' she said. 'It should work, right?' She was desperate for reassurance that everything was going to be OK. 'Everything is set. It should work,' was the best Stephen could offer. Any cast-iron guarantees would have been false and unfair on Diane.

It seemed strange to ask Diane if she wanted to go ahead with something that would hopefully end many months of anguish and reunite her with her beloved son, but there have been cases when the parent has pulled out at the last minute. On an operation in Russia, we had everything set up with a great chance of success so long as the abductor's relatives didn't get to us before we reached the border. On the eve of the recovery day the client walked into our hotel room and said, 'I want to abort the operation.' He was just too nervous to go through with it, knowing his ex's family and that people could get killed.

As Stephen and Diane headed back to the hotel, Peter and I boarded the ferry. The night was beautiful; the cloudless sky a mass of stars and the moon seemingly twice as large as usual. We could see the lights of various cruise ships as we bobbed along towards Kalymnos. As the ferry idled into Pothia harbour, it had to negotiate its way around a cruise liner which had already docked and disgorged a thousand or so passengers.

Since the town was busier than usual, I thought it best to go directly to the hotel and check in. Room eleven wasn't available at Hotel Therme and we were given a different room, on the third floor. At least it had a harbour view. The room was stifling hot so I turned the ceiling fan on and waited for the sound of an Iroquois 'Huey' helicopter. There was no noise because there was no movement. It didn't work. Faced with the stinking hot room I'd have given anything for the noisy fan. It would also drown out the noise of Peter's snoring, perhaps. Ordinarily, you would go down to reception to complain and be moved to another room but these were not ordinary circumstances and we didn't want to attract attention to ourselves. Besides, we weren't going to be in the room until much later when the heat might have dissipated.

The town of Pothia was awash with tourists from the cruise ship but it was quieter closer to the house and we approached the OP carefully and peered around the corner. I could see that the motorcycle was missing and the television was on. I was fairly confident this meant someone was inside watching, probably the grandmother and perhaps Theo, and the father was out, probably down in the town. Considering it was now 11 pm, it was a fair bet that he was in the bars, drinking.

I had been on the road in front of the house enough times to not risk going there again, so I asked Peter to do a casual walk past the lounge window to see if he could see who was inside. For an RV, I pointed up towards the balcony of the vacant, padlocked house I had earmarked as our alternative OP, and then we went our separate ways. Being by myself in the alternative OP was risky, should anyone walk down the alleyway and turn towards it. There was no second escape route and I would be caught acting suspiciously, to say the least. But using the primary OP would take too long to get into.

I found a small patch of grass to the side of the alleyway, with dried leaves and twigs, and gathered as many of them as I could. I placed half of them at one end of the alleyway, 10 metres from the unoccupied house, and the rest at the other end of the alleyway, a similar distance away.

At least if someone were to walk down the alleyway I'd hear them as the twigs and leaves crunched under their feet and I'd be able to walk off in the opposite direction. I checked the padlock and the tape had not been moved, so I stood underneath the stairway under the cover of darkness. It felt like an eternity but moments later I saw Peter walk past the house and continue up the street. A few minutes later, I heard twigs breaking and the cracking of leaves to my right. My heart pumped faster as I quickly exited the balcony, turned into the alleyway to the left and looked to my right to see who it was. It was Peter.

'The grandmother is watching TV but I didn't see the child,' he whispered. 'OK, maybe he's in bed,' I said quietly. 'Let's go down to the esplanade and see if the father's down there.' We approached it from the other side of the road and along the harbour in case he was in the restaurant that we had seen him in before, and we gave the diner a quick check. Lo and behold, he was there, in his usual spot, sitting at the same table, drinking the same drink and smoking the same brand of cigarettes. He spoke to no one or, more precisely, no one spoke to him. He just watched the motorists and the pedestrians passing by.

Peter and I sat inside a nearby bar which gave us a good view of Nick without us being obvious to him. It was approximately 40 metres away and at 45 degrees to his position, away from the road that he was watching constantly. I ordered two colas in small glasses with ice and watched as the barman poured the drinks. The bar had very few customers as it was nearing midnight, but they didn't seem in a hurry to shut up shop so we hopefully had a little while longer for our surveillance. We could both see Nick, but the TV screen in the bar was showing a football match so I asked Peter to glance at it occasionally so that we weren't both looking in the same direction.

After drinking three colas each, we watched the father pay his bill and stagger off to his motorcycle before setting off in the opposite direction from his house. We had watched him do that before and I was curious as to where he was going, but since we had no transportation other than our feet I decided that Peter would go back to the hotel and I would take a walk up to the house and go into the OP to find out what time he returned home.

Approaching the house from yet another angle, I could see from the harbour the empty space where Nick's motorcycle would normally be parked. At the esplanade level there were two houses below the target house and between them was a very narrow stairway leading up to the father's street. At the top of the steps was Nick's favoured parking spot so I sat down on the harbour edge and watched the small gap. It was dark up the steps and I could see something shining from the streetlight outside the house. It intrigued me and, since it was now 12.30 am, I decided it would be safe to take a closer look. I only had to go halfway up the steps before I could see it was a reflection… off the motorcycle. Nick must have got there before me, which meant he didn't go anywhere after the bar. He just took a longer route back home.

On my way back to the hotel I used a pay phone to ring Stephen on the new mobile phone. He answered before the second ring so I clearly hadn't woken him. 'Hello. What's new?' he asked. 'The players and the package are locked up safely. Main player just got in,' I said. 'Right,' responded Stephen. 'But we're not coming tomorrow. The boat skipper's decided he needs twenty-four hours' notice.'

I couldn't believe it. 'What? What the hell for?' I asked. 'I have no idea, mate,' said Stephen with a sigh. It wasn't anything sinister, I was sure, as the boat owner thought he was taking tourists on a jolly. I asked how Diane had taken it. 'What do you think?' said Stephen. 'She's distraught. She'd rung her husband earlier to tell him it was happening, but by the time we got the news it was too late for her to ring him again.' I paused and thought about all the plans we'd put in place. 'Do we still have the blue guys for the following day?' I asked. 'Yeah, no probs,' said Stephen. 'It will be as before, plus twenty-four.' I tutted. 'Bloody hell, eh? Just when things were starting to work out.' Stephen laughed. 'Yeah, I know. You guys come back over tomorrow then.' I said we'd be on the first ferry and hung up.

Back at the hotel, I explained the situation to Peter who'd been dozing in the chair. 'Oh well, it's just another day in Greece,' he said after the news had sunk in. He was right. We both laughed and started to get ready for bed. The room was still stinking hot, even with the windows open, but I had an idea. This room might not have a working fan but, unlike the helicopter room, it had a small minibar fridge. I turned the fridge up to high, taped the light off, left the fridge door open and closed the windows. It worked perfectly as a room-cooler. Now all I had to do to get a decent night's kip was to fall asleep before the wildebeest did. With thoughts racing through my head about what could go wrong tomorrow, it was not going to be easy.

Chapter Twenty

I woke early, around 6 am. I'm not sure whether that was because I'd had a good night's sleep or because the room was freezing. I closed the fridge door, had a long shower and woke Peter up. Once he'd showered and dressed we grabbed our things, placed the room key behind the unoccupied reception counter and walked towards the house. There were plenty of people around even at that time. Peter peered down the street while I waited outside the coastguard building. I could see an officer through the window sitting back on his chair with his feet up on the table, motionless. It was my guess that he was asleep. Peter said that the motorcycle was there so we made our way down to the wharf, bought our ferry tickets and went through our usual boarding routine.

As we stood on the bridge deck a middle-aged man standing next to a utility van kept staring up at us. 'C'mon, let's go sit at the aft,' I said to Peter. 'Some guy is paying a little too much attention to us.' The rest of the journey was uneventful but when we came ashore at Mastichari and had walked halfway down the jetty I stopped. 'We'll just sit down here for a bit,' I said to Peter. 'I want to see what that guy is doing.'

We sat with our legs hanging over the side of the jetty like tourists enjoying the harbour scene and we didn't have to wait long for our man to appear in the queue of vehicles disembarking the ferry. As his utility truck passed, I could see he had a passenger and the men were deep in conversation. Whatever my suspicions, he was clearly not interested in us so we continued to the hotel where Stephen and Diane were eating breakfast on the patio. However anguished she must have been last night, Diane had telephoned her husband this morning and he must have managed to comfort her because she was calm, though still annoyed. 'I can't believe it,' she said. 'If it's not one thing, it's another.' I gave her a sympathetic smile. 'At least we know they're still on the island, unaware of what is going on, and everything else is still in place,' I said. 'Right,' added Stephen, 'The plan sticks. It will just happen tomorrow instead.'

As usual Peter said very little but took it all in. Stephen and I were more determined than ever to get this done and, in spite of the setbacks and the number of people in on the plan, I was feeling confident. I kept visualizing Diane hugging Theo and it gave me a good feeling inside. Stephen was as focused as ever. 'We'll go into town again just to make sure that everything and everyone is ready,' he said. I asked if he thought the Kos police officers would be told of the operation this morning when they come into work but Stephen had already thought that through. 'No, we rang the commissioner in Rhodes last night to put things on hold.' That was a relief.

Before we left the room, I handed Diane the bag with the Snow White wig. 'That's for you to wear under your hat on Kalymnos, tomorrow,' I said. 'For extra disguise.' She peered into the bag. 'Really?' she asked, pulling a face. 'Yes, really,' I replied. I was determined, as much as possible, that no one locally should know who we were and why we were there until the very last moment, which is why what happened next came as such a shock. The young male receptionist had rung for a taxi for us and we were walking out to the front of the hotel when his words stopped me dead in my tracks. 'You found 'em yet?' he asked.

My blood froze and, by the startled looks on the faces of the others, they shared my alarm. 'Huh... found who?' I asked in my fake British accent. 'The bird-watching spots you were interested in,' he replied. 'Oh, right, yes,' I said, trying to disguise a massive sigh of relief. 'The bee-eaters are amazing. But we still haven't seen a long-legged buzzard,' I added wracking my brain for the names of the birds I had read in the book I bought. 'Oh, well good luck,' he said.

Another hell ride in a Mercedes to Kos Town and within minutes we had arrived. I noted with some satisfaction that we must look like tourists, to the taxi drivers at least, because we had been charged four different fares to make this same journey, ranging from 8 to 20 euros. The four of us entered Nikolas' office and waited until the 'ex-Special Forces' guy got off the phone. 'That was the public prosecutor wanting to know why this wasn't happening today,' he said. 'I told him the reason and he is willing to let it go another day.' Stephen asked about the police and Nikolas reassured us they would be fine about it and ready to go tomorrow as soon as the commissioner on Rhodes gives the order. 'What was wrong with the boat skipper?' I asked. 'He wants to clean the boat up and make it look presentable for you,' said Nikolas. I shook my head in bewilderment. 'He really didn't need to,' I said, but Nikolas gave me a look that said he knew better. 'Yes,' he said. 'But you want him to think he is taking you as tourists to look around the island, so he wants to make things look good for you.'

It wasn't an argument I was going to win, or even one that mattered. 'Oh well, whatever,' I said. 'It is what it is.' It was Diane's turn to chip in. 'How much should we pay him?' she asked. 'That is up to you. Whatever you think is fair. He can only take two people, though,' replied Nikolas. What? When the hell was he planning on telling us that? Stephen got in first. 'That's crazy,' he said. 'That boat can take more than two people.' Nikolas shook his head. 'Sorry. The owner said he will only take two people.' Now this was a setback. We had arranged to have six people taken over – Diane, Stephen, Franco and three policemen – and five coming back – the four of us plus Theo – and the skipper had agreed. Now he was saying he could only take two. Since he would earn more money transporting six, why had he now changed his mind? Something wasn't right.

It was approaching midday and Nikolas had to go to court again so we decided to have some lunch at a nearby restaurant. It wasn't the best of restaurants as there were homeless kittens all over the outdoor seating area, wanting to jump up on the tables. As I've said, I'm no fan of cats, but Diane thought they were cute and, despite the latest hiccup, they were calming her down as much as they were winding me up. When she took off her hat to pet a couple of them I reacted more gruffly than I meant to. 'What are you doing with your hat off?' I hissed. 'Oh, it's alright,' she said. I couldn't agree. We had come this far with the element of surprise in our favour, and the last thing we wanted to do was compromise the operation because someone recognized her. But I had made the recommendation, I could do no more. She was the client, and maybe it was just the cats putting me on edge. Diane, however, looked relaxed during the meal, and was smoking less. I guess she could sense we were close to the recovery.

Up to this point, it had been normal for me to order an entrée and a main meal, like the others, but I decided to cut back to one course, to save on operational costs. With all the delays, I was starting to feel guilty about living at Diane's expense, especially knowing that she would be repaying the loan for the next fifteen years. Besides, the more money left over at the end of the operation, the more chance of a bonus… if we were successful.

We went back to the office and Diane checked her email at the receptionist's desk. Peter went to the bank to get more money and made some more phone calls. Stephen and I sat in Nikolas' office to go over the plan. An hour later Nikolas returned. 'Everything is settled then, yes?' he asked Stephen. 'Yeah, it looks like it,' Stephen replied. 'You know, they may shout at you and you may get pushed and shoved,' Nikolas added sternly. Stephen looked stunned at the 'ex-Special Forces' guy's concern. Shouting and shoving was the very least we expected. 'Oh, yes, they could do this to you. You need to know what you may be up against,' said Nikolas in all seriousness.

I could have pissed myself laughing. I felt like turning to Stephen and saying, 'You didn't tell me I might be shouted at. I'm out!' I don't know what line of business Nikolas thought we were in but we were preparing to take a father's son away from him, on an island where we were told everyone had been protecting them. I was more worried about metre-long things with red cartridges than a bit of pushing and pulling.

At 4 pm we made our way back to the hotel in another grand prix taxi when the inevitable happened. Well, if you're travelling at 100 kilometres per hour through a built-up area you will eventually hit something or someone. We had not left the town when our Mercedes ran into the back of another vehicle, which had stopped to allow a pretty female tourist to cross the main road nowhere near any pedestrian crossing. The impact nearly put me through the windscreen and I felt Peter's head hit the back of my seat, but our taxi driver simply raised his arms in disgust and both drivers continued on their way.

Back at the hotel, I was still annoyed by Nikolas' view of how the recovery might get a bit rough. I couldn't help but think he was worried about what was going to happen because it was getting close to reality and he didn't like the fact he was being assisted by us in bringing it to fruition. He was escorted off the island by the police once before regarding this case. Was he bothered that we might succeed where he failed, even though he would have helped considerably? Perhaps. And I wasn't happy about the boat situation at all.

Stephen decided to stick to the main plan with some minor changes. He and I would go over on the ferry this afternoon and Diane and Peter would come over on the speedboat in the morning. The police would come over on the ferry and be met by Stephen at the harbour side in Pothia. The ferry was due to leave at 9 am and the speedboat would leave thirty minutes later as it would only take fifteen minutes to make the crossing. We packed our bags so that they could be grabbed at a moment's notice and checked that we had our passports on us should we find ourselves in a bad position with the authorities.

'How are you feeling?' I asked Diane when she came into our room. 'I actually feel OK,' she said. 'Good. I'll go over what you need to do again.' Diane grimaced. 'I hope I can remember it,' she said. 'You will. Just remain calm and focused on what you have to do.' I took a deep breath. 'You will be met by Stephen and me at the harbour where we will point the old guy to where we want him to moor up. You and Stephen will then go to the police station with the Kos officers and organize the Kalymnos police. When that is done we will approach the house. Make sure that your hair is under your wig and your hat and sunglasses are on so that no one recognizes you. As soon as you see Theo you are to grab him, turn around, and walk away with him. I will be directly behind you and will escort you to the boat and we will leave quickly for Mastichari. It is important not to get involved in a screaming match with the grandmother. You must compose yourself and grab Theo. You must not collapse on the floor or start crying because you see him, just grab him. We will surround Theo to make sure that he doesn't run away. Do you understand what you have to do?' She nodded slowly. 'Yes, I think I can do that,' she replied but I wanted to be sure. 'Parents and children react very differently to these situations and it is important that you do exactly what I have explained. You can give hugs and kisses later. The important thing is to get him off the island, and quickly, before anyone calls Nick.' This time Diane nodded more vigorously. 'Yes, I totally agree,' she said. 'I will do exactly that, Darren.' I smiled. 'OK, good,' I said. 'You need to go over it in your head all tonight to make sure that is exactly what happens.'

Diane went back to her room and Stephen and I went over the operation some more. Peter was off calling someone yet again, to update someone on our progress, I guessed, in spite of our every warning. As Stephen and I brainstormed what could go wrong we even thought of cutting the main telephone line to the Kalymnos police station to ensure no one there tipped the players off on our arrival, but that was obviously not a good idea because of other emergencies that might occur on the island at the same time – maybe even our own. Stephen said he would instruct one of the Kos officers to watch anyone who made any calls while they were in the station, and I would jam the father's mobile phone signal shortly before the recovery.

Everything was in place when Peter arrived back but Stephen wanted to go over the plan for the last time with everyone present, so as soon as all four of us were in the room he began. 'This is the brief for the recovery,' he said. 'Darren and I will go over tonight to make sure that they are still on the island. Tomorrow morning, Peter and Diane will be met at the wharf by the boat guy who will bring his craft to Mastichari. The Kos police officers and Franco, the court orderly, will leave Kos Town at 0800 hours and make their way to Mastichari, in plain clothes and in a taxi. They will board the ferry for Kalymnos and leave on the 0900 hours sailing. Thirty minutes later, Peter and Diane will leave the harbour in the speedboat. Peter, the onus will be on you to provide protection for Diane from the moment you both leave the hotel until you are met by us in Pothia. The idea is for you to arrive after the ferry to minimize the risk of exposure for Diane. I will meet the ferry and give a brief to the police officers and to Franco. Darren will meet Peter and Diane in the speedboat and direct the owner to where we want him to moor the boat. Diane, Franco and I, and the Kos police officers will go to the police station while Darren and Peter conduct surveillance to locate the players. When Diane, Franco and I and the police have finished in the police station, we will make our way to Darren and Peter's location – probably the house – to conduct the recovery. Darren, you will jam the father's mobile phone moments before the recovery, and then we go in. Diane, you will grab your son, turn around and one of us will escort you to the speedboat.

'Us four and Theo will then leave on the speedboat while the police officers and Franco deal with the legal situation. We will use the police's authority to get the boat owner to take the five of us. We will then go directly to Mastichari at full speed and once we have arrived there, you, Diane, and Theo and I will go directly to the airport. Darren, you will grab the bags from our room and Peter you will check us out. Diane, make sure you place your bags in our room before you leave tomorrow morning. I will arrange tickets for the next flight out and Peter and Darren will meet up with us at the airport. We should be safe when we arrive in Athens but we will need to get you, Diane, and Theo out of the country on the first available flight.' We all had a complete picture of how the recovery was to take place and knew of each other's roles and responsibilities. Should it all turn to mud, Stephen and I had contingency plans.

It was now approaching 8 pm. Stephen and I didn't pack our day packs as we wanted to go 'clean skin' to make a fast getaway. We grabbed our passports and the four of us went to have dinner after selecting a restaurant facing the harbour. We could see the ferry already docked, ready for the 9.30 pm crossing. I asked Diane again what she had to do the next day. 'Grab Theo, turn around and walk towards the speedboat,' she said. 'Don't get involved in any screaming match or conversation with anyone.' She was noticeably stronger and more determined than before. 'Just keep going over it tonight and you will be fine,' I said. And then her mobile phone rang.

'Hello? Oh, hi Nikolas. What? When? How? Oh, no, are you serious?' The tears began to flow. 'Oh my God! What do I do? Should I ring her? Oh no. OK then. Thankyou. Bye.' We stared at Diane. 'What's the matter?' asked Stephen. 'That was Nikolas,' she said, gulping. 'He said that Nick's second wife had just rung him and said she saw me in town this morning with three guys and wanted to know what I was doing.'

Shit! That bloody hat! But Stephen was one step ahead. 'Why did she leave it so long to ring Nikolas?' he asked. 'I don't know,' sobbed Diane. 'Why didn't she walk up and talk to you?' he pressed. 'I DON'T KNOW, STEPHEN,' Diane yelled and then softened. 'What do we do?' she asked. Stephen was firm. 'We'll just stick to the plan and hopefully she hasn't said anything. She's not exactly on good terms with Nick, apparently,' he said. He turned to me. 'Darren, if the players are gone we know the game is up but, Diane, as soon as we lay eyes on Theo we will call you to let you know, OK?'

The time had come to board the ferry. 'Good luck tomorrow Diane,' I said. 'You too, both of you, and please be careful,' she replied. We all embraced and I held Diane a little longer and tighter. 'Be strong. Good luck,' I repeated. Stephen had the final word. 'Everyone knows what they're doing,' he said. 'Don't worry too much about what Nikolas said… it sounds suspicious to me. See you tomorrow.' Maybe he was right. It was a little suspicious. Why did the ex-wife ring so late in the day to ask Nikolas? Why did she ring Nikolas in any case? Why didn't she approach Diane and speak with her? They were apparently on speaking terms. They both had issues with Nick. Then again, what if Nikolas was right. Would she go to Nick? Would she tell him anything? Or was Nikolas making things up, hoping we would abort? Yes, maybe now I was thinking in the right direction, the same as Stephen, I suspected. Maybe Nikolas realizes that this recovery is a reality and he doesn't want any part of it, so he makes this up in the hope that we don't go ahead. But Diane should have kept her hat and glasses on.

Stephen and I boarded the ferry and made our way to the bridge deck, hopefully for the last time. I looked at Diane as the ferry made its way out of the harbour, twenty minutes late, and she got smaller and smaller in the distance. I knew that tomorrow was D-Day and I wanted it to be successful for her. Her story had touched my heart. Soon enough we were out of sight of Mastichari and sailing into the inky blackness. This would hopefully be our last time on this slow, two-town vessel.

We were silent for a while before Stephen spoke. 'He is full of shit, that guy,' he said. I nodded in agreement. 'There are things that just don't add up.' Stephen was now thinking out loud. 'Why would she leave it to ring him nine hours later? It just doesn't make sense.' That might have been the case but we needed to be on our toes for whatever lay ahead, and we would find out in not much more than forty-five minutes whether the operation had been compromised. I half expected the father, plus assorted relatives, to be waiting for us at the wharf.

The ferry pulled into Kalymnos harbour and I scanned the foreshore and the harbour side. Everything appeared normal so we disembarked, cautiously approached the shore off the jetty and headed straight to the hotel. We were given the keys to yet another room and, thankfully, this time the fan worked. Not that we were staying in the room for long. As soon as we checked it was OK, we left to conduct surveillance. Down on the esplanade we noticed the father was not at his usual drinking spot, which wasn't good. We pressed on and Stephen approached the churchyard while I continued to the OP. After settling into my hide I could see the motorcycle was missing. Shit! Could he already know we were there and have left with the kid to go into hiding?

The house looked locked, with no lights on. The television was not on either. It was approximately 11.30 pm, but on other nights we had seen them up and about later than this. I had a bad feeling. With nothing happening at the house, I decided to go down and check on Stephen.

I crept into the churchyard, walked around the corner in the shadows and found him lying on the concrete peering through the railings up towards the house. I tapped my foot and he turned around. He crawled away from the fence and then walked over to me. 'You seen anything?' he asked. 'No, nothing. The motorcycle is missing, the house is locked up tight, no windows are open, all lights are off and the TV is off too,' I replied. 'Nothing down here either,' he said. It was as if they had disappeared off the face of the earth. My heart sank. We had come so far. Now what?

Chapter Twenty-One

The silence was deafening; the darkness was claustrophobic; but it was the realization that the father had possibly flown the coop, taking the boy with him into hiding that was making me feel sick. 'Any clues where he could be?' Stephen asked. At that moment a motorcycle entered the street from the barricades end and we went to the open gate, halfway down the stairway and looked down. The father had gone past at a tremendous speed. 'Shit! Quick, the OP!' said Stephen. We hurried back up the stairway, turned left into the small alleyway and stood outside the OP, peering around the corner at the house. We couldn't get into the OP as the father was standing outside the house and would have heard us.

Two more motorcycles appeared, and then another. They parked up and now there were four males standing around, talking. We were too far away to hear what they were saying and it wouldn't have helped much if we could, because they were talking in Greek, but key words such as 'Diane', 'Australian', or 'Mastichari' might have stood out. The best thing we could do was stay put and observe each person's body language, except there was none. The men hardly moved and were pretty much expressionless, but all of a sudden lonely Nick seemed to have friends. Was this a coincidence or had the game been given away? I feared the latter.

It was now 12.30 pm. We had been here nearly every night around the same time and there had never been signs of visitors. Indeed, we had never seen the father in the company of anyone but the grandmother and Theo. Now he had three men with him in the dead of night and he had ridden past at a great speed to arrive at the house, which was locked up tight with no sign of movement. I was prone to paranoia at the best of times but now it was setting in big time.

After fifteen minutes, the three men left, two up the street and one down. The father calmly walked into the house and locked the door. His bedroom light went on and, after a few moments, it went off. Stephen and I looked at each other with puzzled faces, not saying a word. We sloped away from our position and made our way up the stairway, sort of relieved that the father was back, but confused as to what had gone on. And was the boy still tucked up in the house or was he now in the care of a monastery somewhere?

We had just reached the street at the top when we heard a motorcycle heading in our direction and we pressed ourselves up against the wall to get out of its headlight beam. A male with a female passenger riding pillion went past and the female turned to look down the stairway. She must have seen us but the bike carried on its way. After it passed we walked along the street and down towards the hotel. 'He can't know anything if he's in the house right now,' I suggested before adding, 'Unless he's already moved Theo away.' Stephen sighed. 'We'll just have to wait and see,' he said.

'We have another problem, though,' he said after a pause. Oh shit, what now? 'I went to the esplanade to look for the father and rang Diane from the phone box while I was there,' he explained. 'Apparently Peter told her that he had rung his brother in California, told him the operation has been compromised and asked him to ring the US Embassy to get him out of the country. He said he had used the last of the phone cards. Diane broke down and cried when he told her and then he just walked off and left her!' I couldn't believe what I was hearing. 'You're joking!' I said. 'No, that's what she told me,' he said. 'I couldn't even reassure her that we'd seen Theo. It was all I could do to calm her down. I have no idea what is going on in his head or why he would think the embassy would give a damn.'

I knew Peter had been ringing California and updating someone about our operation. It was the night before a recovery, which might already have been compromised, and now this. I was not a happy camper. We didn't know if the father knew something was going on or not; we didn't know how many of his relatives might also know; we didn't know if we could trust the police, Peter or Nikolas and we had a boat that, in all likelihood, wouldn't take us all off the island if, miraculously, we were able to pull off the recovery.

Out of habit, Stephen opened up the hotel phone to check for bugs before putting it back together and ringing Diane. He reassured her that we had seen Nick return home and go to bed and that, in all likelihood, Theo was already in bed asleep. He didn't tell her about the posse of late night visitors. There was no point inviting unnecessary worry considering the state she was already in. With that we turned in for the night to rest up for whatever dramas the next day had in store for us. Success or failure, life or death. We'd find out tomorrow.

Chapter Twenty-Two

D-Day. Thursday, 5 September. This was it. We were ready. Stephen and I were awake at 0600 hours and the morning was beautiful. The sun, not yet glaringly harsh, bathed Pothia's maze of white houses in soft light and the exquisite blue sea was like glass. There was not a breath of wind. We went to the cafe at the bottom of the father's street to have a bite to eat and allow Stephen to have his caffeine fix. Everything in the town appeared to be normal. Some shopkeepers were opening up their stores to commence the day's trading while others were hosing the dust off the walkways. Everywhere people were greeting each other with a cheerful *'Kalimera'* or a simple *'Geia sou'*.

We walked towards the church and looked in the direction of the house. The motorcycle was parked in its usual spot so we climbed the stairway behind the church, turned into the small alleyway, entered the alternative OP and stood beneath the next stairway. At exactly 0700 hours the father came out of the house wearing work shorts, flip-flops and a buttoned shirt. He walked down the stairs from the patio, jumped on his bike and, as he started it, the child ran on to the patio wearing nothing but his underpants and a beaming smile. As Nick rode off, Theo ran behind, waving and shouting 'bye, bye'.

It struck me that neither of them knew this goodbye might be their last for the foreseeable future as the touching scene was being watched by international security operatives ready to snatch the boy away. I pushed the emotion to one side. From our point of view, the situation was looking good. The father had gone to work while the child and the grandmother were in the house. The sense of dread from last night had dissipated. Nothing, it seemed, had been compromised. Happy that we knew where the players were, we returned to the cafe at the end of the street. If the grandmother and child were to leave the house they would have to walk past us in the cafe on their way towards the esplanade.

It was now 0900 hours and Stephen went across the road to the public phone to telephone Diane and reassure here that her son was still on the island and that our plans were intact. All we could do was sit tight and wait for the cavalry to arrive. In the distance we could see the slow ferry making its journey towards Kalymnos. Stephen returned to the cafe to look out for Theo and the grandmother and I walked around the harbour to look for a suitable mooring place for our speedboat, where it would be easy to return to. Most of the spaces were full except for one location at the other end of the esplanade. It was a little further away than we would have liked but it would have to do. I walked to the end of the wharf and waited for the ferry which was getting closer.

A small boat without a canopy could be seen on the left-hand side of the harbour, heading towards the wharf with three people on board. Surely that couldn't be our boat? They weren't due to arrive until after the ferry had docked. As the boat got closer, I realized it was them. What the bloody hell were they doing? How hard is it to follow simple instructions? Peter spotted me and the boat headed to where I was standing. When it came alongside me, I stepped on board and pointed out to the elderly owner where we wanted it moored. At least Diane was unrecognizable beneath her dark glasses, floppy hat and the wig which didn't look too bad under the hat and which, after last night's scare, she had thankfully chosen to wear.

'Why are you here now?' I asked Peter. 'He wanted to go,' he said, pointing to the boat owner. 'Well now I have to hide you both until the police arrive,' I replied, disgruntled. Once the speedboat was moored I helped Diane out on to the wharf. 'What shall I tell him about waiting? How long will we be?' she asked. 'Tell him to stay here,' I said. 'And tell him we'll be about thirty minutes.' I knew damn well we would be longer than that but I didn't want him thinking he had plenty of time to kill and wandering off somewhere because when we needed to move we would need to move fast. 'When shall I pay him?' asked Diane. 'Don't worry about that now,' I said. 'Let's worry about getting you out of sight.' I also knew the boat owner was less likely to get fed up and disappear if he hadn't been paid.

I had no safe house to take Diane to as it wasn't part of the plan and I was having to think on my feet. Peter put his arm around her as they walked from the boat and they looked like a loving holiday couple. I was pleased he was using his initiative. It wasn't until we started walking down the esplanade that I thought of the hotel room. We crossed the road and entered the hotel reception area. No one was around and the key to the room Stephen and I had used was where we had left it behind the counter. Since we didn't officially need to check out until mid-morning there was nothing stopping us from using it so I led Peter and Diane to the room and made sure they were settled in, taking the opportunity to give Peter one of my phone cards, since the last information we'd had was that he'd used all his.

'OK guys, just stay here for the time being until I come to get you,' I said. 'Diane, just stay away from the window.' She nodded and I could see how nervous she was. 'How are you feeling?' I asked. 'I'm fine,' she said. 'You remember what you have to do?' 'Yes,' she replied confidently. 'I went over it last night and on the way over on the boat.' I smiled. 'Good. Then don't think about it anymore until you need to. Peter, don't open the door to anyone, and I mean anyone, but me. I will knock on the door with a three-one-two code.' I demonstrated the knock code to Peter, shut the door behind me and went to the wharf to meet Stephen.

He was briefing the police officers and court clerk Franco who had just disembarked from the ferry. The police looked like regular Greek guys in jeans and shirts. One had a small day pack while the other two wore bum bags facing the front (a tell-tale sign of carrying a weapon). I hadn't been there for five seconds before Stephen turned to me. 'Where's Diane?' he asked. 'In our hotel room,' I said. 'Well, go get her, we're going to the police station.'

I knocked on the door to the room with the pre-arranged knock code and Peter opened the door. We made our way downstairs and I placed the key behind the unattended counter again. Stephen was waiting with the officers outside the hotel to escort Diane to the nearby police station with the order from the Rhodes commissioner of police. Peter and I turned the other way and made our way along the esplanade towards the house. The cat would be out of the bag very soon.

Chapter Twenty-Three

The beads of sweat trickled down the small of my back as Peter and I moved into position to watch the targets. The tension was ratcheting up as the moment of truth drew closer. Happily, there had been no sign of the grandmother or Theo while either Stephen or both of us had been sitting in the cafe so they were still safely at home. 'You sit here on this concrete pillar facing up to the house and I will sit outside the motorcycle rental shop,' I told Peter. 'You bet,' he replied.

Peter sat down facing directly up the hill while I sat on a window ledge outside the rental shop looking over a tourist brochure I'd found inside the shop. I was wearing grey Louis Vuitton trousers instead of my usual jeans, a smart white collared shirt, black Magnum boots and sunglasses. I didn't look like a regular tourist today because I wanted to look semi-official in front of the players and the police officers.

Peter and I had eye contact and I could see the corner of the esplanade where Stephen and Diane and their police escort would soon walk round. There was nothing to do but wait as everything was going according to plan. However, the longer we waited, the less it felt like it. Five minutes soon became ten, became thirty and then an hour. It was now approaching 1130 hours and still there was no sign of Stephen. They had been in the police station for one-and-a-half hours. What was taking so long?

I flicked over a page in the brochure for the umpteenth time then looked up and my heart skipped a beat. In front of me were the grandmother and the child. They were dressed to the nines; she in a blouse and skirt and he looking like a little sailor with a white shirt and navy blue shorts. Theo's hand was in his grandmother's as they passed by me. I turned around pretending to look inside the rental shop but studied their reflections in the window. Shit! They're mobile, and there's no sign of Stephen, Diane or the police. All I could do was follow them, which I did at a distance of approximately 20 metres behind.

As we passed level with Peter's position I made eye contact and held my hand up to my face with my thumb and little finger extended, making a telephone gesture so that he would ring Stephen and warn him that we were mobile and let him know our location. The only saving grace was that the players' progress was slow. The grandmother stopped to talk to nearly every shop owner along the way and the shop owners would grab Theo's cheek in a sign of affection. I had no trouble believing that many people on this island knew the family very well, knew all about Theo and were complicit in him being kept here illegally. At the same time I kept thinking, where the hell is Stephen? What is taking him so long?

We rounded the corner and continued along the esplanade until the grandmother and child turned down an alley. I glanced backwards and could see Peter 20 metres behind me. He certainly had not had time to ring Stephen and be back behind me in such a short space of time. I stopped and made the telephone gesture to him again but Peter had sat down on a bench, was looking towards the harbour and didn't see my signal.

I looked back up the alley and could still see the grandmother and child walking slowly hand in hand. It was decision time. Should I go ahead and follow the players or go back and physically tell Peter to ring Stephen? He was just not paying attention to me. If I went back to tell Peter, there was a high risk I would lose sight of the players but if I followed the players, neither Stephen nor anyone else would know where we were and I could be gone all day, out of contact.

I decided to go back and tell Peter, then rush to catch up with the players. I walked as fast as I could back to where he was sitting without drawing attention to myself. 'Ring Stephen immediately and tell him we're mobile, that we've lost them and where,' I told him before rushing back up to the alleyway. I'd been gone a matter of seconds but there was no sign of the grandmother and child. I couldn't find them anywhere.

In something close to panic, I searched every store and every stall in the alley and they were nowhere to be seen. It was then I realized what a labyrinth of alleyways, walkways, shops, markets and streets they had wandered into. I had no idea how I was going to find them in that maze. My best bet was to wait across the road from the entrance to the alley, at the esplanade, and hope that they came out the same way they went in, but I reasoned that the end of this market district finished at the edge of the mountain and they could walk home via the rear exit there.

However, I gambled that it would mean walking up steep stairways and then back down to the house, and that this would be a tall order for the grandmother and the young child. In addition, I had noted them to be creatures of habit so my logic told me that they should come out of the alley where they went in. But when?

I was absolutely furious with Peter. He was supposed to have been conducting surveillance. How could he not have been looking at me? How could someone not know what a telephone gesture means under the same circumstances? Now things were messy and this time we couldn't blame it on anyone but ourselves. I joined Peter and told him to go back to where he had been at the end of the street, looking up towards the house and phone Stephen if he saw the grandmother and child. I kept it short otherwise I would have lost my temper with him. I was fuming. Where the bloody hell are Stephen and the police?

I returned to watching up the alley from the esplanade with the harbour at my back. It was lunchtime now and the esplanade was a mass of diners. A marked police car drove by. On the back seat were Stephen and Diane and following them was an unmarked police car with the Kos officers. They didn't stop or look towards the esplanade or look for me. That seemed odd. Peter's phone call should have given them my exact location, but the vehicles went around the corner and down towards where Peter was, or should be. Not long after that the vehicles reappeared and drove directly in front of my location. This time Stephen was frantically looking up and down the esplanade towards the restaurants as if looking for me but he didn't see me. The vehicles did a U-turn and drove past again, with Stephen scanning the esplanade. Finally, the vehicles stopped at the other end of the esplanade and I saw Stephen get out and walk towards another alley.

As quickly but as calmly as I could I walked towards him and he spotted me. 'Where are they?' he asked. 'They went up the alley behind me,' I said. 'We lost them.' Stephen was looking as furious as I felt. 'How did you lose them?' he demanded. 'I had to go back and get Peter to phone you,' I explained. 'I went up there and they had gone.'

We went up the alley and Stephen could see for himself that it was like a maze. We searched every shop, stall and alleyway again, with no luck. It was now twenty minutes since I had lost sight of them. They must have gone inside a building. Stephen and I walked back out of the alley and while he stood on the esplanade watching, I walked towards the police cars to explain the situation to Diane. 'How did you lose them?' she asked in a panic. I told her they disappeared in the maze of shops and stalls. 'So what now?' she asked urgently. 'You and the police go to the cafe at the end of the street, while Stephen and I search the area,' I said. I asked her if one of the officers had a spare mobile phone and the driver handed one over to Diane. She gave me her own mobile and I saved the number of the police phone she now had.

The police cars made their way towards the cafe while Stephen and I went to conduct another search. Like all our previous efforts, this proved fruitless, so we sat on the bench opposite the alley and waited. 'This is our fault that this has happened,' Stephen said firmly. 'I had the police ready to go. How the hell did you lose them?' I explained the situation again and told him everything that had happened with Peter. 'I can't believe him! What the hell was he thinking?' said Stephen. I asked if he'd spoken to Peter when he drove down in the police cars. 'Yeah,' said Stephen. 'He said that you had the child and you were sitting out the front of the esplanade.' I couldn't believe it. 'What!' I shouted, startling a couple nearby. 'He was supposed to tell you that we were mobile, that they had been lost up an alley, and the location.' Stephen looked at me. 'He just said that you were with them both out the front of the esplanade,' he added.

I was stunned. Not only was it Peter's fault we had lost the players, he didn't tell Stephen what had actually happened. Stephen had lost all patience with him now. He was totally unreliable and Stephen feared he would lose his temper if he spoke to him, so he wanted me to give Peter his next instructions: maintain sight of the front door of the house and alert the police if he should see the grandmother and child return home. The police should, in turn, call us on the mobile I now had.

I went to the cafe and gave Peter this information. The police officers were sitting in the cafe, drinking cola, and Diane was sitting in the back seat of the marked police car that was parked in front of the coastguard building. She must have been sweltering under her nylon wig. I explained to her that we had to play the waiting game and reassured her that the grandmother and Theo would surely reappear soon. She asked if it was alright for her to get out of the car, considering how hot it was. I agreed and sat her down with the police officers in the cafe. The police were asking me where the child was and I asked Diane to explain the situation for me because I needed to be back with Stephen.

Chapter Twenty-Three

'What if they don't come out?' asked Stephen when I joined him. 'They will,' I said. 'How do you know that?' he pressed. The truth was, I didn't. I was relying on logic. 'The only roads leading out from that jungle in there go up the mountain, to the other side of the island, or right in front of us,' I explained. 'The grandmother won't go up the mountain, I don't think, on a hot day with a 5 year old, and they're not about to head off to the other side of the island, on foot, so they will come back out here. She's probably just shopping.' Stephen chewed the inside of his cheek. 'I hope so,' he said. 'I bloody hope so.'

Chapter Twenty-Four

Diane's stomach had been churning since early in the morning. Only determination and adrenaline had got her this far. Now, as she sat at the cafe surrounded by policemen convinced that the operation was a dud, her world was in turmoil. Earlier, her main disquiet had been the sense of guilt she felt that the elderly, unsuspecting boat owner was about to become embroiled in the drama of a child snatch, and the worry that he might not let them back on board. Now things had escalated way beyond that. There was a very real danger that there would be no child snatch for the boat owner to be caught up in and that, if the boys had lost Theo and the operation had to be aborted, she would have lost her last chance to be reunited with her son. The thought all but paralyzed her.

She tried to stay calm and clung determinedly to Darren's reassurances that her ex-mother-in-law would soon reappear with Theo. She was desperate to believe it but, as she waited, a new fear gripped her. The owners of the cafe where she was now sitting, twitching beneath a nylon wig and floppy hat, had once been good friends of hers. Though they were much older than she was, she had rented a room from their family when she had first been courting Nick and living on Kalymnos. They had been very kind to her then. Would they recognize her now, through her disguise, and would they still be kind if they knew why she was there?

The policemen were relaxing in the sunshine with nothing to do but wait for a call to action that might not come, but Diane could not sit still. She was aware of how much she was fidgeting, but the harder she tried to stop, the more restless she became. What if all her efforts to recover Theo had come to nothing? How would she break the news to her husband? How could she go on living without her son?

The police mobile phone she had borrowed burst into life and she almost dropped it in shock at the shrill ring tone. She recognized the incoming call number as her own and her heart was in her mouth.

*Oh God! Was this Darren calling to say they had found Theo? 'Hello?'
she said, nervously. 'Diane, it's Darren,' she heard, as if in a blur of sound.
'I hope I didn't alarm you but I just took a call for you on your phone from
Linda Hiddins, from the Australian Embassy in Athens. She wanted to
know what progress we were making. 'I told her there should be a result
soon.' Diane felt numb. A result had never felt as far away as it did now.*

*It was approaching 2.30 pm and her former mother-in-law and her
son had been lost from sight for nearly three hours. There had to be
a danger that the police would give up on them and then they would
be stuck. Then she saw Darren walking towards the cafe from the
esplanade. What had happened now? He gave her a reassuring smile,
but she wasn't convinced, especially when he approached the policemen
to ask how long they would be prepared to stay. She could feel her world
falling apart as they told him the latest they would stay was 3.15 pm
because they wanted to catch the 3.30 pm ferry. 3.15 pm? That was just
forty-five minutes away!*

*The most senior of the Kalymnos policemen pinned Darren with his
eyes. 'You lost them, uh?' he said with a smirk. 'No, we haven't,' Darren
insisted. 'I think you have,' said the policemen, enjoying the situation
rather too much. Diane could feel Darren's pain and embarrassment
but it was true, wasn't it? They had lost her son. She watched Darren
chewing his lip, struggling to keep his dignity as he walked away to
approach Peter, with the policemen sniggering behind him at something
the senior officer had said.*

*Peter looked exhausted. 'Hang in there mate. Not long to go now,' she
heard Darren tell him. She couldn't hear the rest of their conversation
but if Darren had meant they would soon complete the operation, that's
not what Diane was thinking. They were running out of time. Their
chance of snatching Theo would soon be over. She tried to picture, as
she had several times over the past week, the moment when she would
grab Theo in her arms and give him the biggest cuddle ever, but try as
she might she couldn't conjure the image. It didn't exist. Behind her
big sunglasses her eyes were welling with tears, but she poked a tissue
behind the shades to dry them and struggled to stay positive. What else
could she do?*

Chapter Twenty-Five

'We may have to abort, mate,' I told Peter with a heavy heart. The look on his face suggested a mixture of sorrow for the failure and relief that it would soon be over. I pepped him up and reminded him to stay focused on the operation while there was still hope. I was desperately trying to maintain my professionalism in the middle of this disaster but deep down I just wanted to throw Peter in the harbour. I could feel the gloating eyes of the policemen boring into me as I made my way back around the corner to where Stephen was waiting. As I walked, a lot of 'what ifs' flashed through my mind. There was a real danger that Diane would not get her child back and that the rest of her life, and Theo's, would be blighted, but that was a secondary consideration for me. Of major importance to me was the company's reputation and mine. We were meant to be stand-out specialists in this field but we had stuffed up. It wasn't that I didn't care about Diane, but this was business.

I approached Stephen and asked if anything had happened. He shook his head. I told him that the police would stay until 1515 hours only and then they would be gone, at which he let out an expletive. 'This will not look good for us,' he said. 'They WILL show up,' I insisted. 'We'll be the laughing stock of the industry,' Stephen continued. 'We had them, but you lost them!' His words struck me like a dagger and I could feel my eyes stinging. I didn't feel like reiterating what had actually happened, so I concentrated on my vigil, scanning the alley and the esplanade. I looked at my watch. It was 1500 hours. Fifteen minutes to go and the police would smugly disappear and the whole operation would be aborted.

I scanned the crowd, left to right, right to left, background to foreground and back again. Suddenly the movement of a small boy running on the stage caught my attention. 'Shit! It's him,' I said almost with a squeal. 'Where?' Stephen asked. 'On the stage, in the blue sailor's top,' I said. 'And there's the grandmother walking towards the stage. They must have come on to the esplanade through an alleyway I don't know about.' It was now 1505 hours.

I rang Diane on the police mobile phone. 'Now, remain calm Diane,' I told her. 'And do exactly what I tell you.' I could hear the wobble in her voice. 'We have them,' I said, trying to keep my own voice in check. 'Please, remain calm Diane, and follow my instructions,' I repeated. I asked her once again if she was sure she wanted the recovery to go ahead and her response was unequivocal. 'OK then,' I said. 'We will proceed. Now, tell the police that we have them in our sights and calmly move towards the vehicles, get in and then wait, OK?'

She sounded like a nervous wreck at the other end of the phone, in spite of her efforts to stay calm. I could hear her repeating what I said, in Greek, to the police, struggling at times to remember the right Greek words, which was another sign of her anxiety. Stephen and I rose from our sitting position and I made my way to a souvenir shop on the path towards the police while Stephen walked directly across the road and sat down on a concrete pillar with the package between us. I noticed for the first time that there was an additional player – a girl of about 8 who was close by the grandmother. I positioned myself behind and to the side of a postcard stand, pretending to look at the postcards. The package and other players passed directly in front of me, not more than 5 metres away. Ironically, the picture on the card I was looking at was of the Pothia harbour, looking towards where our getaway speedboat was moored.

As the players passed my position I casually slipped behind them and followed at a distance of around 10 metres, with Stephen joining me. We were now only 300 metres from where the police were waiting. As the gap closed I phoned Diane again and instructed her to get the police to bring their vehicles towards the corner. We were now close enough to see them. The grandmother stopped to look in another shop window as the children jostled around her. Stephen moved to one side of her and I moved to the other. The police vehicles, with Diane in the back seat, stopped at the side of the road approximately 10 metres in front of us. The trap was set.

Chapter Twenty-Six

Diane had been thrown a lifeline with the news that Theo had been spotted. She struggled to think straight, becoming tongue-tied as she tried to translate the messages from Darren for the police. Now as Theo and his grandmother walked towards them, the policemen burst into life. 'Go! Go! Go!' they said in Greek. 'Go! Go! Go!' Diane found herself shouting as she leapt from the car and suddenly, from the confusion, everything began to work like clockwork, as if in slow motion.

The plain-clothed policemen put on their bright green fluorescent 'Police' vests and approached the grandmother to talk to her. Darren moved in behind Theo to stop him going anywhere. With her role drilled into her, Diane took no more than ten brisk steps and came up behind her son, who had turned in Darren's direction. She scooped him up in her arms and span to face the police car. As she did so, the policemen formed a human barricade to block the efforts of the grandmother who launched herself at Diane and grabbed at the back of her shirt. 'Get off me!' Diane heard herself cry as she wrenched herself from the older woman's grip with a lash of her arm.

The grandmother and the small girl were shouting and screaming but Theo was silent as the black-haired woman with huge beetle eyes and a floppy hat strode with him towards a waiting car. With Darren right behind her, palming her head down to make sure she didn't smash it against the car roof, she threw Theo on to the back seat and jumped in after him. She was all too aware that they were surrounded by tourists, sitting in cafes, eating ice-creams, walking back from the beach or buying postcards, and all of them were open-mouthed in disbelief at the drama unfolding in front of them.

As the policemen who had restrained her ex-mother-in-law got into the front of the vehicles, Darren jumped into the car's back seat beside Diane and motioned to the driver to put his foot down, but the senior

170

officer motioned equally urgently for Darren to get out. 'This… our vehicle,' he insisted. He did as he was told and the two police cars sped off towards the wharf with Darren sprinting beside them. Legs pumping hard, he was so determined to get to the waiting speedboat and prepare it for a quick getaway that his trousers ripped from backside to knee. Inside the car, Diane looked down at her clearly startled son and pulled off her hat, wig and glasses. 'Oh, Mummy!' he squealed. 'Yes, it's Mummy. It's Mummy,' Diane cried and gave him a huge hug. 'You, Mummy! You and your blue eyes!' Theo said in Greek when she finally released her grip and gave him another hug.

When they arrived at the boat, Diane found Darren already on board, untying the mooring ropes and manically trying to start the engine, but there was no sign of the boat owner. Diane was frantic. 'Start the engine! Start the engine! Start the engine!' she yelled in Greek with Theo in her arms. She could see the driver hurrying across the road towards them, eating food. Stephen and Peter had also arrived but, with three policemen and the court clerk Franco already on the boat, as well as Diane and Theo, the officers not only stopped them from boarding, but kicked Darren off as the petrified boat owner was ordered to jump on and cast off. The disgusted security operatives could only look on as 'their' boat idled away from the mooring with Diane crying with joy, hugging Theo and waving goodbye to them, not really taking in that they were being left behind and this was not part of the plan. Beyond the harbour walls, the owner opened the throttle and the powerful 200 horsepower engine propelled the boat in the direction of Mastichari, surging through the water until it was up 'on plane' and bouncing across the waves.

On board, the confused little boy was now finding his voice, albeit in Greek. 'Captain,' he said to the driver above the noise of the engine and the thump, thump, thump of the boat on the water, 'You turn this boat around. My name is Theo Kavouklis and I'm going home.' It was as if he'd been programmed to say that if this occasion ever arose. 'It's OK, you're with Mummy,' Diane told him, but he was firm and unflustered. 'Where are you taking me? Turn this boat around! Do you know where I live? I live here,' he said, reciting his address robotically. The policemen who had seemed so unconcerned about the operation before, now smiled benevolently at the small boy. 'You're with your mummy now, and we are taking you back to Kos,' said one. But they knew they were not home and dry yet.

Chapter Twenty-Seven

I looked on as the speedboat receded into the distance. So much for the owner saying it could only take two passengers. There were now seven people aboard, and we weren't among them; we were left abandoned on the quayside. We had just conducted a highly visible and very noisy child recovery operation and we were now at the mercy of a soon-to-be hostile island. It didn't take long for a large crowd to gather on the harbour behind us, with people arriving by cars, on motorcycles and on foot. This was not a good situation to be in but the two Kalymnos police officers seemed unconcerned. The sergeant who had so enjoyed my discomfort earlier walked over towards his vehicle and started the engine as if nothing had happened. Stephen, Peter and I walked towards him before he could drive off and, pointing out the obviously inflammatory situation, asked if they could house us in the police station until the ferry was set to depart. He looked at us with undisguised contempt. 'No, I will not take you to the police station. It has finished,' he said.

There was no time to argue as a large group of people were coming towards us, but Stephen had no intention of staying put. 'We need protection until the ferry is ready. So let's go,' he told the sergeant and with that we opened the doors and jumped in. The officer now had a dilemma. If he forcibly ejected us he would be deliberately throwing us to the mercy of the fast-approaching crowd and a very likely breach of the peace. Instead, he gave a shrug and drove slowly through the gathering mob, past the esplanade and towards the main jetty. 'I take to coastguard. They help you,' he said. 'Thanks for nothing,' I thought. The police were fully aware of the situation and the danger we were now in and were dumping us at someone else's doorstep. My throat was dry and not just through nervousness about what might happen next. I was feeling the effects of dehydration and needed water. The sergeant drove up to the coastguard station, dropped us at the door and sped off.

172

We glanced down the jetty to see if we could run for the waiting ferry, which was due to depart in ten minutes, but the entrance to the jetty was filling with hostile islanders watching every boarding passenger to see if they fitted our description. We were trapped. Stephen, Peter and I made our way up the stairs to the entrance of the coastguard building, knocked and explained our situation to the duty officer. Starting from the beginning would have been too time-consuming so Stephen just gave the basics. While the officer pondered, I asked if they had any water, but was met by a shake of the head. Eventually we were allowed in and while Peter and I sat in the waiting room, Stephen and a coastguard officer, who could speak a little English, talked to the commander. After a couple of minutes, all three of us were taken upstairs and ushered through a door which was slammed shut behind us.

The room was small, with bunks and a thick door with a tiny window and a large locking device. It took a second or two before I realized it was a cell. Whether we were being detained or held for our own protection was not clear but the effect was the same and, at that moment, on a particularly hostile island, I wasn't too unhappy. Just how hostile the situation was becoming was brought home to us as we heard a man climb the stairs, shouting and screaming at the coastguard officers. We knew this had to be related to what had recently gone on. Curiosity got the better of me and I peered through the small window in the door, then ducked back down again. 'What is it?' whispered Stephen. 'It's the father,' I replied quietly. It hadn't taken long for word to be passed to Nick that his son had been snatched back and now he was just a little more than the thickness of a door away from the people responsible.

The three of us listened intently and awaited our fate. As we did so, the shouting stopped and we could make out the clear, firm instructions of a coastguard officer and the sound of more footsteps on the stairs. I dared to peek again and breathed a sigh of relief as the father appeared to be leaving. For now. 'What do you think is going on? What did the commander say to you?' I asked Stephen. 'I don't know any more than you. They just said to wait in here,' he replied. We exchanged looks that confirmed we were thinking the same thing. Something was not above board.

There was another window high up on the outside wall and since I was the tallest I climbed on one of the bunks to try to peer out. I could just about make out a small crowd at the entrance to the coastguard building, shouting and screaming in Greek. I had no idea what they were saying and I'm not sure I wanted to know. I was pretty sure they weren't after a cup of coffee. To the rear of the cell was a glass panel, behind another set of bunks and a curtain. I climbed down from the bunk and pulled back the curtain a little, looked through it and saw another cell and inside it a large group of people, possibly Turks detained for not having the correct papers. They seemed generally unhealthy, with several scared-looking children with them, and all of them were packed into the small room like sardines in a can. Like us, they weren't going anywhere in a hurry and there was certainly no way out for us that way.

The door to our cell opened and a coastguard officer walked in. 'Your passports,' he ordered. There was something in his voice that suggested things were not going to go in our favour. We handed him our passports and he took them away, shutting the door on us again. I looked through the door window but couldn't see where he had gone. Then his face was at the window and I just had time to move out of the way before the door opened and he handed back our passports.

'What's happening?' asked Stephen. 'Wait!' the officer ordered, then left the cell again, slamming the door behind him. I could see it wasn't locked. I peered through the window and saw a hive of activity at the other end of the corridor, with officers on the radio. It wasn't filling me with confidence and nor was Peter. He was as white as a ghost and very quiet. He was clearly shit-scared and I couldn't blame him. The door opened again and another coastguard officer walked in, this time with three small water bottles under his arm. He smiled as he handed me mine. There was something familiar about him and then I realized it was the officer I had twice seen on night duty, sleeping on his watch.

I slammed the water into my body and felt good again but I could have done with more. At least I could now think straight if we were about to be quizzed but, if we were about to be put through the third degree, why would they bring us water first? It was now 1530 hours and the ferry, our last hope of escape from this island on our own terms, was due to leave. Whether we were detained or held for protection was immaterial as we clearly weren't going anywhere. There was an angry crowd waiting for us outside and God only knew what was going to happen next. I was worried, too, about Diane and Theo. The recovery had been successful and Diane was on her way to Kos with Theo, but we weren't there to look after them. I should have been comforted that they were in the care of the police, but that filled me with no confidence at all.

I took another look around the room, studying the contents and the structure of the wall. The door was unlocked but the corridor beyond was crawling with officers and the entrance to the building was besieged by baying locals. There was no obvious way out. 'Shh! What's that?' asked Stephen. We fell silent to listen but all I could hear was my own heart beating. Gradually I acclimatized and could hear a male voice, commanding in its style, making an announcement. The voice was coming from outside. I climbed back on the bunk and peered through the window. The crowd, which was larger than before, was silent and looking towards the entrance of the building, where the voice was coming from. All of a sudden the crowd dispersed, dejectedly, walking off in all directions and muttering among themselves. What the hell was going on?

The door flung open and an officer rushed in, motioning us to follow him. 'Hurry! Hurry!' he said. We followed him along the corridor and down the stairs which he was taking three at a time, so we ran to keep up. At the base of the stairs, at the back of the building, was a waiting coastguard SUV, its motor running and a driver at the ready. 'In! In!' the officer shouted. We dived into the vehicle and before the officer could close his door properly we were speeding off towards the jetty. At the jetty entrance, another coastguard officer was standing by the closed gates with a radio in his hand. The officer in the front seat spoke into the vehicle radio and got an instant reply. With that, the officer at the entrance opened the gates and our vehicle shot through. At that speed I feared we would be going over the edge and into the water but to my surprise I could see the ferry, waiting approximately 40 metres offshore. It had left the jetty but not the harbour and, as we watched, it made its way back towards the jetty and the ramp was lowered. The coastguard officer got out of the SUV, opened the door and ushered us out, then motioned for us to get on the ferry. We were not about to spurn this invitation.

Before the ferry ramp had even touched the jetty I leapt on board and Stephen and Peter followed suit. The coastguard officer gave us a quick salute then jumped back into the SUV and was driven away. I could feel the eyes of other passengers upon us as the ramp was raised and the ferry made its way belatedly out of the harbour. They must have wondered who on earth we were that the ferry, and their journey, had been delayed for our dramatic arrival. The three of us climbed the steps to the bridge deck and we could see the captain smiling to himself as he sounded the ferry horn and moved to full steam ahead. We were safe, at least for now.

Stephen and I could hardly believe it. One minute we thought we were in serious trouble, the next minute we were being given VIP assistance off the island. On all our visits to Kalymnos, we had never seen the jetty closed before, but it all fell into place now. We had been placed in the cell to hide us while they were organizing our evacuation and presumably they told the angry locals we had already left in order to disperse them before they could get us out of there. The jetty had been closed and the ferry positioned slightly offshore so that no one who meant us any harm could get on board.

As we began to come to terms with our narrow escape, I could see that the ferry was full of tourists who continued to look at us and whisper among themselves, doubtless coming up with wild speculation about these strangers important enough to hold up the ferry. What they would have seen was not three international men of mystery but three utterly exhausted blokes. Peter still looked haunted; Stephen and I had bags under our eyes from the previous four nights' surveillance; and my ripped trousers were showing more cheek than was decent. We looked more like fugitive criminals than rescuers.

'That was impressive,' said Stephen after a while. 'Yeah. You couldn't ask for any more than that,' I replied. 'It's just a shame we didn't have time to thank them.' Stephen smiled. 'People wouldn't believe us, you know,' he said. I agreed, grinning in spite of my tiredness. Even Peter started chatting, clearly relieved that 'the three of us' had pulled it off. With the ferry well clear of the harbour and out into the open Aegean Sea, Stephen and I slumped into our chairs next to the bridge while Peter started filming us and asking questions about how the recovery had gone. We weren't in any mood to answer but did so anyway since he was recording. Meanwhile, other passengers sidled a little closer to try to hear what we were talking about and to get a better look at us.

'Well, we've made it so far, mate,' said Stephen. 'Yeah, but it's not over yet,' I reminded him. 'Don't forget what happened in Ecuador.' Stephen's smile dropped. In Ecuador, we had successfully completed an extraction operation and the package was on an aircraft back to the USA. But before we could get out of the country ourselves we were being chased by armed gunmen, with hostile surveillance waiting at the airport. Fortunately, our pursuers were not too diligent and we managed to slip past their guard and on to a flight out of there.

The ring of the mobile phone jerked us back to the here and now. 'Where are you?' asked Stephen, mouthing to me that it was Diane. 'Yes, that's the plan. We're on our way, on the ferry.' A look of concern came over his face. 'Don't worry. Stay where you are and we'll be there soon,' he told her before ending the conversation in case the phone call was being monitored. 'They're safe at the Antimachia police station,' he told me. 'She wanted to know if we could get her bags.' His words hung in the air and it was clear that it was not the full extent of their conversation. 'And?' I probed. 'And,' Stephen went on, 'She said that she had rung Nikolas who told her that, according to the police, we are currently being chased by people from the island in speedboats. With guns.'

Chapter Twenty-Eight

It felt as though a dark cloud had suddenly covered the sun and a shiver went down my spine. 'Peter, go check out the back of the ferry and see if there are any boats following us, would you?' I asked. Stephen had his game face back on. When Peter returned and said there were boats in the distance that were coming up fast, Stephen went to take a look himself and confirmed it, though they were too far away to see what boats they were and who was in them.

Fortunately, the ferry was close to Kos by now. As it docked in Mastichari harbour we wasted no time in getting off and made our way quickly to the hotel. 'You check us out, Peter, and get a taxi, while Darren and I get the bags,' Stephen instructed. He and I went up to the room, grabbed all the bags between us, and went back downstairs in time to see the taxi pull up. '*Astynomia – Antimachia, efkharisto,*' I told the driver after loading the bags into the car, adding, 'Police station at Antimachia, please,' in case my phrasebook Greek was not understood. The taxi driver seemed to weigh up why we might want to go to the police, and whether he should avoid getting involved, then nodded.

Less than ten minutes later we pulled up outside the police station. The Kos officers who had been with us on Kalymnos were now stationed on the steps to the front entrance, as if providing protection for Diane and Theo inside. Funnily enough, they seemed surprised to see us. As Peter paid the taxi driver, Stephen and I grabbed the bags and ignored the officers as we made our way past them into the building. They were the last people we wanted to see.

Diane's face lit up when she saw us. She greeted us with hugs and thanks while Theo looked on warily. It was our first speaking encounter with him and he seemed shy initially, though it didn't take long for him to warm to us. The police inside the station were congratulating us on a job well done, but I didn't feel like offering them the same pat on the

178

back. 'Thank you so much, guys. Is everyone OK?' said Diane. 'We're all OK,' said Stephen. 'But the police left us on the island to fend for ourselves, which was definitely not the agreed plan.' He spoke loudly enough for them to hear.

Diane was sympathetic – she'd always been vocal about her mistrust for the Greek police – but right now, quite rightly, her overwhelming mood was joy at having Theo back. We just felt betrayed and I couldn't wait to get out of there but that would be our next challenge. Before we had a chance to speak to the commanding officer about how we would achieve that, the phone rang in the reception area and a police officer indicated that it was one of Nick's relatives asking about Theo. The commander ordered us to take our luggage into a back room where they drew the curtains and told us to get down on the floor and keep quiet. What kind of mob was coming for us, I wondered, that the police would rather hide us like fugitives than instruct the crowd to disband and arrest anyone who did not obey?

It was 1650 hours and we stayed silent on the floor for what felt like an eternity. We weren't allowed to stand up, because of the windows, and with the curtains closed we were sweating profusely. Theo was sitting between Diane's legs on the floor, under a desk, and she took the opportunity to show him a photograph album she had put together; a collection of photos of him with her and with her husband Peter and of their life together in Australia before he was abducted. When he had finished looking at them with wonder, she produced a few toys for him and some colouring books and crayons. Occasionally one police officer, who had taken a shine to Theo, would enter the office and keep us up to date with what was happening. We were told that some of Nick's relatives had come into the reception demanding to know the whereabouts of Theo and Diane. Nick's lawyer had also come into the police station and all the while, we were told, officers were trying to work out a way to get us on a flight out of there.

By 2100 hours we had been sweltering in the office for four hours and I was sick of being treated like a dog. Earlier, I had rebelled against being forced to lie on the floor and had sat at the desk, and Stephen, Peter, and Diane had followed suit. But we were still having to talk in whispers, with no water or food provided. Yet again an officer explained in broken English that they were in the process of getting flights for us and said that the commissioner of police for Rhodes had requested that we leave

Kos immediately. We certainly weren't going to argue with that and were glad to have him on our side. Without his pressure, I wasn't confident that the Kos police or, God help us, the Kalymnos police, would manage to make any arrangements. If we'd been allowed to take the speedboat that we'd arranged, we'd have been back at Mastichari in no time and at the airport waiting for a flight instead of stuck in this hellish safe house.

At 2200 hours the same officer returned and said that another officer would be in shortly to explain the plan, but it was half an hour later before he showed up with a sidekick and explained the plan in English: 'The mother and child will fly out on the 2310 hours flight to Athens. An undercover police officer will sit directly behind them to ensure their safety. The aircraft will be delayed to ensure she is the last one on. You three will leave on the same flight but travel separately. The mother and child will leave in a police vehicle five minutes before the flight is due to leave. The vehicle will drive through a side gate to the airfield then pull up in front of the aircraft stairs. You three will leave in an unmarked police car and enter the front entrance of the airport, but not together. There is a young girl with blonde hair behind the airline counter who is aware of the situation and will check your luggage through quickly. It is important that you do not make eye contact with each other and keep a low profile. You must check your luggage in, but not together. You enter the aircraft, but not together. It is important that you are split up, not together.'

It sounded like a reasonable plan and we got the message that they didn't want us to be seen together. Since the relatives had left the police station and were probably waiting at the airport for us, and looking out for Diane and Theo with three men, this seemed like the only plan we could rely on, bearing in mind that the police had previously left us to fend for ourselves on Kalymnos.

To our surprise, Diane's lawyer Nikolas appeared with some paperwork. Unknown to us, he had been in reception for some time organizing things and now he wanted Diane to sign a document. It was in Greek and Diane was not in the best frame of mind to start translating. 'What is this, Nikolas?' she asked. 'It is a detainment notice,' he replied. 'What?' we exclaimed in unison. 'It is to detain you, but do not worry because the station commander will release you after you have signed it.' Diane looked across the desk at me for some sort of approval that she should sign it, but I couldn't help. I didn't trust Nikolas, or anyone or anything else in this country for that matter, but what choice did we have? Diane signed the letter and Nikolas left the office with it.

It was approaching 2300 hours and we couldn't wait to get out of the police station and out of Kos. A police officer came into the office and ordered Diane to follow him, with Theo, to a waiting vehicle. So far so good. Diane and Theo were on their way and soon we would be too, I hoped. Moments later the same police officer entered the office and the three of us jumped to our feet to leave. 'How are you getting to the airport?' he asked. My jaw almost hit the floor. I looked at Stephen who was about to explode and when Stephen explodes hospitals become busy. I walked over and stood between the officer and Stephen. 'What do you mean how are we getting there?' I demanded. 'We were told we would be in an unmarked police car.' The officer shrugged. 'There are no vehicles. You will have to get a taxi,' he said, and walked out of the office. 'Bloody pricks!' Stephen yelled after him. Peter stood there with that pale look on his face and Stephen and I stared at the ground.

The door had barely closed behind the officer when Nikolas walked in. 'You guys need a lift to the airport?' he asked. 'Yes please, and fast!' I replied. He agreed but added, 'I am fearful there will be relatives of the father waiting at the airport who know me. I will have to drop you off up the road.' I figured that was our best bet and we needed to be at the airport in a hurry. One more delay and we would surely miss the flight and be stuck on Kos with numerous members of Nick's family out for our blood. 'That's fine,' I said. We stepped out of the office and were headed for the exit when we were stopped by one of the policemen. 'The commander needs to see you,' he said. 'In his office.' We didn't have time for this and I felt certain it meant more problems, but the officer was blocking our way out, so we had little choice but to comply.

Chapter Twenty-Nine

The commander was on the phone and another officer was in front of his desk as we stood willing him to hurry up and tell us whatever it was that was so important. I glanced at my watch and felt that horrible sinking feeling. Were they about to betray us again? Were we about to be arrested? I wouldn't put anything past them. They wouldn't need to delay us for long in order for us to miss the flight. The commander looked like his phone call was going to take a while and he waved for us to step out of his office. That was enough for Stephen and me. We left the office and kept on going, ushering Peter with us as we headed for the door. 'Quick, Nikolas, let's go!' Stephen hissed. As we grabbed our luggage and went out the main entrance, a police officer smoking a cigarette on the steps turned to us. 'Did the commander speak with you?' he asked. 'Yes, he did,' I said. 'He said we could go.' We threw our bags into Nikolas' vehicle, jumped in and told him to put his foot down.

I glanced over my shoulder as we sped away from the police station and saw the officer who had been standing in the commander's room running out of the entrance, waving his arms at us. I tapped Stephen on the shoulder and nodded in the direction of the station so he saw it too, but we said nothing to Nikolas who was nervous enough as it was. The airport was five minutes' drive away and the three of us did our best to keep ourselves out of view from any passing motorists while I kept half an eye on our rear to see if we were being followed.

'I will drop you off up the road because people know me,' said Nikolas with fear in his voice. 'Yeah, that's fine, whatever,' said Stephen. We needed to split up before the terminal building anyway. Nikolas dropped us off behind some bushes approximately 300 metres from the airport entrance. It was now 2305 hours. Our aircraft was due to take off in five minutes, we hadn't checked in our luggage and we had to hoof it 300 metres with our bags. At this stage I was feeling very pissed off.

No sooner were we out of the car than the three of us darted off in different directions. Stephen went towards the perimeter fence on the right-hand side of the terminal, Peter headed directly for the front entrance and I headed for the left-hand side of the terminal building. As I crossed in front of the building, a safe distance from the main entrance, I scanned the area and saw very few people around, apart from a handful outside with luggage. I could see cleaners polishing the floors inside the building, unattended and unlit check-in counters and airport security staff standing around an X-ray machine in a jovial mood. The coast looked fairly clear.

I walked along some scrubland for cover then headed for the left-hand edge of the terminal where it was relatively dark. I stopped behind a large tree around 5 metres from the building to contemplate my next move. A dull red glow appeared – a lit cigarette. I could make out the figure of a man wearing coveralls who appeared to be on a break, whether authorized or not, and beside him was the frame of a door. I decided that was my way in. The man flicked his cigarette butt in my direction then opened the door, sending a beam of bright light shining towards the tree I was behind. As he went through the door I ran silently towards him and as the door closed behind him, I reached it and jammed my foot between the door and the frame. I left a few seconds and then walked in.

The corridor consisted of cleaning, maintenance and employee facilities and at the end was a door leading into the terminal proper. I walked down it confidently, trying to look like I belonged there, opened the door at the end and walked into the terminal. As I approached the Olympic Airways counter I could see Peter standing there waiting for service. Stephen was just walking in on the opposite side of the terminal. The three of us were reunited without incident, but the counter was unattended and the aircraft was waiting on the tarmac.

A quick look around suggested things still appeared normal, though I was waiting for a police vehicle to turn up at any minute to arrest us. Finally, a female Olympic Airways employee appeared behind the counter. 'Can I help you?' she asked. 'Yes, can we check in for the flight to Athens, please,' said Stephen. She looked surprised. 'I'm sorry but that flight has closed.' Stephen tried again. 'Perhaps you could get the girl with the blonde hair, please. Apparently, she is aware of our situation.' The attendant looked puzzled. 'There is no girl with blonde hair that works here,' she replied. 'Well, we need to get on that plane right now!'

said Stephen angrily. 'I'm sorry, but it is ready to leave. You are too late,' said the attendant. 'You don't understand,' continued Stephen in a loud voice. 'That aircraft is waiting for us. We need to be on it!'

The girl picked up a telephone. 'I will need to contact my supervisor,' she said. 'That's fine, but please hurry,' responded Stephen. So much for the girl with the blonde hair the police had said would be waiting for us. Thankfully the supervisor did seem to have knowledge of us because the attendant quickly checked us in. 'Next time, you need to be here early to check in,' she said. 'No kidding,' I thought. We ran to the gate and boarded the aircraft whose crew did appear to have been awaiting our arrival. The passengers stared at us accusingly as we walked down the aisle looking for our seats and there, sitting on the right-hand side, were Diane and Theo. 'Where have you guys been?' asked Diane, the relief obvious in her voice. 'Don't ask,' I said shaking my head.

An air hostess was standing in front of Diane's seat and I apologized and moved past her to sit next to Diane. 'Excuse me sir,' the hostess began. 'It's OK, he's with me,' said Diane. It was nice that the air crew were looking out for Diane but I didn't see any sign of an undercover police officer sitting behind her. The row was vacant until Stephen and Peter occupied it. As the plane taxied and took off, Theo chattered away while looking out of the window. Behind me, I knew Peter would be going through his Hail Mary routine. Diane couldn't help but look adoringly at her son every so often to check that he was really sitting next to her, then give him another hug and a kiss to make sure.

As the plane reached its cruising altitude I turned round to Stephen. 'How did you get into the terminal?' I asked. 'I jumped the perimeter fence, then entered the terminal through the baggage handling area,' he said. 'You?' I told him I had entered through a side door following a male employee. As I thought about it, I was grateful for the lax security that had so annoyed me when we had first landed at Athens what seemed a lifetime ago. I told Diane about our dash to the airport and my utter disgust at the way we had been treated. She was astonished and apologetic.

'The police were great with us,' she said. 'They were expecting an angry mob at the airport so they put us in the back of the police car with baseball caps on and took us round the back of the airport and straight on to the tarmac. Because some of Nick's family were at the airport, they arranged for tourist buses to be parked in front of the windows so the people inside the terminal couldn't see on to the tarmac and they drove us round to the back of the plane, right to the steps and we ducked out of the car and bolted up the steps. Then we sat in the plane, slouched in our seats with our heads down, hoping not to be seen by the rest of the passengers as they got on. The police had told us you'd be on a later plane so I was just thinking, come on, come on, come on, let's go! Let's get this plane out of here, but the staff told me this was the last plane so you couldn't be on a later plane. I had no idea they were messing you about like that!'

I shook my head. 'What is wrong with these people?' I said. 'Maybe they feel intimidated,' Diane suggested. 'You know that I previously gave a contract to the local police to recover Theo and they failed completely. Now I hire you guys for much more money and you succeed. It's pride. It's a Greek thing.' It made sense. It was as if the police who abandoned us to our fate on Kalymnos were saying, 'If you're so bloody clever, get yourself out of this without our help.' Then the police on Kos made arrangements for us to fly out, because they had been ordered to do so, but seemed to go out of their way to make us fail, as if they wanted to see us fall flat on our faces. To me it was the lowest of the low. Coming from the military, where real men sort out their grievances face-to-face, I regarded their behaviour as spineless. I didn't have long to think about it as Theo wanted me to play games with him. It reminded me of what was important in all of this, and it felt good that we had got him.

No sooner had the aircraft finished climbing than it began its descent and at 0005 hours we touched down in a balmy Athens. We were all exhausted after a very long day, full of drama and emotion, but for Stephen and me, the job was far from finished. The child was recovered but now we needed to get him and his mother out of the country as fast as possible. For the rest of the mission, the child recovery specialists would have to become bodyguards.

Chapter Thirty

We entered the arrivals terminal at Athens on high alert, and left the airport even more cautiously in case anyone from the father's family was waiting for us. Stephen and I escorted Diane and Theo to a taxi while Peter retrieved all our luggage. 'Where are we going, Darren?' asked Stephen as we got the taxi driver to wait for Peter to join us. Diane answered before I could. 'I know of a good hotel which was recommended to me by the Australian Embassy. It's in the centre of the city, at the base of the Acropolis,' she said. The taxi ride at that time in the morning was a fairly quick one and twenty minutes later we checked into the Hotel Nefeli in the trendy Iperidou area.

Diane and Theo were in a room on the third floor while we three blokes were in a room on the ground floor, right next to reception. We booked under Peter's name and Stephen gave instructions to Diane: 'If the phone rings, don't answer it. If we need to speak to you we will come upstairs and get you. If reception want to contact you they can leave a message. If there is a knock at the door, don't answer it unless it is our knock code of two-one-three. It will be either Darren or me. If you want to speak to us, telephone us. Do not leave your room. If you think you are in any danger, telephone us immediately. Keep the door locked at all times and try to keep Theo fairly quiet. We don't want any loud laughter, crying or screaming. We will arrange food for you and if you have to leave the hotel one of us will be with you. Darren will be with you to go to the Australian Embassy tomorrow to get an emergency passport for Theo.' With everything in place, we turned in for the night, utterly exhausted.

Stephen's watch alarm woke us at 0700 hours after a welcome six hours of rest. Stephen and Peter wanted to arrange their flights out of Greece as soon as possible so jumped in taxis to the offices of the respective airlines they had flown in on. Diane, Theo and I set off for the

Australian Embassy to arrange a passport for Theo. His father still had his and Diane had her British passport so when we reached the embassy and found a long queue at the security entrance I went straight to the front, held up my Australian passport and told the security guard we were in danger and in need of immediate assistance. He ushered the three of us inside and I breathed a sigh of relief. The father and his family would know we would have to go to the embassy to arrange a passport for Theo in order to get him out of the country and I didn't fancy waiting like sitting ducks in a queue on the street.

We met Linda, the consular official Diane had been speaking to for the past fourteen months without ever having met. As soon as the three of us walked into the main office area they knew exactly who we were and all the staff stopped work to catch a glimpse of us like we were minor celebrities. 'You must be Diane, and this must be Theo,' said Linda, crouching down to give Theo a smile. 'Please come into the office.' She rose to her feet. 'And you must be Darren,' she said, turning to me as we walked with her. Linda smiled again. 'Thank you very much for your terrific efforts. You look exhausted.'

Did I look that bad? I guess I did, with the bags under my eyes and a sense of indignation burning within me over the way we had been treated by the Greek police. 'It's been something of an ordeal,' I confessed. 'But at least we have Theo.' That prompted Linda who asked: 'Diane, did you want to ring your husband?' She pointed to a phone. The rest of us tried to melt into the background and give Diane space as she made the call, but we couldn't help overhear. After a couple of rings the phone was answered and Diane yelled: 'We've got him! We did it! I've got him and he's fine, he's safe. We're all fine.' Tears streamed down her face as she told her husband: 'We're coming home!'

When Diane finished her call, Linda pressed an intercom button and requested someone to come into the office. 'Are you ready to get your picture taken?' she asked Theo, who gave a shy nod of the head. A young man entered and Linda introduced him. 'Diane, this is Arthur who is with our consulate section and Arthur, this is Darren. Arthur's going to take Theo's passport photo.' I shook Arthur's hand and watched as he led Theo away to the main office area and a photo machine, which I could see from my position in Linda's office. 'I'm sure you're glad it's all over, eh, Diane?' Linda asked. Diane gave her a tired look. 'Oh, Linda, you've no idea what a relief it is to finally hold Theo in my arms,' she said. 'We lost them for four hours and it looked like we would never get Theo back and then Darren rang me and said he had them in his sights.' Diane looked pained at the memory. 'Well, I'm just glad it has all worked out,' replied Linda with a smile.

Theo was still having his photo done when Diane went to use the bathroom and I found myself alone with Linda. I explained to her the difficulties Stephen, Peter and I had encountered with the local police and she didn't seem in the least bit surprised. When Diane returned, I asked Linda about having both Nick's and Theo's passports flagged to alert the authorities should Nick decide to abduct Theo again and she said that would be a good idea and set the process in motion. I was surprised that I'd had to suggest it and that they hadn't already considered it themselves. When Arthur returned with Theo, and the other staff had finished making a fuss of the little boy, Linda asked if there was anything else they could help us with and I prompted Diane to mention something I had suggested to her on the way to the embassy. 'Would it be possible to have an escort to the airport and for someone to be there in case I have any problems getting out of the country?' she asked. Linda hadn't been expecting that request but after hesitating she said: 'Yes, I think we can arrange that. Give me a ring tomorrow before you're ready to go.'

Tomorrow? I would have liked to have been on the first flight out of the country that afternoon but there was no availability using the tickets Diane had already bought, which would take us back to Melbourne via Cyprus, Dubai and Singapore, so the earliest we could leave would be 1400 hours the next day. I couldn't help but feel that everyone at the embassy was behaving as if the job was over, but I knew that until we were actually on a flight out of Greece and the package was safely on its way to Australia I would not be able to relax. The father's family would know that we would be flying out of Athens International Airport and might well try to stop us. I didn't think it was just a possibility. I was expecting it.

Chapter Thirty-One

It was around 1500 hours and ominous dark clouds loomed over the Acropolis by the time we left the embassy and went to a ticketing agency to reschedule our flights. Theo decided that he was hungry for a McDonald's which made me nervous. I wasn't keen to have him exposed in such a public place and said to Diane that we ought to go straight back to the hotel, but she pleaded his case. 'Oh, but Darren, the poor thing hasn't even seen a McDonald's for such a long time,' she said. Theo looked up at me with tears welling in his big eyes at the thought that he would be denied his treat. It wasn't my decision. I could only advise, but I felt like the big bad wolf for counselling against it. In the end, I agreed to escort them to the nearby McDonald's.

We were all sitting eating when there was an enormous bang and Diane and Theo jumped in fright. Thunder! It was probably the loudest clap of thunder I had ever heard and was followed by a torrential downpour that turned the streets of Athens into instant rivers. It was still teeming down by the time we made our way back. We did so in fits and starts, ducking for shelter under shop awnings whenever we could. There appeared to be no end to the rain and when we finally arrived we were drenched from head to toe, but at least Diane and Theo were safely back in their room.

I had a shower, placed my wet clothes in a plastic bag to be packed in my rucksack and relaxed. Stephen and Peter were in the hotel bar, nice and dry, having a drink and, when Diane rang our room to say that she and Theo were ready, I went up and escorted them down to join the others. 'You get an earlier flight?' I asked Stephen. 'The earliest is tomorrow at 0600 hours with Delta,' he replied. 'I'm on standby for tonight at 2010 hours,' volunteered Peter. 'And you guys?' asked Stephen. 'Tomorrow at 1400 hours with Emirates,' I said.

We had a couple of drinks until we were sure it had stopped raining and then we three guys went out to have dinner and to get something to bring back for Diane and Theo. 'So, you interested in going to Hawaii?' Peter asked as we sat in a nearby restaurant. 'Will you be there?' I asked, trying not to make it sound like my decision would be dependent on his answer, which it was. 'No, I'll be back in the US,' he said. 'Sure, why not?' I replied. 'You have any problems in me going?' I asked Stephen. 'No mate, go for it,' he replied. 'Just fly directly back to us when it's done.' Peter looked happy to have recruited me. 'Just get a ticket to Hawaii and I'll reimburse you. I'll let the guy in Honolulu know you'll be arriving.'

We headed back to the hotel with food for Diane and Theo, and Peter went to get his bags ready as, by now, it was nearly 1800 hours. There was just the small matter of money to be sorted out before he left. Diane had given Peter $30,000 for the operation and Stephen and I had each received $2,000 in advance but costs had mounted as the operation had overrun. Now there was just $8,000 left. If that was split between Stephen and me, we would each be $4,000 short of what we were owed for the job, but Diane's case had already touched Stephen's heart and seeing her reunited with Theo had clinched it. He decided that the $8,000 should be returned to Diane and, though she said she would rather Stephen and I have the money than Peter or his company, I was not about to object. Hearing her joy as she told her husband on the phone that she had Theo safely in her arms had been priceless.

Reluctantly, Peter returned the $8,000 but, going through the costs for the operation, Stephen also found another $2,000 unaccounted for and he told Peter to pay that back to Diane as well. Peter said he would have it wired via Western Union and would organize for me to pick it up for her. He said his goodbyes and jumped in a taxi to the airport. I can't say I was sorry to see him go. He was a nice enough guy but it was one thing less for me to worry about in this final stage of the recovery. It was only after he had gone that I realized he had not given me a confirmation number to enable me to receive the money. Just one more task stuffed up.

Having allowed enough time for Diane and Theo to eat, Stephen and I went back to their room and we sat chatting about anything and everything before Stephen turned in for an early night ahead of his 0400 hours departure for the airport. I turned in not long after. It was a peaceful sleep but around midnight I was awoken by a loud thump and an echo. In my drowsy state, it sounded like a large cannon going off and I wasn't sure if I was dreaming or if it was real. In any case, I fell back to sleep only to be woken by Stephen's alarm going off at 0300 hours and the noise of him packing his things. 'I'll see you in a couple of weeks,' he said. 'Make sure you're back from Hawaii in time for that course,' he added. 'Yeah, no problems mate. I'll let you know when I'll be arriving,' I said. Stephen turned out the light and went out the door. 'Good job Skippy. Well done,' he said, closing it behind him.

I was asleep almost instantly but moments later I was woken by a loud knock. It was Stephen again. 'Peter rang the hotel and left a message for you,' he said. It was a confirmation number for the money transfer. I had perhaps misjudged Peter. I went back to sleep satisfied that I would be able to get some more money back for Diane. I didn't wake until 0800 hours the next morning, still exhausted but pleased that this was the day I finally got to leave Greece after thirteen days of operations. I checked on Diane and Theo, arranged some breakfast for them and then left them in their room as I went to the Western Union office to collect the money Peter had transferred.

My patience had worn pretty thin by now with all things Greek so when it took half an hour for the female employee to check the transaction I was getting fidgety, frequently looking at my watch. Then she explained that she couldn't give me the money. 'I am sorry, sir, but I have a different name for the person receiving it,' she said. 'What name do you have?' I asked. She looked at me sympathetically and said: 'I am sorry, sir, but I cannot give that information out. The name I have here does not match the name on your passport.'

I remembered Peter saying that he would get his mother to arrange the transfer from the US and, being Mexican, I wondered if she had perhaps transposed my first name and surname, as I had often had happen when working in South America. 'Try Mr Franklin Darren,' I suggested. 'I am sorry sir, but I have to go by the name in your passport,' she said. Diane would not be getting her $2,000 soon after all and I was seriously annoyed as I returned to the hotel to give her the bad news. 'How could he not get your name right?' Diane said angrily. 'I think his mother was confused by the name,' I said. 'Bloody hell, if it's not one thing it's another,' she sighed.

It was now almost 1100 hours and I had wasted nearly an hour and a half trying to get Diane her money. She telephoned Linda to arrange for transportation to the airport and Linda said she was leaving on a later flight herself and would see us at the airport. We packed our bags and went downstairs to check out and to wait for the embassy vehicle. As we sat in reception, I noticed how happy Diane and Theo were together and I decided to take a photo of them; a personal snap to capture the moment. Seeing their smiling faces made the operation all the more worthwhile. I felt content that I had contributed to doing what was right for the mother and ensuring the best possible future for the little boy.

I was basking in the glow of success when Diane's phone rang. It was Linda saying the embassy driver could not reach the hotel due to the traffic in the one-way streets and asking if we could meet him at a corner down from the hotel nearer the city centre. I wasn't happy being out on the street in broad daylight but Diane wrote down the street names and we made our way to the requested corner. I was carrying my rucksack on my back, Diane's suitcase in one hand and another pack of hers in the other hand, while she carried my day bag and held Theo's hand. It was already hot; the noise of the heavy Athens traffic was deafening and the crowds of people on the pavements were making me feel claustrophobic as we tried in vain to find the street corner we had been told to wait at. Diane telephoned Linda again to check the name, ask where the driver was, and to give our location. According to the information we had been given, the driver was supposed to be right in front of us.

I noticed, some distance away, parked on the other side of the road to my right, a vehicle with registration plates bearing the initials CD, the common identification for vehicles of the *Corps Diplomatique*. 'Come on, let's take a look. It's better than standing still here,' I said to Diane. We crossed the road, with some difficulty and, as we got closer to the car, I could see in the bottom corner of the rear window a sticker of an Australian flag. The driver was nowhere to be seen but a well-dressed man was running towards us. It was either some relative of Theo's father, who had tracked us down, or it was the driver. If it was someone coming to snatch Theo back then I was not in a good position to react, weighed down as I was with bags. Fortunately, the smile on his face gave away that he was the latter as he ran to open the doors for us.

'Where have you been?' I asked. 'Sorry sir, I went for a paper,' he explained. I was furious. We had been walking needlessly around the central business district of Athens with a recently recovered child who was, in all likelihood, being sought by his Greek relatives. I was not happy about the risks we had been forced to take, but once in the safety of the air-conditioned embassy vehicle I felt a little more at ease. Linda phoned Diane again and asked where we were and Diane told her that we had finally been picked up and we were travelling to the airport. I leaned over so that I could be heard by Linda on the other end of the line and said: 'If you see anybody who looks like they might be connected with Theo's father's family, please let us know straight away.'

She agreed that she would but, even so, as we pulled up at the airport, I scanned the drop-off area for any suspicious characters and there were plenty – all of them policemen. 'Don't leave just yet,' I told the driver as we headed directly for the Emirates counter to check in. Linda was waiting for us and Diane presented her passport, mine and Theo's while I stood with my back to the counter to watch the departures hall. Soon we would be through immigration and a step closer to safety.

The concerned look on the attendant's face as she scanned the passports and read some text on her screen didn't look good when I turned around to see why it was taking so long. Still reading, she lifted the telephone handset and requested security. 'What's the problem?' I asked. Diane looked terrified. 'It's nothing. I just have to verify something,' said the Emirates attendant. Within seconds an officer from the Airport Police arrived and was handed all three passports. Another officer positioned himself between us and the door. The first officer looked at the passports and looked at each of us in turn, checking the photos against the faces he could see in front of him, then finally he broke the silence and put his hand on Diane's shoulder. 'Please come with me,' he said.

Chapter Thirty-Two

The junior officer took a step nearer, just in case we were not about to obey his sergeant's summons. 'Excuse me. I am with the Australian Embassy,' said Linda, showing her identification. 'I would like to know what's going on.' The police sergeant was unmoved. 'Please follow me to the office,' he insisted, this time including Linda in his demand. We went with him into a rear office next to the start of the immigration area. Linda continued to ask what was going on but the sergeant was saying nothing. As I followed, I turned to give the departures hall another look but all I could see was blue – the blue uniform of the other officer who was now right behind me, blocking any backward move. We entered the office and, without waiting to be asked, I placed all the luggage in one corner. I was sweltering under the load. Diane was almost hysterical with worry; Linda was frustrated with being blanked and I was thinking to myself, 'Here we go again. Bloody Greek police!' Finally, the sergeant spoke. Theo's father had filed a police complaint that his son had been kidnapped and Diane's passport had been flagged as a potential abductor.

'You are free to go on your way,' he said, turning to me, but I explained that I was not going anywhere without Diane and Theo. 'Show him the court order giving you custody of Theo,' I told Diane, but she looked at me in desperation. 'I can't,' she said. 'My paperwork fell out of my back pocket during the scuffle on Kalymnos.' The sergeant didn't seem interested in Diane's explanations and went to the nearby desk, picked up the phone and, I gathered later, telephoned a number he had been given for Nick's lawyer to notify him that the mother and child were located inside Athens International Airport. There was very little I could do as I couldn't understand a word of what was being said. Linda and Diane were now conversing in Greek with the police officers and there was a lot of shouting and yelling going on.

Linda rang the Greek Ministry of Justice and got through to the director who asked to speak directly with the police sergeant. As they spoke, Linda attempted to interrupt the conversation to point out the outrage of this hold up and the fact that our flight would soon be leaving, but the sergeant was not interested and turned his back on her so he could continue the phone call. 'You are bloody ridiculous,' she said to him in English.

Diane broke down in tears and Theo also started crying, doubtless scared by all the shouting and by the sight of his mother being so upset. I was totally confused as to what was going on and what was being said. 'Why don't you have the Ministry of Justice fax the police here with copies of Diane's sole custody authority, which they have?' I asked Linda. 'That is what they are doing right now,' she told me. I didn't understand why it was taking so long. 'Can't you use your diplomatic status?' I asked, but she insisted that was only for emergencies. Well, here was a 5-year-old Australian citizen under threat of being re-abducted by a hostile father, with the assistance of the police. If that wasn't an emergency I didn't know what was.

What was clear to me, as the police refused to release Diane and Theo even as the legality of the situation was explained to them, was that we weren't going to make our flight. Since I was not personally detained, I told Diane and Linda I was going to try to find another flight for Diane, Theo and me. Linda joined me later and told me that Diane and Theo had been moved to the police staffroom for their safety because Nick would be arriving soon and some of his relatives from Athens were already in the Airport Police office.

Now we were in danger because the police sergeant had called the father's lawyer rather than listen to Diane's and Linda's explanations and check out Diane's sole custody paperwork. 'I will call Arthur and get him to come to the airport to help you because I have to catch a flight in an hour,' Linda said. 'OK,' I told her. 'I have found an alternative flight but it is not until tomorrow. It may have to do.' Because it was still the summer holidays in Europe, all the flights were full and it was difficult at short notice to find three seats, assuming that we were going to need three seats and that the police hadn't handed Theo back to his father by then. I found a flight with Olympic Airways to London, then Singapore Airlines to Singapore and on to Melbourne. I couldn't consult with Diane to see if she agreed with that because she was seeking shelter in the police staffroom, so I went ahead and booked the tickets for 0900 hours the next morning.

As she stood behind me at the Singapore Airlines ticket counter, Linda's mobile phone rang. 'No, she is still in the airport... she's in with the police... no, she is not arrested... at this stage tomorrow,' I heard her tell the caller. 'Who was that?' I asked when she had ended the call. 'That was Diane's lawyer,' she said. 'Nikolas?' I asked. 'Yes,' she replied. 'No, no, no!' I said. 'Ring him back in ten minutes and tell him that they are just walking down to the gate now and that they are about to leave.' Linda looked puzzled. 'Why?' she asked. 'Because I don't trust him, Linda,' I said. 'I don't believe he would be deliberately obstructive but I don't know who he is talking to and what he might let slip. If everyone starts thinking that we have left the country, then people will stop pursuing us.'

Linda waited for ten minutes and then rang Nikolas back and told him that we were walking down towards the aircraft and would be departing soon.' Minutes later, two men and a woman walked out of the Airport Police office and left the airport. They were relatives of Theo's father. Arthur from the embassy arrived a little later and Linda said goodbye as she had to catch a flight to Sweden to be reunited with her husband. I brought Arthur up to speed before we headed to the police staffroom where Diane and Theo were waiting and where Arthur continued negotiations with the Airport Police which, finally, were beginning to bear fruit.

After what seemed like an eternity, a police officer entered the room and summoned me into the office, or so I understood when Arthur translated. 'Darren, the police want to know what flight you have booked yourselves on,' he explained. 'Why?' I asked, suspiciously. 'They want to provide protection for the three of you tomorrow and need to know the timings. Then they will release Diane and Theo and you will all be free to go.' I thought for a moment then told him: 'OK, it's tomorrow at 1100 hours with Lufthansa direct to Frankfurt and then we will have to get a connecting flight to Australia from there.' With my experience of Greek police there was no way I was going to tell them the truth. I didn't trust anyone anymore and the one ally I could trust, Stephen, was out of the country. I was now the sole member of the team.

Arthur and I returned to the back room where Diane and Theo had been lying low for two hours. 'What's happening? What's going on?' Diane asked nervously. 'It's OK, we're free to go,' I said. 'Oh, thank

God for that,' she said. 'I can't take any more Darren, my heart's not strong enough.' I smiled at her. 'It's OK. No one's going to stop us now. Tomorrow we will be out of here, but we need to remain vigilant, OK?' She nodded and gave me a hug. 'I just want it to be all over,' she said. 'Well, it's not over yet,' I replied. 'But we're almost there.'

Arthur helped me pick up the bags, which had been moved with Diane, and asked if we wanted a lift. 'Oh yes please,' Diane started, but I cut her off. 'No thanks, Arthur, but could you do something for me?' I asked. I should have been pushing back my seat and relaxing with a pre-meal drink at 35,000 feet by now, safely on the way home. Instead we were stuck in Athens for another night and I was loaded down with luggage creating wet patches on my shirt where it weighed against my body in the sticky evening air. More worryingly, we were still running the gauntlet of the father's family who would not be fooled for long by reports that we had already left. 'What is it that you want, Darren?' he asked. 'I need you to book us into the Sofitel across the road, under your name,' I explained. 'And you're not to tell anybody that we are staying there tonight.' 'OK, Darren, I understand,' he said.

The Sofitel was situated directly across from Athens International Airport. I knew that it would be expensive but it would save a lot of hassle with taxis and I could check in the bags in the morning and get the tickets without Diane and Theo having to show themselves, then go back and escort them straight through immigration. Arthur booked us in to a room on the eighth floor next to the fire escape. Perfect! The cost was 375 euros a night.

We checked in and said goodbye to Arthur who had been a great help and could understand why I didn't trust any locals anymore despite him being a Greek Canadian. I had a much-needed shower after giving Diane and Theo a short evacuation brief: 'We open the door to no one and I will answer any phone calls. If we need to evacuate tonight, we will exit via the fire escape which leads downstairs to the base of the airport car park. We will then go over to the Airport Police office. Once you are safely inside there I will return to the hotel room to get the luggage and check out.' At this stage I was one exhausted guy. It had been nearly two weeks since I'd had a decent long night's sleep.

After my shower, I nodded off in an armchair only to be woken by Theo throwing projectiles at my face. Diane berated him for waking me up and ordered room service while I drifted off to soldier's heaven in the chair again. I was in a deep sleep until I heard a solid knock on the door and I opened my eyes in time to see Diane walking towards it. I was awake in a split second, caught her attention and motioned to her to go back into the room with Theo and stand around the corner. I peered through the spy hole and could see it was a room attendant with a tray. I opened the door and let him in and, as he placed the tray down on a table, I grabbed the complimentary copy of a local English language newspaper. I scanned the headlines of every article to see if the recovery was mentioned, but found nothing. The only item that did catch my eye read, 'Earthquake Rocks Corsica'. So that was the cannon I thought I had heard the previous night.

My body was aching so I decided to sit in the huge bathtub while Diane and Theo were in the bedroom eating their evening meal. I sat there for around an hour and at one point drifted off to sleep. After my bath I watched television for any news reports of the recovery. Again, there was nothing. Diane and Theo fell asleep in the bed and, after setting the alarm for 0530 hours, I fell asleep in the armchair. I'd never looked forward to an early alarm call so much before as I couldn't wait to get out of this country. Surely nothing could go wrong now.

Chapter Thirty-Three

I slept surprisingly well but woke with a stiff neck when the alarm roused me. I washed and woke Diane and Theo. I left them to get ready while I grabbed the three passports and walked across the road to the airport and checked our luggage in at the counter. The departures hall was quiet. Very quiet. 'Where are the other passengers?' asked the Olympic Airways attendant. 'Oh, they're downstairs having breakfast,' I replied. 'We just wanted to get rid of the luggage.' I watched her eyes as she scanned each passport in turn. Theo's passed with no problem; mine was next with whatever notes were on there from my frequent travel, and I knew there were a few. I had been detained earlier in the year at San Juan Airport, Puerto Rico, after doing a job on the Colombian border. I had been travelling light and there were a number of passport stamps in a short space of time, in and out of South America, and I'm sure they thought I was a drug dealer. They held me for interview for hours, including a lot of questions about my surveillance book – a novel I always carry to pretend to be reading while conducting surveillance. Their suspicions were heightened because I had no idea what the book was about, but after telling them I was a university drop-out, that my father was a leading heart surgeon in Australia that my mother was an anaesthetist and they funded my round-the-world travels, there was no reason for them to hold me any longer and they let me go.

I held my breath as the attendant scanned Diane's passport but whatever flagging had led to yesterday's detainment had either been removed, or an explanatory note had been added. 'There you are, Mr Franklin, boarding time is at twenty past eight at gate number four,' she said as she handed me the passports and boarding cards. I did a visual sweep of the departures hall again and then returned to the hotel and checked out at reception. I went back upstairs to bring Diane and Theo down, handed in the room key, and escorted them across to the airport.

There were no suspicious characters at the front entrance or in the departures hall and we walked directly to the immigration area where the desk officer scanned our passports again, mine first, then Theo's then Diane's. 'Travelling all together?' he asked, having just seen three different surnames. 'Yes, this is my family,' I replied. A Scottish female, an Australian male and an Australian boy who looked nothing like me and whose Mediterranean complexion was very different from Diane's fair colouring... but the officer didn't bat an eyelid, stamped the passports and we passed into the airside area.

I could feel my pulse quickening with excitement and Diane looked ecstatic. 'We made it. We made it,' she said under her breath. 'When the aircraft lifts off I will feel calmer,' I replied, trying to stop her showing any premature signs of celebration which might attract attention. We had breakfast at McDonald's, at Theo's insistence, and as we sat there I noticed a police officer walk past and then return, this time walking much slower and scanning the passengers. I knew exactly who he was looking for and directed Diane's attention to something behind her so that she would be looking away when the policeman's gaze fell on us, but it didn't work. He walked directly up to our table.

'Excuse me, Madam, could I see your passport, please,' he said. Diane looked at me nervously as she reached for her passport in her handbag and I gave her a comforting wink. Well, the police had said they wanted to provide an escort for us this morning. We were about to find out if that was genuine or not. 'When are you leaving, Madam?' he asked. 'In thirty minutes,' she replied. The police officer took another look at her passport and boarding pass, then handed them back without saying another word. He looked at me warily as he left the table. I didn't like the way he looked at me, but then I didn't like the way any Greek policeman looked at me. As we returned to our breakfast I wondered about the contact from the Australian Embassy who was supposed to meet us. Apart from the police officer there appeared to be no one else looking for us, but I wasn't unhappy about that after days of feeling hunted.

We made our way towards the boarding gate but as we got closer I told Diane we would walk past it so that I could see if anyone was waiting for us. Everything appeared normal except for a small guy standing to the side of the gate. He wore an identification card strung around his neck but I was too far away to see what it said. I presumed that he was our embassy contact. We walked for another 50 yards, past three other gates, and sat with a lounge full of people waiting for a different flight. Diane was playing with Theo when the small man I had seen at our gate approached the lounge where we were sitting and made a beeline for Diane. As he got close enough I could see his ID was indeed from the Australian Embassy. 'Hello, Diane is it?' he asked. 'Um, yes, who are you?' she replied. 'I'm Harley, from the Australian Consulate,' he said. 'Oh, thank God,' said Diane, 'I thought you were someone from the Greek authorities.' He smiled. 'No, no. I was informed to meet you here. I hear you've been through a stressful time.'

We spoke to Harley at length about our ordeal while he played with Theo from time to time. He assured Diane there would be no further hold-ups but I couldn't help visualizing police cars pulling up on the runway, stopping the plane from taking off over some legal discrepancy, not least because our departure time came and went with no sign of us boarding. The sight of a Greek Mr Bean lookalike among the waiting passengers provided some light relief and we all laughed but it was a nervous laughter. Finally, twenty minutes after we should have taken off, it was time to board and we said our goodbyes to Harley and thanked him for his assistance. I took one final look around the gate lounge and we walked down the ramp to our aircraft. With every step, I felt a little more confident that we were actually getting out of the country.

We found our seats and sat down with Theo between us and me beside the aisle. Diane couldn't hide the smile from her face while I looked out of the windows and up the aisle for any sign of police officers. The aircraft taxied to the runway and we sat at the holding point for what seemed like an hour as we waited for other aircraft to clear the area. My uneasiness must have rubbed off on Diane as she was no longer smiling. Then the aircraft lined up on its take-off line and with a surge that pushed us back into our seats hurtled down the runway, the nose lifted and all the wheels were off the deck. Then, and only then, did I breathe a huge sigh of relief and I turned to Diane and extended my hand. 'Congratulations, Diane, you are now safe,' I said. 'No one can get you, or Theo, now.'

With that she burst into tears, disregarded my hand and, leaning over Theo, gave me a big hug. 'Thank you,' she said. The relief on her face was obvious. Her fourteen months of stress and emotional strain were over and she gave Theo another hug. 'We're going home! We're going home!' she told him excitedly. As the plane climbed higher into the sky,

I settled into my seat and promptly fell asleep, only to be woken by an almighty thump. Theo had decided to punch me in the nose, which was now bleeding. 'So that's the thanks I get for rescuing you, eh, little man?' I thought, but it did occur to me that Diane faced a battle ahead to repair the damage of an itinerant lifestyle and apparent lack of discipline that Theo had had for fourteen months.

I shrugged it off and played with Theo who enjoyed the attention. Diane and I had a whisky to celebrate and as Theo dozed off, and Diane did the same, I had another and another. When we landed at Heathrow in London, we had a six-hour wait until our connecting flight to Singapore so Diane and Theo wandered off to look in the duty-free shops and I arranged to meet them at TGI Friday for something to eat before the flight. Diane was keen to buy her son some clothes whereas I was quite content to sit in an English-style pub, sink some ales and reflect on the previous two weeks.

By the time we met up again at the restaurant, Diane was weighed down with gifts she had bought for Theo. At least he had plenty of toys to amuse himself on the fifteen-hour flight to Singapore. Diane put him in the window seat, away from me, in case I fell asleep again and Theo decided to wake me in his inimitable style. At Singapore we had a short stop over and while Diane and Theo went for a shower, I took a free bus tour ride from Changi Airport to Sentosa Island for a look around. On my return, I called Qantas to arrange my ticket from Brisbane to Honolulu, via Sydney, before we boarded the aircraft for Melbourne.

I spoke to Diane about the next step in her life, what to expect and how to handle things from thereon. I told her to make sure Theo's passport was kept in a safe place and to request that the Australian authorities kept a flag on both his and his father's passports. I also suggested that she inform Theo's school principal, teachers and local police of the situation so that they would be alert to any repercussions. As Theo had been through a traumatic experience, I suggested that she also take Theo to a counsellor as soon as possible as a preventative measure.

It was the morning of Sunday, 8 September 2002 when our aircraft finally touched down at Melbourne. Diane was excited about arriving home with Theo by her side and was fixated on making herself and Theo look good for her husband who was picking them up. I was just pleased that this job was almost over and that it had been a success. 'You were in Greece, I see,' said the immigration officer as I showed him my passport.

'Yes, that's right,' I said. 'And what were you there for?' he pressed. 'Oh, vacation,' I replied, showing off my suntanned arms. He scanned all our passports without problems and we collected our luggage and passed through the automatic doors into the arrivals hall.

There was a lump in my throat as Diane spotted her husband among the crowds of people waiting and Theo rushed to give him a hug. Diane was not far behind, with me in tow. I stood back like a spare groom at a wedding as Peter hugged his wife and his stepson with tears in his eyes. The poor man had gone through the same fourteen-day ordeal as the rest of us, but had done so feeling utterly helpless thousands of miles away. 'Darren, this is my husband, Peter,' Diane said at last, ushering me forwards. 'Hi Peter, Diane has told me a lot about you,' I said. The tears welled in his eyes again. 'Thank you, thank you, thank you,' he said. The moving moment was interrupted by a messenger from Australia's Channel Nine arriving to claim the surveillance film we had shot and I took the opportunity to say my goodbyes to Peter, to Diane and to Theo and wished the whole family all the best for the future before I slipped away.

It had been an arduous, often frustrating and frequently stressful couple of weeks but it had ultimately been successful. As I walked away I looked over my shoulder one last time to see Diane hugging and kissing her family and Theo meeting his baby sister for the first time and I afforded myself a smile of satisfaction at a job accomplished. Then I climbed on the escalator from the arrivals hall towards the departures hall for a flight to Brisbane, the first step of my journey to Honolulu and the next child recovery mission.

Index